Wisdom
The Absolute is the Adorable

Wisdom

The Absolute is the Adorable

by

Nataraja Guru

PRINTWORLD

Publishers of Indian Traditions

Cataloging in Publication Data — DK
[Courtesy: D.K. Agencies (P) Ltd. <docinfo@dkagencies.com>]

Nataraja Guru, 1895-1973.
Wisdom, the absolute is the adorable.
Includes bibliographical references.
Includes index.
ISBN 13: 9788124600337

1. Wisdom. 2. Knowledge, Theory of (Hinduism).
3. Philosophy, Indic. I. Title.

First published in India, 1994
Second Impression 2012
ISBN 13: 978-81-246-0033-7 ISBN 10: 81-246-0033-3

Published and printed by:
D.K. Printworld (P) Ltd.
Regd. office : *'Vedaśrī'*, F-395, Sudarshan Park
(Metro Station: Ramesh Nagar)
New Delhi – 110 015
Phones : (011) 2545 3975; 2546 6019; *Fax* : (011) 2546 5926
E-mail: indology@dkprintworld.com
Web: www.dkprintworld.com

Preface

THE present title is one of the most important works of Nataraja Guru. He wrote all his works according to a scheme in his mind to systematize the major epistemological, methodological and axiological perspective of man's search for truth.

In the present book we got a comprehensive picture of the frame of reference and the normative notion of the Absolute presented in all his previous works. Being a scientist, a philosopher and a *yogi* in the correct sense of the term, his chief concern is to bring certitude in the mind of his reader. A serious student should know what he wants to learn, why he seeks wisdom and how he can arrive at the unitive conclusion, which is self-evident to the reader. A careful study of *'Wisdom — the Absolute is Adorable'* will amply prove how efficiently Guru takes us to the joyous realization of the Self.

On February 18, 1995 Nataraja Guru is attaining his birth centinary. To celebrate his glorious contribution to Science, Philosophy, Psychology and Poetry, we are brining out his major works in the form of deluxe library editions. His major works are :

1. The Integrated Science of the Absolute (in three volumes).
2. The Life and Teachings of his mentor Narayana Guru, whom Nataraja Guru succeeded next in the heirarchy of Gurus.
3. An exhaustive commentary on the *Bhagavad-Gītā* of Vyāsa.
4. His vision of one-world philosophy which includes:
   a) Manifesto of one world education;
   b) Manifesto for one world government;
   c) Towards one world economics; and
   d) A monograph on the Elements of thought in search of a Unified Language.
5. His main contribution to Aesthetics is his commentary on Śaṅkara's *Saundarya Lahari*.

6. His adventure of spirit in the search for the Absolute is presented as the Autobiography of an Absolutist.
7. The present book 'Wisdom' marks the last of the series he contributed to Philosophy, Science and Aesthetics.

We are much pleased that D.K. Printworld is bringing out *'Wisdom — The Absolute is Adorable'* to commemorate the hundredth birth-anniversary of Nataraja Guru, our beacon and the founder of the Narayana Gurukula Foundation. We are very much indebted to the publisher and it is with warmth of joy we present to the readers who earnestly love Truth and Wisdom.

Fernhill,
30-7-1994.

Guru Nitya Chaitanya Yati

Contents

Part III
GURUHOOD

Part IV
INTEGRATION OF THE SCIENCES

Part V
HINDU ORTHODOXY

PART I

The Absolute is the Adorable

1

Wisdom's Frame of Reference

WISDOM refers to finalized knowledge. Such knowledge could result when the mind is properly focused. The focusing involves a methodology, epistemology and theory of values (axiology) proper to it. Cosmology, psychology and theology are all implied together in wisdom. Physics and metaphysics, ethics and aesthetics lie within its scope. In its applicability a vast range of subjects of higher study, such as sociology, economics or politics come naturally within its range. Besides the searchlight of introspection, the worlds revealed to the telescope, spectroscope or the microscope can clarify wisdom and determine its limits or possibilities. Wisdom knows no distinction of personal attitudes such as optimist or pessimist, liberal or conservative, orthodox or heterodox, contemplative or active, Eastern or Western. The *a priori* and the *a posteriori*, analytic and synthetic tendencies, harmonize in a central norm in the wisdom-seeker's way. Ends and means tally unitively and universally when wisdom is fully finalized in terms of a self happiness which aims at general well-being at the same time.

Having covered certain specified aspects of wisdom, keeping in mind this unitive approach it remains for us in the present article to sum up the subject-matter and object-matter of wisdom, taken together. A scheme of correlation or a frame of reference is here suggested, not to be looked upon as a fetish or magic key for all wisdom, but merely to serve as an aid for the guidance of seekers, so that thoughts may hang together coherently, comprehensively and completely. The apologetic hesitancy of the sceptic is here replaced by the confident hope in the highest possibilities of the Self in Man.

Wisdom which covers both science and philosophy has suffered from excess of departmentalization and specialization in recent years, especially in the West. There is, therefore, a legitimate cry for the unification and integration of the sciences. Some like Russel, who stand for such, limit themselves to an empirico-logical attitude. There are others who, like Niels Bohr and Schroedinger, wish to bring both *a priori* and *a posteriori* fields under the aegis of a unified science. Bohr wrote: "... science is, according to its aims of enlarging human understanding, essentially a unity... above all it may help us to balance analysis and synthesis".[1]

A formula to bring both these disciplines within the scope of one schema is still only vaguely understood at present. Even those who adhere to empirico-logical reason have their orthodoxy which stresses the pragmatic as against the dogmatic predilections of those who can afford to wait longer for results. These lurking rival orthodoxies have to be brought out and fitted into a common frame of reference. This hard task is what we set before us here.

There is no use in rival schools calling one another various names such as solipsists, syncretists or eclecticists. An easy lapse into any of these attitudes would be detrimental to the cause of unitive wisdom. Besides such labels as optimist, pessimist, hedonist or hylozoist, philosophers have been too easily open to attack by such expressions as pantheist, pluralist, animist, conceptualist, transcendentalist or personalist. These terms in their proper contexts need not necessarily be deprecatory. A unitive outlook would help to view the whole field without mutual mistrust.

When we remember that all wisdom is for man or even *vice versa*, and put the human personality in its proper central and neutral position without egocentric evil accruing to our modes of thinking and when we begin to view the whole matter of wisdom from its proper perspective round the normative notion of the Absolute, wisdom can then attain to the open, dynamic and public status of a Science of sciences as against static closed random aggregates of esoteric doctrines, however old or respectable they may be in themselves. Such an absolutist outlook would reveal through wisdom that high value named Truth, the Truth which shall make us free. Existence, subsistence and values would meet in such a central Value in the name of common human happiness.

The Total Content of Wisdom

Wisdom concerns what humans feel, think or understand. Cognition, conation and affection come into its frame. An initial examination of the content of philosophy or contemplative wisdom shows that when completely reviewed in any methodological order it comprises the following items at least, in any attempted inventory. We can take the list given by Prof. A.N. Whitehead for a basic consideration of the 'components of experience':

> In order to discover some of the major categories under which we can classify the infinitely various components of experience, we must appeal to evidence relating to every variety of occasion. Nothing can be omitted, experience drunk and experience sober, experience sleeping and experience waking, experience drowsy and experience wide awake, experience self-conscious and experience self-forgetful, experience intellectual and experience physical, experience religious and experience sceptical, experience anxious and experience carefree, experience anticipatory and experience retrospective, experience happy and experience grieving, experience dominated by emotion and experience under self-restraint, experience in the dark, experience normal and experience abnormal.[2]

Śaṅkarācārya's method is more thorough-going still in this matter of determining the content of consciousness. Anything not given to any of the three states of waking, dreaming or deep sleep has for that reason to be omitted from the true content of experience. If we should turn to another Eastern source we find in the *Bhagavad-Gītā* an enumeration which is more realistically and less solipsistically conceived. Here the levels of personal life are touched in a graded order in two sets, in the second of which personal attitudes rather than conscious reason count. In all the three sources cited, contrasted states like waking or sleeping are brought in and we see that antinomian pairs of another order, such as fear and fearlessness, honour and dishonour, figure at least partially in the *Bhagavad-Gītā* and wholly as in the list of Whitehead above.

The scale of personal values from the positive head-end to the negative heart-end of consciousness conceived vertically, and in two sets, reads as follows in the *Gītā* (Chapter X, verses 4, 5):

> Intelligence, awareness, unerring clarity, persistence, control, calmness, pleasure-pain, being-nonbeing, fear and fearlessness;
>
> Non-hurting, equality, pleasantness, discipline, generosity, honour and dishonour too

Are the various states of living beings as they refer to Me.

Through a close scrutiny of the two lists enumerated, the one by a modern Western thinker, and the other by an ancient sage of the Orient like Vyāsa, it should be possible at least to concede initially that consciousness is the meeting place of two sets of value-experiences. There are some that admit of conflict as between antinomies of the same order, and others more unitively understood. Pure awareness, which is identified with the Absolute Self in Śaṅkarācārya, is more solipsist than the other two cases referred to above. As between the series of items of the modern Western philosopher and the Eastern sage we should also notice that Vyāsa reduces antinomies to the minimum while Whitehead retains dual possibility of experience throughout the series. The Eastern analysis is more contemplatively conceived.

Two Intersecting Axis of Correlation

Even to justify such broad generalizations as the above, it is necessary that a frame of reference for the whole of wisdom should be visualized simply and even schematically to start with; hence its justification. The map helps a navigator, and geometry and graph, by designs, the symbolic world that mathematics builds up through actual counting or measuring things or movements. Second or third degree abstractions of different mathematical arguments, operations, functions and equations help relational coherences. Propositional calculus and syntactical analysis of language have also now entered the field to analyse the strange 'togetherness' of things or concepts in consciousness.

When we remember further that all the words of the dictionary of any language are capable of being arranged in two columns of synonyms and their antonyms, as has been so ably demonstrated for English in Roget's *Thesaurus*, we can generalize initially here with justice in saying that a polarity underlies thought generally.

Further, when specific and generic counterparts of a concept show the same dialectical or ambivalent inter-relatedness, the stage is set for us to think in terms of a frame of reference within which to fit all types of events, movements or tendencies in experience together in what constitutes experience or consciousness which is none other than Wisdom itself.

When the mind is focused more clearly, it is possible to discover two sets of pairs, some that refer to pure antinomies and others belonging to the world of practical values. The former may be said to refer to the vertical axis and the latter to the horizontal axis. There is a principle of contradiction with a possibility of unity which neutralizes these pairs of antinomies where the two axis meet. The 'Being' of Parmenides and the 'Becoming' of Heraclitus may be said to have common ground at this core of experience.

Limits of Empiricism

Empirico-logical reasoning may lead us to the limits of scepticism which can perhaps have its own uses like the uses of adversity which Shakespeare refers to. Bertrand Russell concludes his book on *Human Knowledge*[3] with a whole chapter devoted to "The Limits of Empiricism" wherein he admits finally:

> . . . it must be admitted, empiricism as a theory of knowledge has proved inadequate, though less so than an other previous theory of knowledge. Indeed, such inadequacies as we have seemed to find in empiricism have been discovered by strict adherence to a doctrine by which empiricist philosophy has been inspired: that all human knowledge is uncertain, inexact and partial. To this doctrine we have not found any limitation whatever. (p. 527)

In short, Russell here relies on a certain type of philosophical inspiration to deny the limits he himself admits. Empiricism failing by its strict standards justifies itself by a form of reasoning which resembles the problems such as that between being and becoming of Parmenides.

Dialectics to the Rescue

Plato treats of the implications of such a way of philosophizing, bringing out its full dialectical implications through examination of paradoxes such as between the one and the many, motion and rest, "These are like yet unlike, in contact yet not in contact". The idea of the moment is postulated. It is defined as "something out of which change takes place into either of two states" of motion or rest, being or non-being.[4]

We know this same type of reasoning in the *Tarka Śāstra* of India where non-being (*abhāva*) itself is treated as a substance (*padārtha*). The five other systems besides the Nyāya system to which this style belongs accept this way of reasoning overtly or tacitly. Without full recognition this way of thinking has never been abandoned by man and even to the present-day philosophers lapse into it inadvertently, as it were. Let us quote from Prof. Whitehead again to see how highly reminiscent of the tradition started by the paradoxes of Parmenides and Zeno it reads:

> A pure physical prehension is how an occasion in its immediacy of being absorbs another occasion which has passed into the objective immortality of its not-being. It is how the past lives in the present. It is causation. It is memory. It is perception of derivation. It is emotional conformation to a given situation, an emotional continuity of past with present. It is a basic element from which springs the self-creation of each temporal occasion. Thus perishing is the initiation of becoming. How the past perishes is how the future becomes.[5]

Dialectics not Old, New, Eastern or Western

The same author admits the essentially dialectical nature of this kind of approach to wisdom which is both modern and ancient and common to the East as well as to the West when he writes:

> European philosophy is founded upon Plato's dialogues, which in their methods are mainly an endeavor to elicit philosophic categories from a dialectic discussion of the meanings of language taken in combination with shrewd observation of the actions of man and of the forces of nature.[6]

The *yoga* of the *Bhagavad-Gītā* and the dialectics of Plato, which later Whitehead himself comes to the verge of accepting, have thus their common ground in Wisdom which is the highest knowledge of *homo sapiens.*

Thus understood, Wisdom could be taught and should be taught in all universities of the present-day if the human heritage is not to perish. Unified Wisdom as a science could be formulated better when the general plan, scheme, pattern, structure or frame of reference which relates aspects of wisdom conceived both subjectively and objectively become better visualized globally or unitively. Empiricism and the scepticism it upholds need not be adhered to as a modern surrogate of religion for its own sake. Wisdom rises above more orthodoxies and soars above all limitations of thought.

Common Knowledge vs. Modern Theories

How the common-sense notion of the nature of the physical world has been rudely displaced by modern theories and totally distorted out of all shape is amply evidenced in a single paragraph from Eddington's work, *The Nature of the Physical World:*

> I am standing on the threshold about to enter a room. It is a complicated business. In the first place I must shove against an atmosphere pressing with a force of fourteen pounds on every square inch of my body. I must make sure of landing on a plank travelling at twenty miles a second round the sun — a fraction of a second too early or too late the plank would be miles away . . . the plank has no solidity of substance. To step on it is like stepping on a swarm of fleas . . . if unfortunately I should slip through the floor or be boosted too violently up the ceiling the occurrence would be not a violation of the laws of Nature, but a rare coincidence. These are some of the minor difficulties. I ought really to look at the problem four-dimensionally as concerning the intersection of my world-line with that of the plank. Then again it is necessary to determine in which direction the entropy of the world is increasing in order to make sure that my passage over the threshold is an advance, not an exit.
>
> pp. 467-68

The man of common-sense is sure to feel bewildered but if he is clever enough could still ask the scientist some very simple, seemingly silly, yet fully pertinent questions, three of which could be put down as examples here at least to show how a revised scheme of reference where the expert scientist could converse with the man-in-the-street may still be possible.

1. How could be Empire State Building of New York still stand if the Euclidean geometry and Newtonian physics on which it was built have been replaced by relativistic notions?

2. In the light of the abolition even of the theory of parity of particles in the atom, how is the stability of *terra firma* to be understood at all? Even the picture of the swarm of fleas of Eddington above (1926) has now (1959) to be modified completely.

3. If experimental psychology has displaced faculty psychology, why is it that a waking man cannot pacify a man who is talking in his

sleep and who shouts for help during a nightmare?

Two men in a dark room who ask each other "Who are you there?" can both be equally satisfied with the common response of 'I' coming from either side, revealing the common content of the first person singular, which behaviourists and the experimental or empirico-pragmatic psychologists of the stimulus response school tend to deny: How is this possible ?

Such questions could be multiplied with reference to other branches of science. Even Western philosophers like Prof. Whitehead feel the need for a new doctrine and a revised frame of reference when they go so far as to say:

> The field is now open for the introduction of some new doctrine of organism which may take the place of the materialism with which, since the seventeenth century, science has saddled philosophy.[7]

Platonism and Aristotelianism Really Complementary

The zig-zag course of the history of philosophy in the West may be looked upon as the alternating swinging of the pendulum as between the truth understood by Plato and by his disciple Aristotle. They were both dialecticians, the former employing ascent into the intelligible world and the latter preferring descending dialectics entering into the Prime Mover behind both matter and form. The hylozoism of the Eleatic pre-Socratic philosophers was directly continued in Aristotle, and the paradoxes of Parmenides and Zeno entered into the subtle dialectics common to this teacher-disciple couple who, between them, may be said to have set the pattern for philosophical or theological thinking, with their influence reaching down to our own times. Academic, peripatetic, scholastic, and patristic traditions blended with the background of Dionysiac mysteries to shape and direct European thought.

On the Indian soil a corresponding phenomenon in the history of thought is in the six systems (*ṣaḍ-darśanas*) which together constitute a winding staircase of thought divided between what is called *jñāna* (reason) and *karma* (action). Their dualistic treatment was unitively revalued in the *Bhagavad-Gītā* which stated (V. 4-5) categorically that Sāṅkhya rationalism and Yoga disciplines were one, and that those who saw them as two were "children, not pundits".

Once philosophy is properly related to its norm in the notion of the Absolute, and when it refers to self-realization as a high value for man, a certain coherence and order becomes evident. Truth or Wisdom in general would then attain to a unitive status where subjectivity and mere objectivity are merged in the neutral core of the personality of man himself. If we could supply this central notion as a substance, a monad, or as a conscious experience, holding together ambivalent polarities, the task of understanding together both Plato and Aristotle and all lesser philosophers would be easy. In fact such is the task that the schematic correlation suggested here is meant to accomplish.

The Vertical Axis Implied in Plato

In Book VI of Plato's *Republic* we read the following dialogue:

> SOCRATES: Now take a line which has been cut into two unequal parts and divide each of them again in the same proportion, and suppose the two main divisions answer one to the visible and the other to the intelligible, and then compare the subdivisions in respect of their clearness, and you will find that the first section in the sphere of the visible consists of images, and by images I mean in the first place shadows, and in the second place reflections in water and in solid, smooth and polished bodies and the like. Do you understand ?
>
> GLAUCON: Yes — I understand.
>
> S.: Imagine now the other section of which this is only the resemblance, to include the animals which we see and everything that grows or is made.
>
> G.: Very good.
>
> S.: Would you not admit that both the sections of the division have different degrees of truth and that copy is to the original as the sphere of opinion is to the sphere of knowledge ?
>
> G.: Most undoubtedly.
>
> S.: Next proceed to consider the manner in which the sphere of the the intellectual is to be divided.
>
> G.: In what manner ?

> S.: Thus there are two subdivisions, in the lower of which the soul uses the figures given by the former division as images; the enquiry can only be hypothetical and instead of going upwards to the principle, descends to the other end; in the higher of the two, the soul passes out of hypotheses, making no use of images as in the former case, but proceeding only in and through ideas themselves.[8]

The vertical axis with the ascent of dialectical thought thus finds clear description in Plato, which he further finalizes in a later section in the following significant words:

> You have quite conceived my meaning; I said, and now corresponding to these four divisions, let there be four faculties of the soul —- reason answering to the highest, understanding to the second, faith or conviction to the third and perception of shadows to the last — and let there be a scale of them, and let us suppose that the several faculties have clearness in the same degree as the objects have truth.[9]

Further, we read again:

> And so, Glaucon, I said, we have at last arrived at the hymn of dialectic which is that strain of the intellect only, but which the faculty of sight will nevertheless be found to imitate, for sight as you may remember, was imagined by us after a while to behold the real animals and stars, and last of all the sun himself. And so with dialectic, when the person starts on the discovery of the Absolute by the light of reason only, and without any assistance of the sense, and perseveres until by pure intelligence he arrives at the perception of Absolute Good, he at last finds himself at the end of the intellectual world, as in the case of sight at the end of the visible.[10]

We have quoted Plato full length here as by doing so we can cover what is represented by the vertical positive aspect of wisdom with as few additional remarks of our own. If the description could be made to correspond to subjective aspects of self-realization and objective aspects of cosmology, avoiding prejudices arising out of what in India is referred to as *tripuṭi* (tri-basic partiality) of objectivity, subjectivity or conceptualism, the notion of the vertical axis will have been fully described for the schema we have here in mind.

Mathematical Version of Dialectical Descent

Prof. A.N. Whitehead, who has been described as "the latest and greatest of Cambridge Platonists", has a mathematically conceived version of the implications of what we have called the vertical positive of our suggested schema of correlation. Explaining that what he calls "eternal objects" are the 'Universals' as understood in European philosophy generally, and that it is an abstraction, he says:

> By 'abstract' I mean that what an eternal object is in itself — that is to say, its essence — is comprehensible without reference to someone particular occasion of experience.[11]

He goes on to say that an 'eternal object' "is to be comprehended by acquaintance with (i) its particular individuality, (ii) its general relationships to other eternal objects as apt for realization in actual occasions, and (iii) the general principle which expresses its ingression in particular actual occasions".[12]

Explaining the nature of the 'connexity' between grades of 'eternal objects' which form a hierarchy between themselves at different levels, the professor enters into mathematical speculations as follows:

> Any set of eternal objects belonging to the hierarchy, whether all of the same grade or whether differing among themselves as to grade, are jointly among the components or derivative components of at least one eternal object which also belongs to the hierarchy.[13]

We quote below the full paragraph referring to the abstractive hierarchy of eternal objects which is what we have tried to represent in the vertical positive of our schematic representation. The schema is capable of avoiding poetic embellishments of the Platonic language as well as the dry mechanistic logic-chopping of its mathematical version in a manner appealing to common-sense. The mathematically conceived description of the vertical axis of values reads as follows:

> A finite abstractive hierarchy will, by definition, possess a grade of maximum complexity. It is characteristic of this grade that a member of it is a component of no other eternal object belonging to any grade of the hierarchy. Also it is evident that

> this grade of maximum complexity must possess only one member; for otherwise the condition of connexity would not be satisfied. Conversely any complex eternal object defines a finite abstractive hierarchy to be discovered by a process of analysis. The complex eternal object from which we start will be called the 'vertex' of the abstractive hierarchy: it is the sole member of the grade of maximum complexity. In the first stage of the analysis we obtain the components of the vertex. These components may be of varying complexity; but there must be among them at least one member whose complexity is of a grade one lower than that of the vertex. A grade which is one lower than that of a given eternal object will be called the 'proximate grade' for that object. We take then these components of the vertex which belong to its proximate grade; and as the second stage we analyse them into their components. Among these components there must be some belonging to the proximate grade for the objects thus analysed. Add to them the components of the vertex which also belong to this grade of 'second proximation' from the vertex; and, at the third stage, analyse as before. We thus find objects belonging to the grade of third proximation from the vertex; and we add to them the components belonging to this grade, which have been left over from the preceding stages of the analysis. We proceed in this way through successive stages, till we reach the grade of simple objects. This grade forms the base of the hierarchy.[14]

Here the 'ingression' into the 'particular' is a descent instead of the ascent in the method of Plato himself.

The Ascent from Prius Nobis to Entelecheia

From hypothetical constructions reaching upwards to the supreme good we descend into the realm of Plato. It is possible to descend by a process of inverse abstraction into the very heart of the specific prime mover of Aristotle, which would represent his God as the source of all things. What corresponds to the real in Platonic dialectic corresponds to the *entelecheia* in Aristotle. Here the real becomes an abstraction and a universal or unitive concept. Priority and specificity characterize the prime mover. What is anterior to all knowledge is referred to by Aristotle as the *prius nobis*. Before we can attain to this final term of priority we have to pass through what Aristotle would call *prius natura* and *prius natura intendente* (priority of the perfect) where form passes into matter itself in its inmost essence and uniqueness. If we should start the abstractive hierarchy from the 'vertex' of this specific yet eternal object we can ascend through grades of lesser and lesser degrees of specificity to the point where as entelecheia specificity partakes of universality. Entelecheia may therefore be said to lie at the moment where the one and the many change over in terms of each other.

That such are some of the implications of the dialectics in Aristotle's philosophy can be corroborated by a brief quotation from Baldwin's *Dictionary of Philosophy* which explains the notion of Entelechy as follows:

> By this conception of passive power the attempt is made to explain why a specific effect such as melting in the case of wax is produced by the same cause, heat, which produces an opposite effect upon other substances. This ground we conceive must lie in the thing acted upon. It is therefore not inappropriately named a power, since it is an intrinsic state which determines (in part) the effect. Power is opposed on the one hand to actual activity; on the other to the certainty of non-activity. It is therefore a mediating concept between non-action and action.

Between the *prius nobis* and the actualized principle of the entelechy thus understood there is therefore a possibility of a dialectical movement in thought similar to that between the real and the intelligibles of Plato. If the extreme points of abstraction in both are joined by a vertical line, entelecheia and the real may be understood as the point of intersection between the vertical and the horizontal axes.

Such a neutral core of consciousness is implied in the dialectics of "identity and non-identity" or of "one and the many" as explained in the *Parmenides* of Plato where we read:

> The One is neither other than itself nor the same with itself.[15]

> The contradiction involved in ascribing any relation to unity leads to the denial of it.[16]

In terms of pure time this neutral core of consciousness corresponds to the concept of the moment as described by Plato in the same context as follows:

> . . . the moment seems to imply a something out of which change takes place into either of two states; for the change is not from the state of rest as such, nor from the state of motion as such; but there is this curious nature which we call the moment lying between rest and motion, being and non-being in any time; and into this and out of this what is motion changes into rest and what is at rest into motion.[17]

The 'moment' is thus the meeting place of the real and the entelechy of which nothing can be predicated. In short, Western philosophy arrives at the position enunciated by Narayana Guru in the following simple verse:

> Of one thing there are many as in many objects
> One single meaning reside;
> by such knowing we can know
> In consciousness as inclusive of all differencelessly;
> This secret ultimate is not given to all to know.[18]

The Central Locus of Paradoxes

The notion of the Absolute is the locus of all possible paradoxes. As the Upaniṣadic imagery would put it, the Absolute in itself is the hub of the wheel where all predications meet in the living moment at the pure core of life. This core is to be connected peripherally to actual practical aspects through successive concentric zones of concretion, virtual or actual, by means of what would correspond to spokes of a wheel, each of which would have its counterpart on the opposite side of the hub. The primary function of the core of consciousness is to hold the spokes together centripetally, when they tend to be centrifugal. The thousands of possible syllogisms possible according to Aristotelian logic are movements of thought between the general and the particular in the pure and practical domains of life activities, innate or overt.

Such a wheel would be given in a cross-section view, while in a long section view the Absolute, though truly confined to what constitutes a 'moment' as defined above, would reveal a vertical scale of values, the most primary of them based on simple direct sensations where reflex actions and stimulus-response functions hold good. Here man feels rather than thinks. The second level of this vertical axis would contain the loci of all formally logical functions of thought. In the third or final level, mere relatedness to multiplicity of interests yields place to intense attraction or adoration to a unitive and pure value.

The circulation of thought takes place as between the centre and the periphery, solving paradoxes of different degrees of interest. According to life interests there is a movement of the personal interests up or down the scale of general human interests till they find their term in full self-realization. Each such unit of consciousness may be thought of on the lines of a 'monad' — with possible centrally unitive monads belonging to the three levels in the vertical scale.

The Monad Fitted into the Frame

The concept of the monad can be traced back in Western philosophy as far as Pythagoras. Through its successive use by Ecphantus, Aristotle, Euclid, Augustine and many others, it has a sufficiently general and recognized status as a philosophical concept of great antiquity and respectability. Plato himself referred to his ideas as monads. Cusanus and Bruno among later philosophers have led up to its legitimate founder in Leibnitz whose monadology marks an important stage in modern philosophical tradition. Its persistence as applicable to the human personality in Renouvier proves how hauntingly the notion persists.

When we read that, according to Leibnitzian monadology, "God is the monad of monads whose being is in harmony with all other beings, whose pure activity only is the source of all activities, and whose sufficiency is the ultimate ground of reason",[19] and also such descriptions as,

> The monad is a simple substance, completely different from a material atom. It has neither extension, nor shape nor divisibility. Nor is it perishable . . . They 'have no windows' . . . The universe is the aggregate, the ideal bond of the monads, constituting a harmonious unity, pre-established by God who is the highest in the hierarchy of monads. The bond of all things to each, enables every simple substance to have relations which express all the others, every monad being a perpetual living mirror of the universe . . . The highest monad, God, appears to be both the creator and the unified totality and harmony of self-active and self-subsistent monads.[20]

and when we analyse the implications of monadology under items such as (1) continuity of monads, (2) their dynamic substance, (3) their consisting of infinitesimal *petites perceptions* which are subconscious, (4) the interrelatedness of monads, (5) their life as non-spatial, (6) that though finite they are infinite and belonging to a self-representative system, (7) conservation of the energy of the monad, and (8) as leading to perfection, — we are sure to feel the need of fitting all these into a coherent frame of reference such as the one we have been developing.

In appraising the validity or status of such an elaborate system which is perhaps the most intuitively realistic picture combining cosmology, psychology and theology, with a dialectical method supported by the language of universal mathematics of which Leibnitz himself was the promoter in his day, the frame of reference we have employed would be of service. We could sum up our criticism with its aid by simply stating that monadology is stronger on the negative vertical aspects of the Absolute. By its omission of space it has no horizontal axis of reference. The vertical plus side is only vaguely touched upon by such terms as "pre-established harmony" or "self-representative system", which could be clarified further in the light of the dialectics of Plato.

In spite of these drawbacks, monadology when supported by the universal mathematics of Leibnitz, could be looked upon as the best pointer to an integrated or unified notion of reality compatible with notions of modern biology and radio-active matter. In the monad as the specific source of the universe, the monad as the universal goal or term of perfection and, at the same time, as Thilly puts it (above) "God is the monad of monads whose being is in harmony with all other beings", we find three different concepts of God all lying in one and the same vertical scale. The first corresponds to the Prime Mover of Aristotle, the second to the supreme Good of Plato and the third to where the real meets entelechy in the moment at the point of intersection of the two axes of our schema.

Leibnitz himself refers to the three grades as "*in esse, in intellectu, et in re*" respectively. These technical terms of monadology would correspond to the terms *sat*, *cit* and *ānanda* of the Indian philosophical context. The schema could thus be used for comparison of systems of thought as within themselves between rival types or sets. The overall plan and the most intimate structure of thought or wisdom generally conforms to the schema suggested here.

We shall pass on to examine this claim in a certain order as applied to different departments of thought.

Cosmological Correlation

The nature of the physical world has been the subject of theorization and philosophical discussion from the most ancient times. From Pythagoras to Eddington in the West and through chapters corresponding to Genesis in the scriptures of the world, we have had various theories. If you believe in the Bible, some think you should not believe in the Darwinian theory of evolution. Creation of the cosmos at one stroke is opposed to gradual creation, and the co-existence of rival theories is ruled out as totally impossible. Newton and Einstein are popularly thought to be mutually exclusive but then so also is the Cartesian theory of 'vortices' and 'occasionalism' which brings brute matter and subtle mind as dual entities together, giving us a picture of the universe, which is supposed to be basically different from the monadology of Leibnitz. The planetesimal hypothesis and the nebular theory are discredited, one in favour of the other. While the readers differ, it is strange to find that between those who put forward theories themselves there is willingness to allow each theory its freedom to exist by the side of the other. Einstein himself has his own two theories, the general and the particular theories of relativity, both valid together. The Hegelian principle itself is that when a new theory is formulated the truth of the anterior stage in thought is preserved in the posterior. The following quotation from Einstein would be of interest:

> No one must think that Newton's great creation can be overcome in any real sense by this or that theory. His clear and wide ideas will forever retain their significance as the foundation on which our modern conceptions of physics have been built.[21]

The possibility of a vertical scale of theories one dialectically anterior to the other is thus admitted as possible. Theories correctly formulated can co-exist and even contribute to the general over-all epistemological scheme instead of disrupting it. Overstress on the horizontal applicability would tend to place one theory as the rival of the others, but vertically understood they can absorb one another unitively.

Thus from Pythagoras to Eddington we have had a string of theories through antiquity, each to be looked upon as a particular view of verity.[22]

The latest position here can be surmised from the following pronouncement of Dr. A.C.B. Lowell who said in a BBC broadcast dated 15th December 1958: "I do not believe that there exists any observational date which are decisively in favour of any particular contemporary cosmology".

The possibility of such co-existent and equally respectable theories without rivalry has been recognized in the *Darśana Śāstra* of India, culminating in the *Darśanamālā* of Naryana Guru, where it has been shown that all facets of the vision of truth can be strung together so as to make a garland of visions which as an ornament can adorn the fully wise man. The harmony between the vertical and horizontal aspects involved is the secret by which the global relation of theories can be conceived.

Correlation in Particle Physics

The same dialectical revaluation and harmonizing process among theories pertaining to the atom can be noticed in particle physics. Thus we read in Cajori:

> While physicists and mathematicians were busy celebrating the dynamics of the Bohr atom, another atomic model was invented by chemists which was a 'static' atom in contrast to the 'kinetic atom of the physicists'. A compromise was effected between them.

Later in the history of modern physics we read:

> De Broglie's wave mechanics was made the starting point of new theoretical developments by Schroedinger (1926) who raised the question, what need is there in a group of waves, of the mass particle? Thus arose the theory of the 'wave' atom.

From the time the quantum theory came into the field the picture of the material atom has been revised. That a human being can still touch and directly experience something which is described, though even superstitiously it may be, as 'material' remains true. It is therefore necessary to conceive of particle physics as having an empirico-logical or practical (horizontal) principle and a non-empirical or pure (vertical) principle of reference within itself. The theories of Drs. Yang and Lee tend to support such a view.

Biological Correlation

The monad and the living cell conform in many respects to the schema here outlined. The space-time continuum could refer to the life history of an organism in terms of horizontal 'a-periodic' or 'periodic' bodies, the latter containing the principles of continuity. Salt crystals multiply a-periodically while chromosomes supply the factors of continuity of the species. Multiplication of cells and their growth have to be balanced to regulate the general harmony and individuality of the species. Erwin Schroedinger in his book *What is Life*? goes into the difference between periodic and a-periodic solids which multiply in different ways, one of which could be called horizontal (periodic) and the other vertical (a-periodic). The difference is described by the scientist as follows:

> A small particle might be called the 'germ of the solid'. Starting from such a small solid germ, there seem to be two different ways of building up larger associations. One is the comparatively dull way of repeating the same structure in three directions again and again. That is the way followed in a growing crystal. Once the periodicity is established, there is no definite limit to the size of the aggregate. The other way is that of building up a more and more extended aggregate without the full device of repetition . . . We might quite properly call that an a-periodic crystal or solid and express our hypothesis by saying: 'We believe a gene — or perhaps the whole chromosome fibre an a-periodic solid.[23]

We have already gone into other aspects of life in the light of our schema in the *Education Manifesto*. It is interesting to note further that Schroedinger was inclined to call De Vries' theory of mutation in biology figuratively as "the quantum theory of biology" . The integration of life and matter is thus in the minds of scientists themselves. We have suggested also that the latest discoveries in particle physics tend to suggest a vertical axis in respect of the transformations of mass and energy aspects in right and left-handed particles.

Theological Correlation

When God has been called the monad of monads and if the monad covers the common ground with the living unit and the basis of quantum pulsations it should be easy to conceive of an overall frame of reference which would form the basis of comparative theology and reveal the structure of any single religious growth. God is the central normative notion in theology and the problem here is to transcend the paradox as between God and Nature by means of the neutral principle of the Absolute underlying all science.

The theology of John Scotus Erigena lends itself admirably for treatment as an example here along the lines of our schema. The following four divisions relating the subject-matter and the object matter of theology have been presented by Erigena. As combining the best in the Dionysian tradition and that of St. Augustine, Erigena may be considered representative of theologians in general. The four divisions are:

(1) That which creates and is not created — God; origin and principle of things;

(2) That which is created and create — Logos; Primordial causes or types of things existent in the matter of God and co-existent with God;

(3) That which is created and does not create — Phenomenal world of space-time (Platonic reals);

(4) That which neither creates nor is created — God again — but as the end of all things (for Erigena held that just as creatures have emanated from God, so all will return to Him by an ascent).

The correlations will become clear at once if graphically represented as in the diagram on the next page.

Psychological Correlation

Modern psychology, which claims to have abandoned the faculty psychology of classical times, is based on the primacy of the stimulus-response approach depending on various brass instrument measurements and statistical studies. The discovery of the cardio-encephalograph has pushed the possibilities of such a method to extreme limits, but beyond the reaches of such study it is being increasingly recognized that whole unexplored regions still remain to be investigated.

The cardio-encephalograph has revealed the astounding fact that there are two sets of mental activities, some of which show great expenditure of physical energy and others which are sharply different from them. Educationists and philosophers like John Dewey have incessantly complained that "the whole man" has not yet been brought into cultivation or use by educators or psychologists. Dewey says:

> Particular S-R connections interpreted on the basis of isolated reflexes, are viewed as static *cross-sections*, and the factor most important in education, namely, the longitudinal, the temporal span of growth and change, is neglected.[24]

More elaborate implications of psychological correlation along the lines implied in Dewey's complaint have been worked out in our *Education Manifesto*.[25]

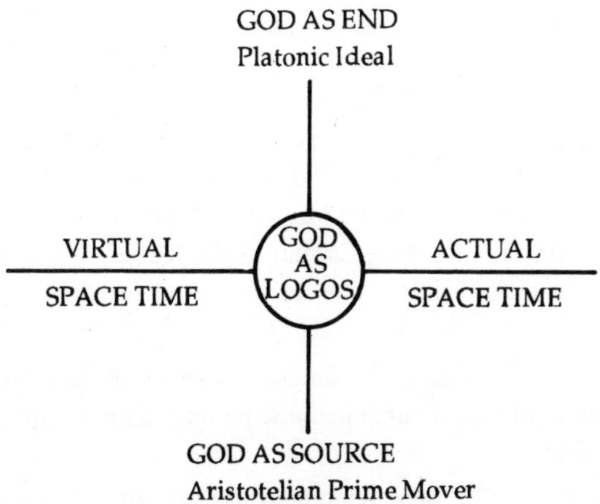

COSMO-THEOLOGICALFRAME OF REFERENCE

Ethical and Aesthetic Correlations

Where value-judgments in life are directly involved as in ethics or aesthetics generally the vertical and horizontal components of morality or art require a subtler insight to discern.

Generally speaking, tragedy has a movement along the vertical axis and plays on human feelings at their negative levels. To avoid tragedy would be the purpose of ethics and in doing so we would have to avoid horizontal interests in life and cultivate vertical interests instead. Such are some of the ideas of the Nichomachean Ethics of Aristotle. The further implications of this statement can be found in Henri Bergson's epoch-making work, *The Two Sources of Morality and Religion* in which the vertical world of open dynamic values is contrasted with the horizontal world of closed static or socialized values where obligations prevail.

Logical and Mathematical Correlation

Two volumes (*International Encyclopaedia of Unified Science,* Univ. of Chicago) of a branch of study which aims at the unification or integration of all sciences into a science of sciences, out of a large series of volumes contemplated, have been published. At present they contain interesting pointers in the direction of effectively correlating all branches of knowledge.

At present all that we can say about such efforts is that when the attitude of empirico-logical orthodoxy still persisting in most of them is discarded in favour of a bolder dialectical revaluation of the two positions round the common norm of all thinking, which could be none other than the Absolute, logistic and semiotics can be expected to usher in an era of truly united science instead of the ideal of a mosaic which its present sponsors including Carnap, Bohr, Russell, Morris, Northrop and others set before themselves as their goal for their International Encyclopedia.

The structure of logical thought, however, is capable of being correlated to conform to our schematic pattern in the meanwhile on the following lines:

The four figures of logical modes, three recognized by Aristotle and the fourth by Galen may be seen to conform to the four aspects of the axes of reference that we have suggested. The descriptions of the four figures are:

Figure I : Middle term is subject in major premiss and predicate in the minor premiss.

Figure II : Middle term is predicate in both premisses.

Figure III : Middle term is subject in both premisses.

Figure IV : Middle term is predicate in major premiss and subject in minor premiss.

When we remember that the middle term is defined as "what occurs twice in the premisses but is omitted in the conclusion, and that syllogistic logic is based on the laws of thought of which the excluded middle is a rule in judgments envisaged by this kind of logic, it is easy to see how it is meant for scientific reasoning of the empirico-pragmatic order. It works best in hypothetical and disjunctive forms of syllogistic reasoning. When we come to categorical forms of the syllogism, the reasoning seems to serve no pragmatic end, but has the nature of a truism merely. The schema of correlation would present the plan shown on the next page.

Logical Syntax and Correlation

"The last word on these matters has almost certainly not been said", concludes the article on Formal Logic by Alonzo Church in Runes' *Dictionary of Philosophy*.[26] That new branches of study such as semantics, semiotic or even logical syntax do not lead us far enough for a bolder attempt at the unification of all science is evidenced by the controversy prevailing over the positions of two philosophers of modern times, Whitehead and Bradley about which the former writes:

> There are various controversies about relations which need not be explicitly referred to. But there is one discussion which illustrates our immediate topic . . .
>
> For example, New York lies between Boston and Philadelphia. But the connectedness of the three towns is a real particular fact on the earth's surface. It is not the universal 'between'. It is a complex actual fact which, among other things, exemplifies the abstract universal 'betweenness'.
>
> This consideration is the basis of Bradley's objection that relations do not relate. Three towns and an abstract universal are not three connected towns. A doctrine of connectedness is wanted. Bradley (*Essays on Truth and Reality* Chapter VI, *On our Knowledge of Immediate Experience*, Appendix, p. 193) writes: 'Is there, in the end, such a thing as a relation which is merely *between* terms? Or, on the other hand, does not a relation imply an underlying unity and an inclusive whole?[27]

Bradley himself answers:

> At every moment my stage of experience, whatever else it is, is a whole of which I am immediately aware. It is an experienced non-relational unity of many in one.[28]

The trouble here is that Western philosophy has not made the distinction sufficiently clear as between the actual and the perceptual aspects of reality

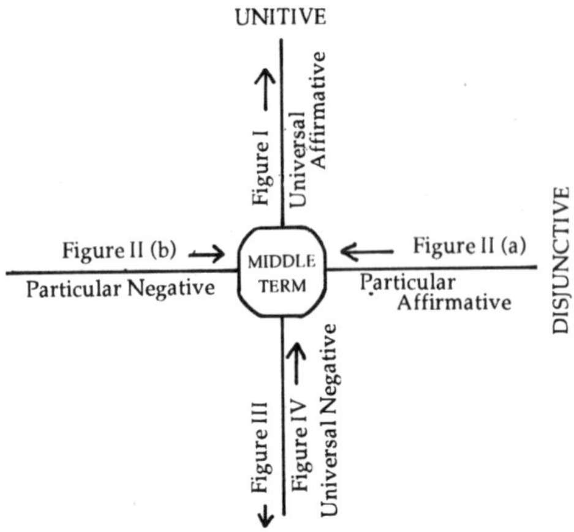

AXIAL FRAME OF REFERENCE OF SYLLOGISMS
Arrows point to major predicate in each logical mode

Prof. Whitehead sums up for us the position of modern philosophy.

> .... each event, viewed in its separate individuality, is a passage between two ideal termini, namely, its components in their ideal disjunctive diversity passing into these same components in their concrete togetherness.[29]

The line joining the two termini referred to above would come most near as can be to the acceptance of the vertical axis of reference in modern philosophy. The double reference required here and the unitive resolution implied is of the essence of dialectics which is higher than mere logical thought. We have already dealt with its implications in our article on *The Absolute and the Relative* in this book.

Mystical or Contemplative Correlation of Wisdom

Our consideration of possible applications of our schema for purposes of correlated factors in various aspects of wisdom would be incomplete without reference to its mystical or contemplative implications. In the following passage quoted from the *Taittirīya Upaniṣad* (1.iii.1-4) we have evidently the foreshadowing of the four aspects of correlation which we have adopted throughout. This is but one of many passages suggestive of a scheme of correlation like our own which can be found throughout the Upaniṣads:[30]

> Now next we expound the wisdom import (*upanishad*) of the togetherness (*samhita*) under five aspects: the world, the luminous, knowledge, progeny, self:
>
> Regarding the world: The earth is the prior; the heaven the posterior; space their medium; wind the link.
>
> Regarding the luminous; Fire is the prior; the sun is the posterior; water the medium; lightning the link.
>
> Regarding knowledge; the teacher is the prior; the pupil the posterior; knowledge is the medium; teaching the link.
>
> Regarding progeny; the mother is the prior; the father the posterior; progeny the medium; sex union the link.
>
> Regarding the self; the lower palate is the prior; the upper palate the posterior; speech is the medium; the tongue is the link. (*slightly adapted from Hume's translation.*)

The principal findings of our discussion here could be set down tentatively and independently of topics, as follows:

That the wisdom-function in consciousness has two axes of reference, the vertical and the horizontal and, with reference to either or both of which thought circulates organically within its normal limits subjectively and objectively at once;

That each of these axes presents a polarity with plus and minus with a neutral point between each;

That a subtle reciprocity or ambivalence relates these with the common neutral point;

That wisdom as subject-matter and wisdom as object-matter should tally to finalize a wisdom experience;

That units of wisdom given *a priori* or *a posteriori* have a dialectical relation between them;

That theories (physical, cosmological, theological, psychological or even mystical) can represent endless dialectical revaluations of aspects of Absolute Truth;

That endless serial inner or outer worlds can co-exist non-exclusively and non-conflictingly, but inclusively absorbing one another;

That the Self and the Absolute can be treated as interchangeable terms; and

That human happiness which is a worthy ideal even for a dispassionate scientist is to be conceived in terms of unitive understanding which is none other than wisdom.

References

1. *International Encyclopedia of United Science*, vol. I, Part I, p. 28. Uni. of Chicago.
2. *Adventures of Ideas*, p.262. Pelican, London, 1948.
3. Unwin, 1948.
4. Cf. *Plato's Dialogues*, Vol.2, p. 126. Jowett, Random House, New York.
5. *Adventures of Ideas*, p. 276. Pelican, 1948.
6. *Ibid.*, p. 265.
7. *Science and the Modern World*, p. 31. Pelican, 1938.
8. Jowett's translation, p. 771. Random Books, New York.
9. *Ibid.*, p. 773.
10. *Ibid.*, p. 791.
11. *Science and the Modern World*, p. 186.
12. *Ibid.*, p. 186
13. *Ibid.*, p. 196.
14. *Ibid.*, p. 197.
15. *Plato's Dialogues*, Vol. II, pp. 102-03. Jowett, Random House, New York.
16. *Ibid*, pp. 112-13.
17. *Ibid.*, p. 126.
18. *One Hundred Verses of Self Instruction* (*Atmopadeśa Śatakam*), verse 73, p. 222. Narayana Gurukula, India, 695145.
19. *History of Philosophy*, p. 55. Thilly.
20. Joseph Maier in *Dictionary of Philosophy*, D.D. Runes.
21. Quoted by F. Cajori in *History of Physics,* Macmillan, 1938.
22. For reference see *Le Systeme du Monde de Pythagore a Eddington*, Jules Sageret, Payot, Paris, 1931.
23. Erwin Schroedinger, *What is Life*?, p. 60. Macmillan, New York.
24. *The Sources of a Science of Education*, pp. 67-68. New York, 1929.
25. See VALUES, Vol. II, No. 12, and Vol. III, No.1.
26. Jaico, Bombay.
27. Whitehead, *Adventures of Ideas*, pp. 267-68. Pelican, 1948.
28. Quoted from *loc. cit.* p. 175 by Whitehead, *ibid.*, p. 270.
29. *Ibid.*, p. 273.
30. Cf. under 'Correlation' in *The Thirteen Principal Upanishads*, R.E. Hume, Oxford Press, 1971.

2

Existence

EXISTENCE (*sat*), Subsistence (*cit*) and Value Dynamies (*ānanda*) mark three graded levels in the vertical axis of the frame of reference that we have developed stage by stage. They are both subjective and objective categories of consciousness understood in the unitive abosolutist manner to which we have adhered in our discussions.

The mind of man is so constituted that it can enter into relation with something second to itself only under these three categories of which the most primary and fundamental is that of Existence.

Truth, belief, fact, reality and faith all refer to the factor of existence which is itself a generalized abstraction. When we think of a particular object in the practical context of everyday usage, the relation has nothing to do with the philosophical notion of existence in a purely idealistic sense. Pure existence has its place in a vertical axis, while the practical reality of a thing when referred to as existing is the product of a horizontal movement in consciousness. The vague generic content of 'this' in a sentence such as 'This is a pot' underlies the more specific content of the word 'pot'. The movement from the generic to the specific takes place within the world of virtuality-actuality.

A still deeper experience of existence as referring to purer factors in consciousness is possible as when we think of the synthetic-analytic movement in thought implied in a sentence such as "This is knowledge".

To distinguish these two movements in consciousness is a very important matter in the methodology and epistemology of all scientific philosophizing. The mixing up in the mind of the pure or vertical aspect of existence with its own horizontal aspect, is the fecund cause of the "metaphysical puzzlement or perplexity" facing even logical positivists at the present-day. According to Morton White, Wittgenstein, the last of the so-called analysts, carried the cure for this 'puzzlement'.

Degrees of abstraction are possible and qualitative abstractions have to be kept apart from quantitative ones if our logic in philosophy is not to lose its way. Epistemological monism, realism and idealism, when they deal with Essence or Existence, have hitherto erred in this respect.

The Vedāntic term for existence is *sat*. This refers to the ontological aspect of the Absolute which has much in common with existence as understood by modern existentialists. *Sat* or existence in this sense should be understood as placed at the base of the vertical axis. It represents the calm, pure or eternal content of Absolute Consciousness both within as without, transcendent as immanent, in a context of Wisdom which is both psychological and cosmological at once.

Existence and Essence

Is the idea of existence to be given priority over the notion of essence? This has been an epistemological problem disturbing the favourite dreams of philosophers throughout the history of thought. However carefully one might read the literature of philosophers who might be classed as epistemological realists, idealists or monists, there seems something elusive as between these two abstract notions.

The idea of essence, as related to the Latin term *esse*, has been much in favour with theologians of the so-called Dark Ages before the triumph of reason or science. God represented this principle of essence while creation itself with its material actuality was existence as God's creation.

The modern existentialists reverse the position between essence and existence, and give primacy to the notion of existence as against essence. Among existentialists themselves there are the believers and disbelievers in God. The believers who began to reverse the primacy of essence in God did not know that God would be dispensed with totally by their own argument by later existentialists such as Sartre. How the changeover from godly existentialism to godless existentialism took place can be gleaned from the following extracts from the writings of Jean-Paul Sartre who, according to editor Morton White "like Bergson has achieved popular fame that far exceeds anything possible for an English-speaking philosopher today . . . He may be criticized but he cannot be ignored".[1] In Sartre's own words:

> What then, is this that we call Existentialism? . . . indeed the word is now so loosely applied to so many things that it no

> longer means anything at all. . . All the same it can easily be defined.
>
> The question is only complicated because there are two kinds of existentialists. There are on the one hand the Christians among whom I shall name Jaspers and Gabriel Marcel, both professed Catholics; and on the other the existential atheists among whom we must place Heidegger as well as the French existentialists and myself. What they have in common is simply the fact that they believe that **existence** comes before **essence** — or, if you will, that we must begin from the subjective. What exactly do we mean by that?[2]

Our interest here is to see in this new philosophy so popular at present in post-war Europe, the tendency to a new form of idealism and subjectivism in which the pendulum seems to swing away from Platonic ideas towards the ontological or real of the here-and-now world of values. What is taken away from the idea of God is given by another hand to the freedom of Man here, raising thus his dignity in the vertical scale of values.

Existentialism

That Existentialism stresses personal subjective values with a dynamism that may be said to move in the vertical rather than in a horizontal axis of relationships, will be amply evident to anyone who by this time has acquired the mental habit of referring all factors correctly to our frame of reference which alone can save philosophers even of the most advanced type from that kind of 'puzzlement' to which we have already alluded. Sartre himself explains the nature of the subjectivism questioned in the previous quotation, and as implied in existentialist philosophy, as follows:

> Man simply is . . . Man is nothing else but that which he makes of himself. That is the first principle of Existentialism. And this is what people call its 'subjectivity' using the word as a reproach against us. But what do we mean to say by this, but that man is of a greater dignity than a stone or a table? For we mean to say that man primarily exists — that *man is before all else, something which propels itself towards a future and is aware that it is doing so*. Man is indeed, a project which possesses a

> subjective life, instead of being a kind of moss or a fungus or a cauliflower. Before that projection of the self nothing exists; not even in the heaven of intelligence. Man will only attain existence when he is what he proposes to be.[3]

Man can thus wish to be like the essence implied in God after his own existence has been first postulated without God. Such is the position of the Sartre school of modern existentialists.

From this school for our purposes it is important to note two things, one of which is that Existentialism has a contempt for things understood as simple utilities. The stone, the table, the cauliflower do not touch the subjective dynamism of the existentialist. Though in favour of an ontology as against any religious teleology, the dynamism implied can be clearly seen to move in a vertical axis of pure values. In the words we have italicized above, "man is before all else, something which propels itself towards a future and is aware that it is doing so", the subjective personal dynamism, not unlike that of Bergson, is clearly evident.

Existentialism asserts the dignity of man and his high destiny although it does so avoiding Platonic, Christian or even Cartesian terminology. The existence here resembles rather that of Aristotle who conceived it as something at the basis of matter and form. Existence as opposed to essence and as consisting of essences subjected to accidents are further clarifications of the notion of existence as defined in Runes *Dictionary of Philosophy* (p. 102).

We shall not be far wrong when we try to clear the puzzlement as between these terms when we say that existence in philosophy strictly refers to a horizontal factor and that essence is strictly a vertical one. In Sartre we have a notion of existence to be understood in verticalized yet negative terms. According to the stricter epistemological frame of reference we have tried to develop, we could sum up Sartrean Existentialism by saying that it is an attempt to rob godly essence by conferring it on free man here and now. Briefly, it refers to a vertical but negative value.

Static and Dynamic Existence

Modern philosophy tends to stress dynamic existence as against merely intellectual fixed concepts of existence. Bergson is well-known as the philosopher of flux, change or becoming. What he says in the following paragraph will help to show how great a family resemblance there is between Bergson's notion of existence and that of Jean-Paul Sartre:

> Human intelligence as we represent it, is not at all what Plato taught in the allegory of the cave. Its function is not to look at passing shadows nor yet to turn itself round and contemplate the glaring sun. It has something else to do. Harnessed like yoked oxen to a heavy task, we feel the play of our muscles and joints, the weight of the plow and the resistance of the soil. To act and to know that we are acting, to come into touch with reality and even to live it but only in the measure in which it concerns the work that is being accomplished and the furrow that is being plowed, such is the function of human intelligence. Yet a beneficient fluid bathes us, whence we draw the very force to labour and to live. From this ocean of life in which we are immersed, we are continually drawing something, and we feel that our being, or at least the intellect that guides it, has been formed therein by a kind of local concentration. Philosophy can only be an effort to dissolve again into the whole. Intelligence . . . consists in an interchange of impressions, which correcting and adding to each other, will end by expanding the humanity in us and making us even transcend it.[4]

Bergson's objection to Plato's view arises from the fact that Platonism lives in a world raised above everyday living necessities, in the world of intelligible essences, like the attributes of a hypostatic entity such as a deity. When, however, Bergson himself refers to an entity called the 'Whole' with a capital letter, and refers in the last part of the above quotation to expanding the humanity within us even so as to transcend it, the dynamism that is in his mind is unmistakable.

In the earlier reference to the fluid that bathes us belonging to the 'ocean of life', the negative ontological idealism, not unlike that of the existentialist is discernible to any but the most superficial philosopher. Being and becoming as applied to something existent which philosophers postulate, are really complementary notions in the context of the Whole which Whole itself can be nothing but the Absolute.

Platonic and Aristotelian realities are poles of an axis where dynamic consciousness can move. Consciousness can be viewed also as a kind of "local concentration" as Bergson puts it in the above quotation.

We could call such a static view of existence a cross-section of the whole, where being and becoming, existence and essence come to a sort of equilibrium, cancelling each other out into a neutral personal state.

Such a hierarchy of states of existence was known to scholastic theologian, but other imaginative or poetic representations of the dynamism of progress in consciousness, in keeping with evolution, have largely displaced this notion. Reincarnation persisting in India contains essentially the same idea of stages of stable existence among beings of different grades. Prof. A. N. Whitehead has underlined for us the primacy given to 'becoming' rather than to 'static being' in the following unmistakable words:

> It is nonsense to conceive of nature as a static fact, even for an instant devoid of duration. There is no nature apart from transition, and there is no transition apart from temporal duration. This is the reason why the notion of an instant of time, conceived as a primary simple fact, is nonsense.[5]

Momentary and Eternal Existence

Being or static existence is generally spoken of as opposed to non-being or the void. Being and becoming are also sometimes referred to as counterparts in the dialectics of the Greek Eleatic school. The Eleatics gave being an absolute status. Plato tended to give primacy to ideological existence while his disciple and complementary philosopher Aristotle, while giving to the notion of being an eternal status, admitted 'ideas' and 'forms' as inseparable concomitants of essential being. Thus throughout the history of thought something elusive has persisted round this question of being and becoming, or between being and non-being. If we were asked to mediate, the position that we should take would be that of the dialecticians. In the *Bhagavad Gītā* we have the famous verse which reads:

> Becoming cannot apply to the non-existing and non-becoming cannot be predicated of something that exist. The conclusive position with regard to both these together has been seen by the philosophers. (II.16)

The statement here bears a family resemblance to the position as stated by Parmenides who put the same problem in the following dialectical form as mentioned by W.S. Weeden in his article on 'Being' in Runes

Dictionary of Philosophy:

> According to Parmenides and his disciples of the Eleatic school, everything real belongs to the category of Being, as the only possible object of thought. Essentially the same reasoning applies to material reality in which there is nothing but Being, one and continuous, all inclusive and eternal. Consequently, he concluded, the coming into being and passing away, constituting change, are illusory, for that which is not cannot be and that which is cannot cease to be.

The last sentence in the above quotation is a distinct echo of the thought in the *Gītā* that we have just cited. A careful scrutiny of the rival theories on the subject will reveal the superiority of the dialectical approach whether in the East or in the West. This approach has a methodology of its own which is different from the merely logical or rational. When this distinction is made clear, the 'puzzlement' here must vanish.

Even when dialectics is applied to the problem of existence, it is possible to have two answers equally valid, one by which we have the notion of the *Dialectical Moment* and the other which may be called the *Eternal Present*. The Dialectical Moment is Being understood as the Void, and the Eternal Present has a conceptual content which can only be the notion of the Absolute as the meeting point of contradictions.

According to Indian *Vedānta* texts we know the Absolute as Being referred to as *sat-asat* (existing-nonexisting) which should not be understood as a contradiction but is a unitive intuitive contemplative vision with a sufficient reason unto itself. Contradiction here is reabsorbed into the supreme unity of the Absolute which stands for all existence. The *śūnya-vādins* and the *kṣaṇika-vijñāna-vādins* of the later Buddhistic context, confronted this very problem and solved it in their own ways by treating *śūnya* (void) and *vijñāna* (practical wisdom) as Absolute Norms, equally valid.

Metaphysical Bewilderment and Overlapping Definitions

Anyone who has tried to follow carefully modern trends in philosophical thought will recognize that from the day Positivism was formulated by Auguste Compte there has been a persistent tendency to discredit all forms of abstract reasoning as baseless, non-factual or sentimental. Darwin's theory of evolution became a natural starting point for a new variety of practical and realistic philosophizing. Factual metaphysics as opposed to abstract doctrines became preferable. Kant, Descartes, Spinoza, leaving aside classical philosophers such as Plato and Aristotle, were boldly criticized and decried as living in their own ivory-tower abstractions.

The true representatives of *the Age of Analysis*, as writers like Morton White called them, include such names as Pierce, Whitehead, James, Dewey, Russell, Croce, Bergson, Sartre, Santayana and Wittgenstein. A practical common-sense view of the universe, as conducive to 'progress' (whatever that meant exactly to these writers as each followed the foot-steps of science), stressing clarity of a certain kind, represents something of the characteristics of the philosophy in common to these moderns. The notion of the Absolute gave place to the admissibility of pluralistic belief. With the advent of the "Logical Positivists" the limits of analytical philosophy seemed somewhat extended so as to admit within its scope logic, mathematics and linguistic studies for distinguishing what they called 'meaningful' from absurd assertions.

When one has reviewed all these philosophers, one notes that the latest of them, Wittgenstein, not only relied on logical syntax and semiotics, but began to question the very possibility of definitions. He is said to have been the most modern and the most puzzling of all analytical philosophers. We shall quote a paragraph from his *Philosophical Investigations* (section 77) to show the nature of the puzzle to which Wittgenstein directs his attention. Taking the case of two pictures, one sharply defined and a blurred one corresponding to it, he says:

> And if we carry this comparison still further it is clear that the degree to which the sharp picture *can* resemble the blurred one depends on the latter's degree of vagueness. For imagine having to sketch a sharply defined picture 'corresponding' to a blurred one. In the latter there is a blurred red rectangle: for it you put down a sharply defined one. Of course — several such sharply defined rectangles can be drawn to correspond to the indefinite one — but if the colours in the original merge without a hint of any outline won't it become a hopeless task to draw a sharp picture corresponding to the blurred one? Won't you then have to say: 'Here I might just as well draw a circle or heart as a rectangle, for all the colours merge. Anything — and nothing

> — is right.' — And this is the position you are in if you look for definitions corresponding to our concepts in aesthetics or ethics.[6]

The impossibility of clear definitions when we follow the way of *looking* rather than *thinking* — i.e., when we conform to an objective discipline in philosophy, is what Wittgenstein labours to make clear. Morton White, the editor of the book, himself estimates Wittgenstein's contribution to modern philosophy in the following words:

> Wittgenstein's passionate interest in describing the use of language without metaphysical presuppositions is reminiscent of Husserl. His interest in describing the role, job and function of words is like the pragmatists'. His hostility to Cartesian dualism and his preoccupation with shared, social linguistic activity sound more like John Dewey than Dewey or Wittgenstein would have dreamed. The notion that each word is embedded in a large linguistic context that swells into a 'form of life' *is certainly not utterly removed from idealism* . . . 'the meaning is the use' was Wittgenstein's most famous slogan and it applied ten-fold to his own words. To understand him one must read him and see the use of it.[7]

A philosopher who insists on seeing the use of words that cannot be defined clearly and depends on what he calls 'family resemblances' recognized by each person between instances of a concept such as 'game' or 'patch of colour' or even those notions such as 'good' etc. implying value, is in short a follower of Wittgensteinism as the latest expression of an idealistic positivism. The vaguer the definition — is taken to be the better the chances for the 'family resemblance' to operate in a useful or progressively scientific way. Such is the position which takes us far beyond the strict limits of empiricism which a Carnap or a Russell would set for modern philosophy. We have every reason to believe in this tendency a sly return to a new form of idealism, as Morton White hints at in the sentence we have italicized in the above quotation.

After stating that 'games' form a family based on certain connecting fibres, as it were, of 'family resemblances' which elude precise definition, Wittgenstein concludes:

> . . . if someone wished to say: "There is something common to

> all these constructions — namely, the disjunction of all their common properties" — I should reply: now you are only playing with words. One might as well say: "Something runs through the whole thread — namely, the continuous over - lapping of those fibres.[8]

The principle of 'continuity' referred to here as opposed to the principle of 'disjunction' referred to above, correspond to the vertical and horizontal aspects of existence as we have tried to distinguish them.

The Notion of Non-Dual Existence

Philosophy as understood in our day tends to be based on common-sense utility. Pure rationalism and idealism, which were considered that true domain of philosophy in the era of Descartes, Spinoza and Kant, have suffered a rude displacement in favour of something that 'works', or is 'provable' or demonstrable as in a laboratory experiment.

This tendency has been pushed to its furthermost limits and the diehards of the empirico-utilitarian school are still maintaining the ground they invaded with the triumph of science in whose wake they followed till now. But unfortunately for them, science itself is now turning speculatively philosophical. The material basis of matter is gone. A mathematical god is being visualized by disciplined scientists who lapse alternately into the language of mysticism or mathematics.

It looks as if the battle will be lost in favour of a new idealism. Such a prospect would be both good and bad. If all normative thinking should be lost, solipsism and sentimentalism would engender a crop of pseudo-scientific superstitions with dangerous consequences to civilization. The opposite danger is equally serious whereby in the name of scientific validity we might stand to lose our bearings in the world of worthwhile human values.

When the rigid experimental foundations of thought are failing on one side, and scientific thinking is invading the domains of pure thought on the other side, looking for new norms and meanings, it would be normal for those who take neither the side of empiricism nor that of mere rationalism, to discover a way to open up the blind alleys leading from opposite directions, by a revised and unitive methodology and epistemology. In this matter the *Vedānta* of India undoubtedly has some suggestive lines of thought to offer to the modern West.

The Existent in Śaṅkara's Philosophy

Vedānta philosophy generally and Śaṅkara's system in particular is built round the primary notion of *sat* or existence. The given, ontological real of here-and-now, although conceived as a unique abstraction along the lines of the 'prime matter' of Aristotle rather than as a hypostatized entity as with Plato, is the basic starting point of all *Vedānta* philosophizing. Prof. Lacombe of Paris in a whole work devoted to the notion of the Absolute according to the *Vedānta*, starts his chapter on Śaṅkara's notion of *sat* with the following bold generalization:

> *Vedānta* is a philosophy of being — *sat*. It is in this that, taken as a whole, its most central point of insertion in the tradition of the *Upaniṣad* resides.[9]

In the *Bhagavad Gītā* we find that this idea of *sat* as the basis of the existent in the strictly ontological sense is extended into notions of value and good or right action:

> In the sense of existence as well as in the sense of the good (the expression) *sat* is used. Likewise when speaking of worthy actions too this same term *sat* is pertinent, O Pārtha. (XVII. 26).

In the next and last chapter, the same vertical series of ontological levels from the most basic or generic to the most specific, expressing itself through possible activities in life, is again referred to as follows:

> The base, the actor, the instruments of action and activities of diverse kinds with God as the fifth here. (*Gītā*, XVIII.14)

A vertical series of ontological factors attaining to supreme specificity in God through intermediate stages in which activity is implied gives us a living picture of the human personality or spirit much after the manner of the moderns such as Bergson, whose words quoted above bear a family resemblance to the ontological approach implied in *Vedānta*.

The inversion of the *Vedānta* approach *vis-a-vis* the traditional occidental approach to the problem of reality is further clearly explained by Lacombe in the following passage from his book:

> The metaphysical problem *par excellence* for occidental philosophy is to conquer the two paradoxes in passing from things finite and relative to the being infinite and absolute.

> Daughters of Plato, the one as well as other, but all the same turning their backs to one another, two great doctrines separate from each other here; Aristotelian Greek and Medieval of being and of the pure act; Cartesianism with all it was followed by, which will soon be a philosophy of action. (p.35).

After devoting some additional paragraphs in which the course of Western philosophy is carefully traced from Descartes through Spinoza and Leibnitz to Kant, Prof. Lacombe goes on to sum up the position of Śaṅkara in respect of his existent reality of *sat* which participates to some extent in the notion of *substance* as known to the West. He then says:

> Thus while all our (Western) philosophy is constructed upon the primacy of Ideas or of "formal causality" the philosophy of Śaṅkara sets the pace deliberately for what we should call fundamental causality or substantial causality. It is not that it is unaware of the fecundity of being nor would it underestimate such, if one would well understand its generosity. But if it is true of other metaphysics than his, and not Indian alone, that the movement of return from the finite to the infinite is more profound, charged with greater sense — even to the extent of setting on one side its saving orientation — than the movement of departure, involution more authentic than evolution, this seems particularly true of the *Vedānta* of Śaṅkara, because for him the term of all evolution definitely coincides with its source: the final cause as well as the formal cause re-absorb themselves in the substance, and by way of consequence, the efficient cause also.[10]

We can now clearly distinguish two distinct trends in philosophy. To use Prof. Lacombe's expression, they are turning their backs on each other. Plato's ascending dialectics led him into the thin air of the world of the intelligibles, while Aristotle by an opposite tendency or trend in the progress of philosophic thought, went beyond matter and prior to it into another world of unique existential factors basic to matter and form.

The notion of substance was meant as an intermediate link between these two poles to which thought was drawn. Modern analytic or pragmatic philosophers who tended to discredit the idealism of Plato, did so because Plato's concept of Ideas, though sound from the point of view of abstract philosophy, could not lend itself as the foundation of a scientific or progressive civilization which believes in action rather than in calm contemplation.

However, with the admission of logic, mathematics and semantics into philosophy in recent times, a new phase in philosophic thought is being ushered in. This has at present the added support of a philosophy of science which itself is becoming more and more non-materialist. We have seen how Russell has long been convinced of the limits of empiricism and its inadequacy for philosophy in all its aspects. Carnap's position brings him to the verge of seeking worthwhile meanings in propositions which have to be demonstrable and useful. As we have just seen, Wittgenstein goes further into the mystery of meanings even of words such as 'game' or 'yellow' and says that no distinct notions can be formed by the mind about these in pragmatic ontological terms when we 'look' and do not 'think'. To him meaning has also to be useful. It is clear that an ontological concept of existence is being formulated afresh in modern philosophy. In such a task human values should not be shut out. The primacy of man's existence has to be conceded. A fresh normative notion for philosophy seems almost ready for birth. In this the notion of *sat* or existence as known to *Vedānta* will have at least a certain 'family resemblance' in the Wittgensteinian sense. Further aspects of this question will be examined when we take up 'subsistence' for consideration.

References

1. *Age of Analysis*, p. 116. Mentor, New York, 1955.
2. Quoted from Satre's *Existentialism and Humanism*, p. 122, *ibid.*
3. *Ibid.*, p. 124.
4. From *Creative Evolution*, pp. 74-75, *ibid.*
5. Quoted from *Modes of Thought*, p. 88, *ibid.*
6. *Ibid.*, p. 235.
7. *Ibid.*, p. 228.
8. *Ibid.*, p. 231.
9. Trans. from *L'Absolu selon le Vedanta*, p. 3. Paris, 1937.
10. *Ibid.*, pp. 37-38.

3

Subsistence

THE Visible world of positive or objective, experience is the world of *existence* which we have covered in the last chapter. Now we have to pass on to the next level of reality as we envisage it more subjectively through our minds or in terms of our consciousness.

Physical reality demands our attention when we are active and want to move about among the things or interests with which we are surrounded. But philosophy implies a more settled attitude. If in our everyday life we should fail to recognize the fact that things exist subject to the laws of mutual exclusion or contradiction, when viewed horizontally, we would be exposed to the danger of knocking against things and hurting ourselves. However, by treating things one after another in a certain intelligent order in time, we are able to circumvent this conflict of the rival claims of things at one and the same time: *One after another* in interests avoids conflict while multiplicity of interests at the same time would confuse us. A well ordered life of interests is one which can harmonize the vertical and horizontal values in life in a graded succession.

At the end of our last article we arrived at a point in critical philosophizing, such as that of a Wittgenstein where clear notions of things or ideas become impossible from the pragmatic angle. When we think of the meaning of such words as 'game' or even of 'a patch of colour', analytical and synthetical tendencies operate through our minds which make strict, cut and dried classifications or definitions impossible. Analysis has to be arrested at a certain point and synthesis established by the mind, for any useful, meaningful value to result from our attitude to even objective realities. Quality has to neutralize quantity. Human intelligence is ever selecting from a multiplicity of possible alternative interests. We balance between opposing factors. The order of interests in things depends on the unravelling of our instinctive dispositions from one stage of life to another.

Whether we picture this process as consisting of seven stages, as Shakespeare did, or into three with Śaṅkara (in his verses on Renunciation *Bhaja Govindam*), meaningful life is an organic process of the matching of outer and inner interests into unitive values prevailing with each person at a given period of his life-span. From the choice of instruments to help our hands to work, to the choice of abstract philosophical values, is the range of this organic process of the harmonious unravelling of human interests. If science or philosophy is not to lose its way in the ramifications of by-paths of possible interests, and if it is to be natural, meaningful or intelligent, then a series of vertical unitive values must be kept in mind, for the sake of methodical thinking within utilitarian as well as in purer idealistic philosophizing. True philosophy must keep an open mind and not limit itself in advance to the confines of any 'ism', however laudable or legitimate such might be in itself.

The Change-over from Existence to Subsistence

As we have seen, existence as understood in the context of the modern philosophy of Existentialism is not concerned with mere things, but is treated as a rival notion to *essence.* It has thus already encroached somewhat into the domain of rational or *subsistent* entities.

An actual chair or table enters into our consciousness by necessary forces of circumstances. The passive contemplative or philosophical mind, which is not committed to pragmatism or to mere utilitarianism, seeks truth for its own sake in a spirit of idealism. When a mild form of subjectivism is implied in such a philosophical attitude, we usually name it rationalism, as against vitalism where activity, and not thought, is the starting point. As more and more of the mind is admitted into philosophy, we get various grades of idealism as represented in Europe between Descartes and Hegel through Spinoza and Leibnitz. The modern tendency is to discredit the rationalists and question the very starting point of methodic philosophizing as understood in Descartes. His *cogito ergo sum* has been subjected to various adverse comments in recent times. Some of the critics are in favour of greater idealism, while others want to take away the 'will' implied, in favour of necessary factors of a work-a-day life. The German idealists after Kant stressed the primacy of the will in various degrees, from the basis of a mere 'presentiment' through the 'will to live' to the 'will to power'. William James and other pragmatists brought it lower down in the scale of human values as a 'will to believe' down to the notions applicable to the generality of working and striving human beings. By doing this they have brought true philosophizing to a blind alley. When closely examined Wittgenstein represents the *cul-de-sac* to which philosophizing is heading at the present moment, as we have noticed at the end of our last chapter.

To set healthy philosophizing on its course again, supported by common human wisdom, we have to put some order into the methodology and epistemology implied. It is here that existence is to be understood as passing correctly into subsistence. The former notion has been located by us as belonging to the base of the vertical axis of our scheme. As thought is not anything that stays put and stagnant within the mind of the philosophical investigator in his search for certitude about reality, it would be interesting to watch within ourselves the dynamism of the thought process which changes over from the levels of necessary existence, rising to the higher stage of subsistence, without any break in the continuity of the transition, as it takes place within us. Thought rises and circulates within consciousness itself and there is rhythm and an alternation implied here which, if we should miss it, would lead us into that characteristic puzzlement in philosophical thought to which we have already alluded.

Alternation

If we imagine ourselves pressing our hands on a table, there are two ways in which this event could be regarded. We feel the resistance of the solidity of the table on our hand, and conversely we are overselves exerting a pressure of which we are also conscious. The tendency among philosophers like Berkeley and Hume has been to give primacy to one or the other of these aspects. Dialectical methodology, however, demands that we show no partiality at all and treat both these aspects of sensation which belong to the afferent and efferent impulses in the nervous system, as meeting and neutralizing themselves as a central experience. Berkeley's idealism and Hume's scepticism could thus be reconciled as sides of the same coin of the central absolute reality.

The rationalist tradition of European philosophy of which Descartes may be said to be one of the greatest of founders, was a bold attempt to put body and mind together into a unitive whole, through the linking bridge of interaction between bodily and mental aspects through the famous idea of 'occasionalism'. This occasionalism was in the hands of a deity who matched inner and outer events. This bridge or link between the two aspects, mental and material, later became the 'substance' as understood in the philosophy of Spinoza. In his notion of the 'thinking substance' we arrive at something which is neither material nor mental but which links both unitively. How Leibnitz carried this idea further into his Monadology is a story which might lead us into an unnecessary digression here. God was the Monad of monads. In Kant's 'Free Will' and the 'Will as Presentiment', the 'Will to Live' and the 'Will to Power' we have further stages of later German idealism which attained full maturity with Hegel's full-fledged absolutism.

If we concede that existence or *sat* as understood in *Vedānta* marks the lowest point in a vertical axis of reality, subsistence may be said to mark the next higher level in the scale of vertical realities which come normally within the scope of a contemplative philosophy. When the last vestiges of the Cartesian duality have been effaced from pure idealistic philosophy, we can see the dynamism implied in the transition of existence in terms of subsistence reflected in Hegel, whose principle of negation (*negativitat*) is explained as follows:

> Negativitat is a principle both of destruction and of production. That which Negativitat produces on the positive and objective side of its work, is first precisely the world that at the outset the philosopher empirically finds as the realm of immediacy, the whole universe of experience. . .Negativitat finally as the 'negation of the negation' appears in a new constructive task, as the process whereby the rational unity of thought and the things of immediacy and mediation, of experience and reason, comes to light in the positive system of the philosopher.[1]

Double Negation in Hegel and Śaṅkara

The mechanism implied in Hegel's notion of the principle of the *Negativitat* bears a family resemblance to the principle of becoming which is implied as between the *sat* (existent) and the *cit* (subsistent) aspects of the Absolute as understood in the context of *Vedānta*. Prof. Lacombe explains for us the method employed by the Vedāntic teacher in dealing with the pupil who is initially only able to see the existent or empirical aspect of reality. The process of double negation, implied here as in Hegel above, belongs, as we can easily recognize, to the context of dialectical methodology:

> The Vedāntic doctor is not yet in the Absolute, or rather, if he philosophizes, it is for someone who is not yet in the Absolute; his whole task is to make it come, in relativistic terms of existence and of nature, so that in the end, one gets oriented towards it and finally discovers it. For the disciple there is but one reality: that of the empirical world; he has but the similar error of according to it that dignity which is too great, for the world is effectively, and in a certain sense, a complex of being and non-being; in any case it is from here that he should necessarily start. The second time will be from negation, negation of the negative of the things that are empirical, not of their positive. . .[2]

The professor goes further to direct our attention more minutely into the implications of the transition of *sat* into *cit* when he writes again *a propos* the philosophical position of Śaṅkara as follows :

> There is without doubt, in the empirical universe, duality of the subject and the object with a marked primacy, though not unconditioned, of the subject. But if the subject emerges from a depth which is indivisibly being and intellectual light — *sat* and *cit* — behind the object also, although the degradation may be more pronounced, there are again the aspects of being and of light which do not separate themselves from each other. In such a way it is that the profound identity of the subject and the object which is reality Absolute, translates itself into relativity by an osmosis and in the form of an exchange of substance as between the two orders, between the two 'attributes', to speak in the manner of Spinoza.[3]

Hypostatic and Hierophantic Substances

The notions of existence and essence have a central coupling notion in the word substance as understood in Spinoza in the West and as *cit* in *Vedānta*. The word substance is derived from the Latin *sub-stare* 'to stand under', which has its corresponding term in Greek *hypo-stasis* which has the same significance. From both words it is clear how the classical mind thought of substance as something that remained as the ontological basis of reality in the axis which admitted of the higher and the lower.

The notion of substance or *cit* supplied a neutral point where ascending and descending dialectical processes in thought met and neutralized each other. Although ascending dialectical thought is what is at first sight implied in the notion of substance, in the light of the dialectical methodology that we have developed elsewhere, it would be permissible for us, especially after the scrutiny of the mechanism of thought implied in the paragraphs quoted from Hegel and from the *Vedānta*, to add that both hypostatic as well as hierophantic entities or realities are to be treated as blending into the central notion of the 'substance' as it is to be understood here. As the process of double negation becomes asserted, substance begins to represent a positive value. When the notion of substance is understood without its positive or negative attributes, on neither of which it depends, we have the notion of substance corresponding to the notion of the Absolute itself which Vedāntins describe as *cin-mātra*, i.e., consisting purely of mind-stuff. Spionza's definition of substance brings the notion as near to the Vedāntic Absolute as the mind-stuff as could be imagined. Spinoza writes:

> By substance I understand that which is in itself and is conceived through itself; in other words, that the conception of which does not need the conception of another thing from which it must be formed.[4]

Elsewhere he makes it clear that God alone is substance, and continues:

> Everything in which there resides immediately, as in a subject or by means of which there exists anything that we perceive, i.e., any property, quality or attribute, of which we have a real idea, is called a *substance*.

If existence refers to a factor that is not essence but could be placed at the bottom of a vertical scale, while essence itself could occupy the top of the same scale, subsistence is undoubtedly a factor that, according to the best of rationalists like Spinoza, occupies the central position between the two extremes. Identified with the notion of God and as a factor sufficient unto itself, it could be no other than the Absolute itself understood realistically.

Ascent into the Specific Essence

When the contemplative has been able to think of substance as the pure mind stuff intermediate between its attributes of existence on the negative side and of essence on the positive side, the ascending dialectics that becomes implied thereby must carry him to interests and values understood both objectively and subjectively. The human personality is where unitive or integral values of import reside.

Starting as we did objectively with existence and rising dialectically into the domain of subsistence we could speak of the world of unique specific or positive essences belonging to the world of the intelligibles of Plato. These essences have nothing objective or substantial about them, but resemble pure ideas such as that of Beauty. Heavenly or celestial values consist of these essences. In the idea of God when monistically conceived, we have the unitive meeting-point of all essences fused into one.

The Beautiful, the Good and the True are attributes of essence, together with omnipotence, etc. The luminaries of the sky, insofar as they represent light, which is dialectically nothing other than the faculty of sight or even intelligence, is the domain where essences reside. In Western philosophy the transition between existence and essence is not clearly understood as a continuous correlating factor that runs through the gamut of all legitimately human values. In the context of the *Vedānta,* however, there is a subtle vertical link between such notions as the sapidity of the waters and the specific attributes of manhood in human nature. The two aspects of reality, the one which belongs to the order of being and the other which belongs to the order of the intelligibles, which is classical Western philosophy tend to be treated as an ambivalent pair of concepts, with a marked primacy in favour of the intelligible, tend to have a more unitive status conferred on them in the *Vedānta*. Existence and essence meet and merge their duality in a central notion of *cit* which is to be identified with *ātman* (the Self) as also with the notion of the Absolute (*Brahman*). We shall content ourselves with quoting one abstract from the pages devoted to this subject by Prof. Lacombe to bring out the nature of the vertical line of correlation that links, in a subtle implicit-explicit ambivalence, the two aspects of existence and essence in the context of non-dual Absolutism (*advaita*) as implied in Śaṅkara:

> The Indian conception of *essence* (the gamut of terms *svarūpa, svabhāva, bhāva, sāra* indicates this by itself) seeks to keep the two aspects together, by giving a philosophical value to the second, and for this, let us state it at once, it accords to the implicitness of being (and not surely to the sensible as such, it

> is not a question here of remaining in the empirical plane) a certain primacy over the explicit.[5]

The vertical line that passes through existent, subsistent and essential values, all with a unitive status, can be gathered from the verse of the *Bhagavad Gītā* where the two ambivalent polarities of the factors are referred to, together with the intermediate linking factors in the following manner. Kṛṣṇa, who is the representative of the Absolute understood in cosmological and psychological terms at once, describes, himself to Arjuna his disciple in the following striking words:

> I am the savour of the waters, I am the light that shines in the moon and the sun; I am the mystic syllable AUṀ in all the *Vedas*; I am the (intelligible) sound in space and what constitutes (specific) human nature in mankind. (*Gītā*, VIII.8).

Explicit and implicit human value-factors are thus treated without duality and with no primacy to one or the other in the epistemology and methodology of the *Advaita*.

Values are more than mere Concepts

In existence, substance and essence we have three grades of concepts lying the vertical axis of pure or absolute being or becoming. However, we have to remember that they are still only philosophical concepts sometimes understood subjectively and at other times objectively. They could also be understood semantically as a meaning common to subject and object. Even when understood in any one of these three possible ways, it does not become a living personal Value which would induce the unitive state of consciousness in its fullest sense. Existence, substance and essence have to fuse into a whole as a central Value that knows to distinction of subjective or objective. Like the kingdom of God which is within and as a pearl of great price and the leaven that leavens the whole lump, this central experience has further to be felt and known as within oneself in the form of a consciousness that is neither within nor without, as a global core of both being and becoming at once.

The realities of Aristotle and Plato have to fuse non-dualistically into a global and central core of personal life with which alone one can establish the most intimate of relations. Thus it is that by a long philosophical detour we arrive at the study of man, which is, as Pope put it, 'the proper study of mankind'. 'Know thyself' as the ultimate term of all philosophizing was also well-known as a dictum marking the term of Socratic philosophizing. *Ātma-jñāna* (knowledge of the Self) an *ātma-lābha* (gaining the Self) and finally *ātma-ārāma* (finding job in the contemplation of the Self) are also equally familiar notions of the Vedāntic context. The cosmological Absolute and the psychological Absolute may be said to be transparent to each other. When the two transparent pictures or schemes are brought one over the other, as it were, under a normative notion of the Absolute common to both cosmology and psychology, we cancel the tribasic prejudice of *tripuṭi* (subject-meaning-object).

Such a notion then attains to the status of the highest of human values. The analysis of this notion of Absolute Value and the dynamism implied in it, we shall reserve for a future discussion.

The point we have arrived at in the present discussion can be summed up as follows:

Existence starting in the mind of ordinary men who are not given to philosophy or contemplation, refers to a multiplicity of empirical entities given *a posteriori* to consciousness. They are there by necessity and imply mutual exclusiveness and they are subject to the principle of contradiction and conflict that goes with plurality of things or interests. Rival interests of men also complicate the situation from the psychological approach. The philosopher begins by negating multiplicity and tries to see existence in the form of global guiding interest in life. To be able to do this he has to see reality divested of its multiplicity and diversity. The savour of water is the subjective and conceptual version of the actual empirical entity. It is in the form of taste that water can find a place in our own subtler being or consciousness. This unitive hylozoic principle called taste in the water has its corresponding factors in the five elements (earth, air, etc.) when looked upon as conceptual principles lying in a vertical unitive scale of values linking the hierophanies of earth, air, and ether etc. till it comes out of the limits of existence and, by the process of an osmosis to which we have referred earlier, gets fused into the notion of subsistence or substance as more realistically understood. Substance itself, as we have seen, has its hypostatic attribute in the idea of essence. Essence as a *rasa* (prime taste or essence) or *bhāva* (state of being, existence) in *Vedānta* is treated non-differently as implicit in substance. Substance thus attains to a neutral and central position like a pearl of great price and emerges as a precious human value. Value itself has to be understood without actual or perceptual prejudices and with a dynamism all its own. To the consideration of Value itself we shall devote another chapter.

References

1. Baldwin, *Dictionary of Philosophy,* p. 458
2. *L'Absolu selen le Vedānta*, translated, p. 58.
3. *Ibid.*, p. 58 fn.
4. *Ethics*, I, Definition III.
5. *L'Absolu selen le Vedānta,* p. 51.

4

Value Dynamics

EXISTENCE and Subsistence between them have an osmotic interchange of aspects of reality. The notion of Substance that we have developed in the last chapter is itself the result of such an osmosis between the aspects of reality of existence and essence.

Now we have to understand how the two polarities involved lead to the emergence of the notion of Value which regulates human behaviour or conduct. Happiness with a capital H is the highest of human values. It is neither wholly mental nor material. If refers to the core of consciousness. This core can enter into bipolar relations with existent or subsistent realities so as to make for the central experience which we feel as Happiness. Within the gold coin of absolute Happiness there is implicit all other items of value, corresponding to small change.

Ranging from sense pleasures to the supreme peace of Self-realization there is a series of values, important or negligible, to the extent that bipolarity is implied in their inter-relations. Now if we should reduce this scale of values in an orderly fashion as being neither transcendent nor immanent, neither perceptual nor actual, we can see that we, in ourselves, represent a golden ladder of values as given to our contemplative imagination.

From the simple relation with a piece of bread to the supreme happiness of Self-realization we have within us a unitive Principle which is neither within nor without. The various objects of interest with which we are surrounded enter into this self-consciousness in the form of value-factors, emergent and neutralized at various levels as they float, rise, change or circulate in a certain organic or living manner. It is to this aspect of contemplative life that we refer when we use the expression Value Dynamics.

In focusing our attention here on such an aspect of the Science of the Absolute we must admit we are treading on very speculative ground.

Within ourselves, however, we shall decide not to overdo this kind of theorization. It requires the utmost mutual adoption between a Guru and a Disciple to be bold enough to tread most delicately on this contemplative ground. If at this stage we indulge in it here, it is by way of making it easy for the student of wisdom to be introduced to the spirit of the writings of the Guru. The present article is but a humble attempt to lead the seeker to the portals of that Wisdom Mansion where there are many apartments.

The Emergence of Value

Lodged, as it were within man, the personal consciousness relates itself to outside objects of interest through the windows of the sense-organs. Afferent and efferent impulses meet and neutralize themselves while the personality gets related to one interest-system after another in a bipolar manner. When the innate or instinctive disposition goes out to meet its own objective counterpart, a fusion occurs between the inner and outer factors, and there emerges unitive entities representing values.

A football on a lawn may be said to represent a whole-hearted item of interest to a boy of ten or twelve whose limbs call for activity. The adolescent seeks the intimacy of companionship in a person of the opposite sex. The sick man might relate himself to food or to an ideology with the tenacity of a drowning man to a straw. The husband represents a value to the wife and the wife to the husband. Their inseparability represents a value which is none other than what is derived from the gold coin of absolute Self-happiness.

When natural interests in the world of actual relations become unavailable or when the interests attain to purer rungs of the ladder of interests normal to life, there is a sublimation of interests at a higher level where purer emergent values are involved. We can visualize a contemplative ascent into the world of hypostatic values, such as the grades of intelligible interests known to the philosophy of Plato. The inverse process of a descent into the Aristotelian worlds of prime or hierophantic realities cannot be ruled out, in principle at least.

Thus within contemplative man there is a rise and fall of value factors which should be understood both realistically and idealistically at once. True philosophy has to take into its survey the whole of truth globally and not in fragments piecemeal. In doing so we have to visualize this rise and fall of value-worlds within ourselves. And this we share also at the same time with every other individual, whether we are conscious of this sharing or not.

The earth value, the water value, the wind value, the fire value, the value of the great etherial void which leads on to the values of the ego, knowledge and mind, by imperceptible gradations, as one level of value yields place to the next, from lower to higher, in a methodologically and epistemologically conceived succession must be brought within the focus of consciousness if we are to attain Self-realization in the full light of the Absolute which is nowhere and everywhere.

Such are some of the aspects of Value Dynamics.

Scale of Values

Values are not just things or mere concepts, but are both. Contemplative methodology must necessarily think of any kind of spiritual progress in terms of the sublimation of values. In the contemplative consciousness there is a circulation of values. This has its phases of positive and negative, actual or virtual, vertical or horizontal. The spotlight of values turns round like a red-hot splinter of wood which one might spin round quickly in circles or figures of eight in darkness. Inner and outer aspects fuse together in such a highly dynamic spot-light within consciousness at a given time.

Now if we should bring this constant movement in the flux of consciousness and conceive of an umbra and penumbra and a focal point in consciousness, as psychologists such as William James have done, as fitting into a Bergsonian picture of absolute reality, we must postulate two value-worlds as overlapping and coalescing. These consist of cosmological entities which, unitively, will yield a vision of a scale of values.

This scale of values is given to the contemplative mind which is interested in expressing philosophy in living terms. The proof of this is in the fact that great thinkers and artists from all over the world have referred figuratively to the higher and lower worlds. *Paradise Lost,* the *Divine Comedy* Goethe's *Faust*, and Jacob's dream of the ladder on which angels ascend and descend exchanging vessels of the elixir of life from which they drink, are all various ways of referring to the scale of values in life. We have further the important contributions of axiology and phenomenology which we must try to understand and fit into a unitive, globally living picture to what we call Value Dynamics. This, when formulated properly, would constitute an important branch of the wisdom of the Absolute as it refers to common human life.

Axiology and Phenomenology

We have seen in previous articles that the notion of Existence as understood in modern Existentialism is of the nature of a philosophical abstraction. Just as the mathematical philosopher by his abstraction and generalization can treat of many particular instances as comprised in a general and comprehensive notion, used as a symbol, so we have seen how terms such as Existence, Essence and Substance stand for perceptual, nominal or conceptual factors with which different writers are able to develop their inquiry into the nature of truth or the Absolute. We can profit by all of them as aspects of truth viewed from a particular point or angle. In fact, with the help of the scheme of frame of reference that we have been developing in these pages so far, we can put them all together into a global whole, so that Eastern and Western approaches to wisdom could meet on common ground.

Such an integration is possible without any patchwork eclecticism, unjustified syncretism or easy solipsism, but in a fully integrated scientific spirit. Existence and Subsistence have been examined by us already as verticalized factors in the scheme of the Absolute. We have just noted also that the emergence of the notion of value needs only the addition of personal interest to be brought to bear on the situation. When the osmosis between Existence and Essence is first accepted, and when the notion of a central Substance as a higher abstraction is understood, then the step to the emergence of a resulting value-factor where the consciousness of the seeker of truth is also included, follows in philosophical order.

Plato's idea of the Good and the scholastic version of this as the *summum bonum*, which is implied in all idealization from Plato to Hegel and Fichte and perhaps culminating in the personalism of thinkers like Max Scheler (1874-1928) imply not only phenomenology conceived in the abstract as the interplay of values, but more particularly personal values.

In order to locate ourselves correctly in the dialectical revaluation which has been taking place down the ages around this notion of personal values, whether theologically located outside man or psychologically within him, we shall mark our latest position by referring to the contributions made by the last-named philosopher.

Writing in Runes' *Dictionary of Philosophy*, Paul A Schilpp says:

> In common with other phenomenologists, Scheler's doctrine begins with the assertion of an inherent correlation of the essences of objects with the essences of intentional experience. His unique contributions lie in the comprehensiveness of his vision; in his interpretation of the value qualities of being; of emotional experience, especially love, as the key for the disclosure of being; of a hierarchy of concrete ('material' as against formal) values; of an analysis of 'resentment' as a thorough grudge, rancour, perverted emotional attitude towards the values of life; of his definition of 'person' as *the concrete unity of acts*; of this acknowledgement of total personality beyond individual persons; of his definition of 'ethos' as a preferential system of values determinative for the validity of any specific thought-forms; of his development of the *sociology of knowledge* as a distinct discipline within cultural sociology; and of his working out of a philosophical anthropology showing man's position in and towards the whole of being. (p. 279).

If we make certain reservations for the present in regard to the notion of the person (as italicised by us above) and the inclination to think of the person in the social context rather than as an isolated person finding satisfaction in himself (in the second phrase italicised), it is not difficult for the reader who goes through it carefully, to discover a striking summary of what we ourselves have in mind in regard to Value Dynamics. Quotations from other phenomenologists, axiologists and personalists could be multiplied. However, we shall resist this temptation and content ourselves by stating here that modern thought does think in terms of the dynamism of value-factors, and that this enables the imaginative and intuitive seeker of wisdom to build up for himself a global picture of the detached Self within as it enters into bipolar relation with its own non-Self, as it were, without.

The interaction of these two factors understood as taking place along a mathematically postulated vertical axis of reference or correlation is what we are at present interested in bringing to view. These poles of Self and non-Self could equally well be referred to as 'knowledge' and the 'known'.

Consciousness 'Of' and 'In' a World

From the *terra firma* on which we stand our consciousness rises into the starry firmament and soars above it into the subtler worlds of ever purer consciousness. We ascend thereafter still, from existent, subsistent or value-factors physically, mentally or intentionally. Our consciousness relates itself to different grades of worlds, some gross, some subtle, while the process of eternal change goes on cyclically like seasons within us. The outer seasons can also be reduced into pyscho-physical terms when we become conscious *of* a world and not as living *in* a world.

Thus there is a nature inside and a nature outside, both of which are of interest to us, sometimes together, sometimes alternately and even separately. Action gains primacy at a given moment and then it is the outer world of horizontal values which occupies the centre of interest in our consciousness. At another moment the spirit relies on itself and rests within a world where there is also a vertical positive and negative polarity.

The phases of alternation and circulation of value-factors as between the inner and outer natures with which the personality is always related, implies a taking over or appraisal of subjective values in terms of objective values, or *vice versa* at a given moment. In the game the ball is passed now from the outside to the inside, and from inside to the outside, and so the circulation goes on. To arrive at such a dynamic picture of the alternation and circulation of values according to a natural vital rhythm, we have only to read pages of the writings of Henri Bergson.

The phenomenology of personal values has to be put together in coherent vitalistic terms, giving credit to the various writers who in recent years have made valuable contributions to the subject. In axiology which is the study of the theory of value, and in phenomenology which starts from the study of what appears to pure intuition, wherein eminent modern writers have broken fresh philosophical ground with notions such as that of the principle called *Intentionalitat*, built up after laborious groundwork of idealistic philosophizing by writers such as Edmund Husserl (1859-1938) we have a picture of Value Dynamics which is coming more and more in line with what has been tacitly accepted in the East for ages.

This new science of Value Dynamics must have the philosophy of personalism added to it to give it coherence and unity. There is room in human nature for the whole of outer nature to be epitomized and contained in a concentrated or verticalized fashion. Theistic or cosmological personalism would also contain immanent and transcendental aspects of a world within with its own levels of immanence and transcendence which could finally coalesce in contemplative thought with the consciousness of the world around. In other words, our consciousness *of* a world outside would mean the same to us as our life *in* a world as understood in pure verticality. Pure consciousness which lives and moves through personal values, intentions and the creative urges of life, would thus have full freedom to relate itself to its highest value *in* and *through* itself by Self-realization.

Personal Intentions and Values Implied in Vertical Living

Existence, Subsistence and Value in the phenomenology of a whole-hearted and fully lived personal life have to be conceived in unitive terms without compartmental treatment. An integral personal life, which is that of a *yogī* in India or of a contemplative wise man as understood anywhere in the world has to be conceived in pure or vertical terms before what we have called Value Dynamism can make any meaning.

Keeping in mind the gold coin of Absolute Value, the personality in Man has its career of spiritual progress in and through the lowest of instinctive and mundane levels of small-change values right up to the highest value within its reach as an intellectual and conscious being. As man thus passes on in pure verticality of attitude from one life intention, interest or value to the next, living in a series of worlds represented symbolically by the five elements (earth, water, air, fire and ether) and then passing beyond them to that world of purer consciousness in a cosmological-cum-psychological sense, man rises from the values at the immanent pole to those at the transcendent pole. The course which is traced in this manner resembles that of a glacier which moves on its course leaving behind it all the grades of stones that it rubbed into shape or which obstructed it in its inevitable and necessarily imperative forward movement of becoming.

In order to help us to enter intelligently into a sufficiently critical understanding of such a Value Dynamism we shall direct our attention to three of its component aspects taken in a methodical order. The emergence of Value from the interaction of Existence and Essence through the notion of Substance is the first step in the understanding of Value Dynamism. Value emergence then takes place.

Axiological Dynamism

After the emergence of the notion of Value, in order to be able to see the rise and fall of values which know no distinction of being inside or outside of purified consciousness, we have to start with positive physical objectivity itself.

The earth conceived as an object is a symbol of all physical or material objects. Matter is a level in our consciousness which is capable of being taken into consciousness as a primary value. The very fact that it can thus enter consciousness is itself proof that it has the same status as consciousness. Otherwise, as a liquid cannot enter into a solid, there should have been no possibility of any osmosis or interchange between subjective consciousness and objective physical entities. The simple fact that we can be related interestingly to a stone or to the ground is evidence to show that some equality of status has been established between the two factors.

This relation becomes all the more evident when a person is able to say with conviction that he owns an object and can be sorry for its loss. We enter into everyday value relations with lands, furniture, or pet animals, not to speak of persons we love such as a child, a casual friend or a serious partner in life. The relation with coins goes without saying.

Modern axiology or the theory of values reaches back to the idea of the Good of the time of Plato. Its later exponents include his immediate disciple Aristotle who developed it in his *Organon, Ethics, Poetics* and *Metaphysics*. Stoicism and Epicureanism were philosophies based on the rejection or selection of right value in life. Theologians conceived of God as representing the highest of values as a *summum bonum*. Later, in Spinoza's *Ethics*, Kant's *Critique* and Hegel's dialectical approach to the Ideal of the Absolute, we have implicitly, various aspects of the modern science of axiology.

R.H. Lotze (1817-81) may be said to be the last of the moderns who still treated axiology unitively. His dictum that "that which should be is the ground of that which is" really brought him to the position of the later phenomenologists like Husserl who, as we shall see presently, introduced the idea of the worlds of intentions in which we live. Lotze's image of the world of values is contained in the following summary:

> Lotze's psycho-physically oriented medical psychology is an applied metaphysics in which the concept soul stands for the unity of experience. Science attempts the demonstration of a coherence in nature; being is that which is in relationship; 'thing' is not a conglomeration of qualities but a unity achieved through law; mutual effect or influence is as little explicable as being. It is the monistic Absolute working upon itself. The ultimate absolute substance, God, is the good and is personal, personality being the highest value, and the most valuable is also the most real.[1]

The changing world of phenomenological intentions and the personalism that refers backward and forward to the self within and to God above are all blended beautifully in the vision of this philosopher who is described as an empiricist in science, teleological idealist in philosophy, theist in religion, poet and artist at heart. His view on the nature of beauty puts the crown, as it were, on his unitive approach to dynamic values in life: "Unity of law, matter, force and all aspects of being produce beauty while aesthetic experience consists in *Einfuhlung* (entering of one's consciousness into that of another — empathy)".

Franz Brentano (1838-1907) in his *Vom Ursprung Sittlicher Erkenntnis* (The Origin of Moral Knowledge), by identifying value with love, gave to axiology a touch of absolutism and unitive coherence.

Phenomenology and Value Dynamics

If we should accept Lotze's dictum that "what should be is the ground of what is" we have already accepted in principle the central notion of the phenomenology of Husserl which he called *Intentionalitat* (German word, from the Latin, *intendere* meaning 'to stretch' — the stretching out of consciousness beyond itself).

Modern axiology leads up to phenomenology which takes over charge of the subject of Value Dynamics as we have tried to develop it here. The nature of the notion of Intentionality will make the contribution of philosophy in general, sufficiently clear to us, at least for immediate practical purposes. We quote here from Dorion Cairns, who writes under the subject *Phenomenology* as follows:

> Under the influence of Franz Brentano (1838-1917) Husserl coined the name *Intentionalitat* for what we saw as the

> fundamental character of subjective processes. The reflectively experienceble part of one's stream of consciousness is, on the one hand, consciousness of subjective processes as immanent in the stream itself and, on the other hand, consciousness of other objects as transcending the stream. The character of subjective processes as consciousness *of*, as processes in which something is intended, is a property they have intrinsically, *regardless of whether what is intended in them exists.*[2]

A careful scrutiny of the above paragraph will make it sufficiently evident that the global image of Value Dynamism that we are trying to evoke in our mind in this article for purposes of understanding contemplative Self-realization in a modern revised setting independent of traditions whether Eastern or Western, is sufficiently justified by the trends in modern philosophical thought.

The expressions 'Intention', 'subjective processes' and the corresponding 'consciousness *of*' such processes as referred to above, have to be put globally together into Self-consciousness as understood in a science of the Absolute. The last phrase in the above paragraph should be particularly remembered here. There is a type of contemplative abstraction here implied in the words "regardless of whether what is intended in them exists".

Phenomenology does not dismiss Existence but includes it in a revised form. We come close to a nominalist or conceptualist position here, but without its one-sidedness. Perhaps we could call it better 'Perceptualist' to avoid suggesting too much abstraction.

When the contemplative has been able to abstract himself correctly in this way, it will be seen that the processes in which intentions are involved as abstract value entities in life rise and fall and change over sides and circulate as in an eternal game. The very ground that is under our feet may be said itself to rise and become something higher in the flux within consciousness. Released from the cruel rigidity of horizontal factors and forces in consciousness itself, the gentle osmotic sublimation and circulation of value-factors in Self-consciousness requires intuitive imagination to visualize with all its implied flux of practical or pure dynamism. The contribution of modern phenomenology is thus of import to us here.

Personalism and Pure Value Dynamics

Placing the personality normatively at the centre of reality so as to view it in its proper perspective, proportion, unity and coherence in order that values in life may fall into a healthy gradation, orderliness or purposefulness, and to regulate thus the Self with the non-Self both in its cosmological and psychological aspects at once is not something new in the history of thought.

From the days of the Socratic dictum 'Know Thyself' and the corresponding 'Thou Art That' in *Vedānta*, and many similar utterances in the West such as that of Protagoras' (480-410 B.C.) "Man is the measure of all things", the tradition of putting together God, Man and the Universe in a single line of dialectical correlation has prevailed in human history.

The recognition of the same principle in the context of theology is found masterfully stated in the beginning of St. John's Gospel in the New Testament which reads: "In the beginning was the Word and the Word was with God; so the Word was divine and was in the beginning with God, and by Him everything had being, and without Him nothing had being".[3]

In modern thought empirical positivist and naturalistic tendencies asserted themselves, but from the time of Descartes we have had the same ancient tradition of personalism explicitly or implicitly contained in the various philosophers who followed the rationalistic leader. Bergson himself may be said to be its representative who lived up to the year 1941. Personalism persists in more recent times in its various varieties of theistic or phenomenological personalism with its many sub-varieties such as vitalistic personalism down to the political personalism (Mounier) of our own times. Borden Parker Bowne (1847-1910) has analysed for us its implications with particular reference to theistic personalism (of which he himself was a representative), in the following terms, from which we can derive the main features of the personalistic attitude applicable to the Value Dynamism. According to Ralph Tyler Flewelling, Bowne's analysis of personalism implies:

Metaphysically: the personal nature of the World Ground;

Epistemologically: a knowledge validated by the common source of thought and thing in the World Ground and mediated through personality;

Logically: the pragmatic assumption that life is superior to logical form;

Ethically: that values are real and based in the Cosmic Nature.[4] The crystallisation of reality viewed in terms of Value basing itself on the notions of Existence and Subsistence, thus occurs at a point where many branches of philosophy converge and focus themselves into a central notion of personality which is a Value to be understood with neither subjective nor objective prejudices. Absolute Self-knowledge given its proper central place in the Science of the Absolute thus arrives at its final phase in terms of a personalistic approach to reality.

The heart may be said to be the seat of this Person which combines the *Logos* and the *Nous* in one. The final stage of actualization or achievement of the still theoretical notion of the Person within each man would become clearer still if we avoid even the two Greek terms above, but simply look upon the Self as the personal entity who is capable of enjoying eating food. This eater of food within each man is a Person who is the same as the Supreme Self, the World Ground or the Absolute, when reduced to most practical and realistic terms. Thus the person is a simple everyday reality and the wonderful Absolute at one and the same time. In the constant interaction of the two aspects of the Absolute and their final absorption into sameness consists the essence of Value Dynamism.

References

1. Huri F. Leidecker, p. 184, Runes *Dictionary of Philosophy*.
2. *Ibid.*, p. 232, Italics ours.
3. *The Authentic New Testaments* tr. from original Greek by Hugh J. Schonfield, p. 451.
4. Runes' *Dictionary of Philosophy*, p. 229.

5

The Absolute and the Relative

THE Absolute and the Relative are terms variable and indefinite in their connotation. They depend much on each other for whatever overtly precise meaning they might each have as distinct expressions taken individually. Usual realistic objectivity is alien to them. They are thought of better with the eyes shut than with any particular concept or object in the work-a-day sense.

Even when one of these terms is allowed to lend meaning to the other by contradiction, contrast, or reciprocal correlation, the resultant certainty about anyone of them suffers to the extent that the meaning depends on or is derived from, the other. The Relative with the capital letter is meant in contemplative language to be absolutely relative, and the Absolute likewise to be so without any trace of the relative adhering to it even as a vestige of import.

They are in reality a dialectical pair of related terms or counterparts which have to be placed in the epistemology and methodology of the absolutist way of thinking, which is dialectical rather than rational. In other words they are dialectical counterparts which, by their very nature, have to be thought of both at once or as nearly together as possible, so that the mind can take in the neutral meaning between them, at one stroke or effort.

The Crowning Gift of Wisdom

A trained dialectician could contemplate both these terms together as belonging to a common context of inward experience. Then there is a vague sense given to the 'inward eye' to use the expression of Wordsworth (when he wrote about the after-imagery of the daffodils in his 'vacant' and 'pensive mood' after he had seen a group of those flowers dancing before his vision). The pale gleam of vague meaning which might float across the consciousness of a sensitive person when thinking of the meaning of these terms together, is in fact the result of a contemplative operation of the human mind or spirit. To have such a contemplative intuition is the privilege of the human mind, and the true dignity and distinction of man depends on this gift of intuition.

This crowning gift of wisdom is what makes human life dignified and superior to the rest of vegetative or animal life, especially when such a gift or higher faculty could be consciously and purposefully employed in regulating human affairs both in the individual and collective sense.

The Absolute has a substantive, and with the definite article prefixed to it, assumed in language, especially in recent years, a definitely recognized and respectable status.

In ancient Greece it referred to the cosmic matrix of the Ionians, the One of the Eleatics, the Being or the Good of Plato, the World of Reason of Stoicism, and the One of Neo-Platonism. In patristic and scholastic Christianity it referred to God, and the God of the mystics of Europe such as Erigena, Hugo de St. Victor, Nicolas of Cusa, and Boehme, was also the Absolute, as a singular and unique entity.

Present Status of the Notion of the Absolute

The recognition of the Absolute as an entity, notion or value factor, both in its cosmological and psychological setting and, generically, in various sciences like logic, ethics, aesthetics, etc., is therefore neither ancient nor modern. Mystics, seers and sages both in the East and in the West have relied and made use of the terms from the most ancient times to the present-day. After the dawn of the age of enlightenment in Europe however, these terms went into disuse and disrepute with the spectacular progress of sciences such as mechanics. In recent years, after Hegel and Bergson, philosophy is again paying attention to these important concepts, without however attaining to any exactitude in regard to them.

In order to indicate roughly where modern knowledge stands in respect of these notions we quote the following from the *Columbia Encyclopedia* (II ed., 1951).

> *Absolute:* In philosophy the opposite of relative. The term has acquired various widely variant connotations in different philosophical systems. It means unlimited, unconditioned or free of any relation; perfect, complete or total; permanent, inherent or ultimate; independent or valid without reference to a perceiving subject. In logic absolute means certain or

indubitable as opposed to probable or hypothetical. As a substantive the absolute is the ultimate basis of reality, the principle underlying the universe. Theologically it is synonymous with, or characteristic of God. Philosophically it may be considered as the unknowable, the thing-in-itself; as that ultimate non-relative which is the basis of all relation; as that ultimate all-comprehensive principle in which all differences and distinctions are merged. The concept of the absolute was present in Greek philosophy. In modern days both realists and idealists have used the term, but it is perhaps most intimately connected with Hegel's absolute idealism. For Hegel and his followers the absolute is the all-comprehensive mind.

Paradox Explained

It is to be doubted if anyone would be the wiser for reading such a description of the Absolute. The paradox implied in one of the clauses above must be striking even to the casual reader, for it is also said to be "that ultimate non-relative which is the basis of all relation". Whether paradoxes of this form are even permissible in modern definitions is also a pertinent question here. Since we find paradox being relied on by even the best of modern writers, it must be taken for granted that it is so, and the only sense in which we can justify it is when we admit that the dialectical way of thinking of two propositions, predications or logical terms at once, which is at the bottom of the dialectical method, is tacitly employed in all thought where pure reason is concerned.

We shall try to justify this in some of the sections that follow. Meanwhile, let us agree that both these vague terms refer to realities of a *contemplative order* and that they have to do with *purposeful living*. Further, they belong to the domain of the *unitive* and the *universal* contexts of *inner* life. The Relative is a given starting point which is natural to man. The Absolute is a target to be reached or a state of plenitude in Wisdom. In the latter case the Absolute is neutral between the extreme poles of the Relative and the Absolute unitively conceived, as both belonging to an axis of reference, dialectically understood. The implied paradox above can only then be justified.

Double Negation and Double Affirmation

Contemplative, mystical or spiritual progress may be said to consist of the transition from the merely relative first to *the Relative* of the absolutist context, and then to the ultimate Absolute of the same context. There is an ascent and a descent involved here which have to be figured out clearly. The first part of the ascent is when the unreality of the multiple values in which life is caught, is consciously denied by the subject. This is double negation. Simultaneous with this, the positive pole of the Absolute, which gets lost in its own specific attributes, descends reflexively into oneself by a process of double affirmation. Even in grammar we know that two negations make a positive, and in algebra two pluses give again an affirmation. Neutral plenitude of the Absolute Consciousness is the term of spiritual progress, where progress itself is, as it were, countered by double assertion.

To What Purpose?

When we realize that the term Absolute has no definite content at all, especially when it is placed between the two poles of the axis comprised by the Relative and the Absolute, we should legitimately ask ourselves why such a term came into vogue at all. What purpose does it serve in human life? We all know that private or relative truth is the most dangerous element in life. It is by virtue of unitive, universal or Absolute Truth that we can understand the interests of a neighbour who might want the same thing as one does oneself at the same time.

To avoid human conflict, as across frontiers, actual or ideological, the absolutist outlook is the only remedy. For this reason it has been said that the truth shall make one free, etc. This is the practical purpose of the Absolute in everyday human life.

We know also that human beings, fortunately or unfortunately, are not mere animals. They crave for what are called contemplative or higher satisfactions and do suffer from spiritual loneliness or from intellectual cravings. Purposeless living leads to frustrations, keener than hunger from want of bread. There are many individuals we can see in common life who are misfits or dissatisfied persons and who would continue so, even when the possibility of a plain life would be open to them. The gambler and the cheat, the dictator and the demagogue, the passionate and the ambitious, the prodigal and the profligate, the fanatic and the martyr, are human beings who behave peculiarly because they are seekers of the Absolute in their own ways.

The evil represented by the devil and the good represented by the deity both mark the range and amplitude of an axis within which human nature seeks self-expression. All are caught necessarily in a process of creative becoming called life. In each case the relative pole within seeks compensation by means of a positive pole which might be 'objective' but yet within consciousness. Inner and outer values cancel out into satisfactions at every stage of human life. After establishing oneself in a unitive attitude on the plane of relative interests, the personality attains to the positive Absolute, and then again by introspection there is a descent into the neutral plenitude of the Absolute when, as Plotinus would put it, the "flight of the alone to the Alone" would be completed. When double assertion in the context of absolutist contemplation succeeds more and more, the tail end of negation dwindles automatically by double negation, simultaneously, into nothingness. Then the full Absolute with a capital 'A' fills the whole of consciousness with its light of Wisdom.

Initiation into the Way of the Absolute

All religions are recommendations to attain the Absolute Value in life. Some are theistic, others are not. Some stress one aspect of absolutism at the expense of others. Sometimes history accentuates some special absolutist trait which gives them a certain necessary colouration or character which is not of their essence. All religions tend to become static, although intended to be dynamic. There is also a closing tendency which invades them all, depending on the balance religions are able to keep between orthodoxy and heterodoxy of a certain spiritual expression, at a given time or place. When these forces are neutralized in the pure dynamism of the Absolute, which is the central value implied in all religions, and when they are stated in unitive, universal or open terms, the essential content of all religions tends to be the same. It is in this sense that the *Bhagavad Gītā* declares that "all paths lead to Me". (III.23, IV.11) Here the personal pronoun is meant to refer to the Absolute as understood systematically in the various chapters of this contemplative text-book of dialectics. In the same sense, the statement, "I am the light of the world" by Jesus is also to be understood.

Religious initiation into the fold of no matter what religion, when scientifically understood, means only affiliation to the unique way of life as conceived by any particular religious growth, as helping to attain the Absolute.

All religions thus come to have the narrow path of the needle's eye through which only those who are chosen can pass. Those who are lost in the multiple interests of relativist life, not within the context of the Absolute, are excluded from the Kingdom of the Absolute. A unitive and universal, open and dynamic attitude, balanced between orthodox and heterodox tendencies, and equipoised between the poles of relativism and absolutism, according to necessities or contingencies of life as it unfolds, is the way that one who is affiliated to the Absolute has consciously and scientifically to follow. All spiritual effort or aspiration could thus be conceived as the same, under the aegis of the notion of the Absolute. It would thus be possible by a science of the Absolute to pave the way for human solidarity even on the basis of *One Religion* for Man.

Einstein and Newton

Modern science is a measurement of objective phenomena, of which motion is a typical instance. Motion takes place in space and time and, when great distances are not involved in any measurement of an event of short duration, Euclidean space and Newtonian ideas of motion tend to hold good one hundred per cent. Thus it is that space and time happened to be treated as absolute factors by classical science, and Gravitation with a capital letter was also naturally raised by the classical scientists to the status of an absolute entity.

In cosmological or astronomical measurements which involved a longer time-span and a larger space-extent, this rigidity had to be relaxed. For one hundred per cent correctness of the measurements of the phenomena involved, a norm based on the velocity of light had perforce to be adopted. The Special Theory of Relativity put forward by Einstein in 1905, which served this purpose, was only meant to be a supplementary *theory* and not a law. It was not intended to displace Newtonian physical notions altogether. On this point we read in the *Columbia Encyclopedia* (p. 1657, II Ed., 1951) the following sentence:

> In most phenomena of ordinary experience, the results from the application of the special theory approximate those based on Newtonian dynamics, but deviate greatly for phenomena occurring at velocities approximating the speed of light.

Without entering into the intricacies of the higher mathematics involved here, it would not be difficult even for a layman with some intuition, to see that Einstein was not abolishing the absolutist standpoint of Newton, but only taking away the emphasis Newton puts on measured Euclidean space and mechanistic units, in favour of giving the same absolutist status to the Velocity of Light. The velocity of light is given the central position as a *norm* in the measurements Einstein was interested in making. In the Unified Theory of Relativity that Einstein put forward in 1950, sub-atomic and electromagnetic phenomena are studied from a relativistic standpoint. To suit his purpose he gave primacy to the *Velocity of Light* as an *absolute* norm of measurement, without expressly stating it to be so.[1]

Need for an Integral Science

The evaluation of the Unified Theory of Relativity is still to be made by scientists. Relativity and absolutism are the two rival standpoints involved here. A correct methodology for any science based on an epistemology that would give to all branches of science their proper place, is here to be envisaged, if the rival claims of scientists are to be fitted into *one* body of higher human knowledge.

The integration of the sciences is what is involved here. When properly formulated, such a science could be called a Science of sciences. Correct notions of the Absolute and the Relative would have to be first outlined before the foundations for such a science could properly be laid. The notion of the Absolute will necessarily occupy the central place in such a science, as a normative principle of all thought.

It is encouraging to note that in recent years the interest in the Absolute and the Relative is on the increase. Human unity and solidarity demand more and more that all knowledge be integrated and restated, and the evils of specialization and over-departmentalization be effectively counteracted. In our own days the pet theories of individual religious teachers, mystics, philosophers and theoretical scientists cannot be expected to remain in particular pockets or preserves, but must tend to be shared on a world scale.

Printing, reading and listening-in to the words of others are becoming more and more common throughout the world. Isolated norms of thought have to banish their barriers and world-wide unity of knowledge has to be made an accomplished fact. Whether in politics, religion, education, economics, sociology, domestic or family life, unitive norms belonging to a Science of the Absolute have to be formulated and fixed.

Each science must have its central absolute notion or normative principle and its proper frame of reference. The age of the earth according to Geology is at present different from that arrived at by calculations based on thermodynamics. The layman does not know whom to believe. Many scientists take upon themselves the role of philosophers, accepting no normative regulating principle between themselves, and much pseudo-scientific literature is being put out to mislead the common man.

Recent Appraisals

A proper notion of the Absolute, with a methodology and epistemology that would properly belong to it, would help us to put the whole house of Wisdom in order. The desirability of such a preliminary step cannot be over-emphasized at the present stage when the whole world needs at least to be mentally integrated even as a mere measure of safety or precaution. Meagre and hesitant as it still remains, the following information, brought together in respect of the Absolute, summarizes recent trends in formulating more clearly than hitherto, this all-important notion, on which the future of humanity depends so much for its solidarity. Continuing from where Hegel and his followers left off, Wilbur Long, a contributor to the *Dictionary of Philosophy* (D. Runes, New York, Indian edn. 1957) writes:

> Until recently, however, it (the Absolute) was commonly incorporated by the Absolute Idealists to connote with Hegel the complete, the whole, the perfect, i.e., the real conceived as an all-embracing unity that complements, fulfils or transmutes into a higher synthesis the partial, the fragmentry and the self-contradictory experiences, thoughts, purposes, values and achievements of finite existence. The specific emphasis given to this all-inclusive perfection varies considerably, i.e., logical wholeness or concreteness (Hamilton), mystical feeling (Bradley), aesthetic completeness (Bosanquet), moral perfection (Royce). The Absolute is also variously conceived, by this school as an all inclusive Person, a Society of persons and as an impersonal whole of experience. (p.2)

After being thus amplified in its scope and content by post-Hegelians, the notion has broadened out still further and grown out of the limits of the particular philosophy of the Absolute Idealists. It is interesting to note for the first time that the contributor referred to in this case, does not omit to allude to Eastern contributions to the meaning of the Absolute. Under the same article he continues:

> More recently the term has been extended to mean also (a) the All or totality of the real, however understood, and (b) the World Ground, whether conceived idealistically or materially. It thus stands for a variety of metaphysical conceptions that have appeared widely and under various names in the history of philosophy. In China: the *Wu Chi* (Non-Being), *T'ai Chi* (Being) and, on occasion, *Tao*. In India: the Vedāntic *Ātman* (Self) and *Brahman* (the Real), the Buddhist *Bhutatathatā* (indeterminate Thatness), *Vijñaptimātra* (the One, pure, changeless, eternal consciousness grounding all appearances), and the Void of Nāgārjuna.

The Scope of Wisdom

While writing these concluding paragraphs on the importance of understanding correctly and more completely the content of these intriguing terms, the Absolute and the Relative, the present writer has before him some press reports about the Roy Jacobsen controversy with Columbia University in which Dean Lawrence Chamberlain, speaking for Columbia, states categorically that wisdom is only a "hoped-for end product of education" and that neither Columbia nor any other institution could teach it. (See *Values*, Feb. 1958, p. 159).

This statement is a pointer that comes to us at this very moment, which is enough to indicate that what Max Lerner, writing in the *New York Post* commented was quite correct and to the point. He wrote: "That solitary and glittering word 'wisdom' is a word that has almost dropped out of the current turmoil *which rages round science and power and the weapons race*". (italics ours). He further complains that the present policy in educational budgeting is "Billions for research but not one cent for wisdom". It would see that humanity should give up seeking wisdom and instead console itself with dangerous toys which might bring about the extinction of the race. No, the heritage of wisdom is of the highest value for even the common man, and human beings have a natural birthright to it. The ends and means confusion in the Dean's statement given in the above controversy in what keeps us from reaching out boldly for what is naturally ours. Let us first decide, like Roy, that we want wisdom, and it will be seen that it is already within reach. Wisdom is not a commodity in the market or to be manufactured in any 'mind-plant' like Columbia, but it is to be sought first within oneself. Teachers have to be found who can establish the correct personal relations in education. Relativistic knowledge is what may be seen in the form of shadows by men who turn away from the bright light of the Absolute. Even to want to know the Absolute takes much wisdom. In discovering what we even want, the distinction between the Relative and the Absolute is important as the merest starting point. It is hoped therefore, that this chapter needs no apology.

Reference

1. Alonzo Church, (article contributed under "Relativism" in the *Dictionary of Philosophy*, D. Runes, New York, Indian Edn. 1957) is seen to corroborate this view when he writes: "But on the other hand, the relativity theory represents as absolute certain things which are relative in the classical theory, e.g., the velocity of light in empty space".

6

The Philosophy of Necessity

PHILOSOPHERS are of two kinds — those who work upwards and dialectically ascend from the given, objective, empirical reality to a supreme or pure reality free from all worldly taint; and those who work downwards digging deep into the potent principle of 'necessary' or given existence.

The dictum of the scientists as seen emblazoned on the insignia of the Royal Society of Science, London says, "We believe what we see". Any philosophy, therefore, that stems out of the scientific outlook gains its impetus from the 'objective' mode of investigation and has a down-to-earth quality which could be included under the philosophies of necessity.

As against such philosophers of necessity there are large numbers of philosophers who approach reality from a high ivory tower of luxury as it were. Rare Platonic concepts and hypostatic entities are postulated by such philosophers who miss the common touch. Such an attitude of the privileged is often open to the charge of trying to run away from the facts of life.

While philosophers tend to ascend into the rare world of the intelligibles or hypostatic entities, there is at the present time a large and growing volume of philosophizing that puts the accent on the existent or the necessary. Rational or ethical religions, such as Buddhism and Jainism, could also be included among those that follow the objective trend of science. When we find such factors as 'suffering' and 'hunger' being treated as the central notions in old schools of thought such as the Buddhist or even in such new ideologies as that implied in the Marxian movement, it is easy for us to see that the trend which distinguishes the 'philosophy of necessity' is neither out-moded nor even new-fangled. Like the Lokāyatika or the Sāṁkhya schools in India which date back to Vedic times, the tradition of the philosophy of necessity has been perennial.

Food as a High Value

The Tamil *Kuṛal* (verse 18) has this characteristic outlook when it states that the gods of heaven would forfeit the offerings made to them if there should be no rain falling on earth. The *Bṛhadāraṇyaka Upaniṣad* (1.iv.10) refers to the jealousy of the gods when philosophers become over-wise. The *Bhagavad Gītā* (Chap. 18) preaches the downright philosophy of Absolute Necessity when it asks Arjuna to 'do or die'.

In the West these two complementary and compensatory movements in thought have been represented by the schools of Plato and his disciple Aristotle. The former may be called the philosopher of contingent ideas and the latter the philosopher of necessary fact.

The philosophy that the Guru represents has been one that follows the middle way of dialectics which neither descends into matter nor ascends into thin air. At the same time it attempts to reconstruct a world philosophy which is not the preserve of the privileged intellectual aristocrat. This middle path is the line which strings vertically or in the form of a garland all unitive, universal and essential human values in a series touching all possible items of human happiness, joy or bliss, from those 'of earth earthy' to those that belong to 'the pure worlds above'. All these values may be conceived serially or could be brought under one supreme head of human Value called Happiness with a capital 'H'.

Let us take the case of food as a primary human necessity. Maṇimehalai, the wisdom heroine of South India, while preaching the high Wisdom of the enlightened Buddha, is described as follows:

> To those suffering from pain of the body,
> Being eaten away by hunger,
> Maṇimehalai appeared with the feeding vessel.

If we should think of a man about to die of starvation, we can easily imagine what a loaf of bread or a bowl of rice would mean to him. His need could attain to the white heat of an Absolute Necessity. The bread on the one hand and the absolute hunger on the other are counterparts in a common human situation or 'moment' which could be subjected to a dialectical philosophical treatment. The two factors could be made to equate to each other, cancelling themselves out into a central human value which could be indicated as 'Food'. When viewed in the universal context of human necessity and unitively understood philosophically or contemplatively, the Food would gain the status of an Absolute with a capital 'F', which would glorify or spiritualize it as a supreme Value.

Such a Value would fill with its content the vacancy implied in the notion of the Absolute understood in any academic philosophy.

Common Need for Happiness

The *Vedāntins* of the Śaṅkara school treat pure being (*sat*) as the content of the Absolute. The Buddhist *Vijñāna-vādins* give the same status to active understanding or conscious will (*vijñāna*). Even the Grammarian school of Pāṇini who approach philosophy through semantics (word or *logos*) have the concept of the *sphoṭa* which gives content to their notion of the Absolute. Those Buddhists who belong to what is called the Middle or Central Way (the *Mādhyamikas*) treat the purer notion of *śunya* or *prajñā* as the core of the content of the notion of the Absolute. If all these precious values could be treated as giving content to the notion of the Absolute, it could be legitimately claimed by us without any violation of the canons or norms of philosophical thought that actual values of everyday life within the framework of a true human situation could fill the same vacancy as that of the Absolute with a more living, real and practical content than in the instances given above.

Thus we arrive at an everyday philosophy of necessity in which a ripe fruit would gain as holy or spiritual or absolutist a status at least as important as a hypostatic entity such as an angel or godhead. The *Upaniṣads* refer to *annam* (food) as *Brahman* (the Absolute) on this same principle.

Ranging from the most ordinary of human values which fall within the domain of necessity, we could enumerate unitive human values which go beyond 'practical' necessity but continue into 'purer' items of necessity that could quench the intellectual or spiritual thirst of man. Knowledge is itself an inevitable necessity that is natural to the human species (*homo sapiens*). Thus the distinction between 'mundane' and 'celestial' necessity would be abolished and all necessities would attain an equal unitive status and fill the same vacancy that the Absolute represents. The *Bhagavad Gītā* (VII.7) refers to such a string of pearls representing all values.[1]

Taking the whole of humanity, if we could think of one general item of necessity which motivates and regulates each and every action or strife of man it could be stated both philosophically and scientifically to be Happiness. Happiness is a supreme necessity and constitutes the common goal of all beings, especially all human beings. The goal of the philosophy of necessity leads us to recognize Happiness with a capital 'H' as the supreme common, unitive and universally necessary Value for mankind. Happiness may even be said to constitute the *One Religion* of mankind.

Reference

1. "All that is here is strung on me as rows of gems on a string."

7

The Absolute is the Adorable

WE have seen in the last chapter how hard it is to fix definitely the notion of the Absolute. But the vagueness, instead of being a drawback, is really a strong point. As seen from the mechanistic angle of life the domain of contemplation is itself vague and nebulous.

Although this notion is as elusive and vague as it has always been, there is a general aspiration on the part of humanity as a whole to reach out towards it and grasp it. The Absolute is the much-prized pearl of potent power in human affairs. All religions are attempts to formulate doctrines about it. A great deal of human energy is absorbed in efforts or aspirations directed towards this end. It may even be said to constitute the one master interest unconsciously or consciously regulating human affairs.

The Absolute would be truly Absolute only when it absorbs the Relative into itself after giving it an equal status under the notion of the Absolute. The Central Absolute that would emerge would then reign supreme in all its neutral glory. It is thus that we arrive at the possibility of the notion of the Absolute as the Adorable.

Such a notion has hitherto been understood as belonging properly to the domain of religion of theology. But this need not necessarily be so hereafter. It would be possible with the help of more modern mathematical and intuitional reasoning or logistic to think of the Absolute even as the Adorable, in a more positive manner without even the limitations of that natural religion that Auguste Compte and others imposed on such a subject. Modern thought has focused itself more precisely on this notion than hitherto, and ancient precedents of both the East and the West can now be relied on for support in this matter.

The normative principle in ethics can also be derived from this norm of all norms as understood in a proper Science of the Absolute. We can go still further and state that values such as the True, the Good and the

Beautiful, as well as Just and even the Holy, can be derived from this central notion.

The state of spiritual perfection, self-realization or of the superman would not fall outside the scope of a science which has the norm of the Absolute as its centre. This can be recognized if we understand initially that the Absolute is neither a thing, a mere meaning, or just a high value. It would come nearer to a simple *trait d'union*, a mere hypen, or a unitive copula connecting dialectical counterparts at the core of human consciousness, consisting of existent, subsistent and value elements within itself as well as in the world of its interests.

The Epistemological and Methodological Home of the Absolute

The notion of the Absolute has to be understood in a setting that is properly its own. It belongs to the world of the unitive and the universal. Mechanistic rationalism can carry us only to its outer fringes. Pluralistic amorphous relativity is the domain proper of the world of conflicting multiple interests which the faculty of ratiocinative mechanistic logic can envisage.

But when we shut our eyes against sensible objects which absorb our mental energies spending themselves among objects of rival interest in work-a-day waking life or in the world of active dreams involving cerebration of some sort, there is still within consciousness room for an inner zone of self-consciousness where the self feels a vague satisfaction or yearning, exaltation, or depression. The self equates itself to its proper counterpart, the non-self, through adopted interests. Grades of reality representing the non-self become interesting to it. From the necessary limitations of the world of actuality or levels of existence, the self can raise itself through contemplation to a more perceptual world which, though still subject to formal logic in the mechanistic sense, can yet free itself and be emancipated. This world of meanings and sounds allows the subjects to use logic or dialectic or both for supporting itself and thereby raising itself to higher and higher contemplative levels.

Beyond even this world of subsistence there is the third stratum within the make up of the self-consciousness of man, which enables him to equate himself to grades of value-systems. Interest in value-systems of the global non-self can make the self elevate itself or climb down from a vertical scale, in which the Absolute itself seen as a *trait d'union* moves, as on a sliding scale. The range of human values and interests can play higher or lower notes in life in any given case at a given time. An alternating process of regression and progression is to be imagined here.

In other words, the Absolute in living terms is a principle regulating inter-relations at the basis of individual and collective life. It lies buried deep in consciousness. It is not concerned directly with the objects that absorb bodily energies. It moves from the levels of reality that are natural and instinctive and is ever reaching out to intersts that are placed higher in the scale of human values. A double movement of ascent or descent is implied in spiritual or contemplative progression, and in adjustment through regression.

The living consciousness of man is ever dynamic. It seeks the open light of Wisdom. Wisdom which is the synonym of the Self and of Happiness, represents the Absolute, depending on the aspect of spirituality in which one is interested at the given moment. Wisdom seeks its own home prospectively or retrospectively, along the axis where pure duration prevails in consciousness. The moment of the eternal present touches the centre of consciousness when contemplation is well established.

Being and Becoming Meet in the Unitive Absolute

Being and Becoming are aspects of the same Absolute that meet unitively in the eternal present. All possibilities of contradiction and mutual exclusion become effaced in the unitive notion. The irreducible paradoxical difference between the Relative and the Absolute will be finally eliminated when dialectical reasoning is correctly employed.

Viewed dynamically and statically, both in the open sense and in the closed, with the finalized notion of the Absolute as the central normative principle, a regular science becomes possible. Such is the subtle mode of operation or the mode of life as seen in a methodological and epistemological setting proper to this most important factor. This is how the Absolute may be intuitively understood as living and moving within its own proper four walls and its own framework of reference.

Degrees of Duality in the Logic of the Absolute

Although dialectics is the proper instrument for the appraisal of such a unitive Absolute, as a Deity to be adored or as a God to be worshipped, in practice certain concessions have been made in order to vulgarize the notion for popular consumption. A subtle form of logic, not strictly logical, has then been consciously employed. The pure and practical aspects of the notion have been juxtaposed and treated together inclusively or exclusively, disjunctly or conjunctly, by various systems of theology or schools of philosophy. Strictly speaking, when dialectics is correctly employed there should be no room for any duality at all. Dialectics, however, is an instrument that only the most versatile can employ. Mythology, fable, parable, allegory and analogy are the other second best alternatives with which to try to bring the notion of this unitive Absolute within reach. Statically codified theologies have tended to get formulated in all climes and at all times in the eternal attempt to place a worthwhile central value and give hope or purpose to human endeavour.

The *Bhagavad Gītā* refers to the difficulty of regulating spiritual life based on pure abstractions although it seems, indirectly at least, to concede that but for the ease, the purer approach would be superior:

> The difficulty of those whose relational minds are set on the Unmanifested is greater, for the way of the Unmanifested is very hard for the embodied to reach.
>
> But they who cherish devotedly this righteous immortal Value, as stated, endowed with faith, with Me for Supreme, those devotees are exceedingly dear to Me. (XII.5 & 20).

Śaṅkara, Rāmānuja and Madhva are three teachers of the Absolute well-known in South India and to the contemplative world, who represent various degrees as between duality and non-duality. The *Bheda-abheda* (difference-non-difference) as also the *Syādvāda* (doctrine of may be-may be not) of Jainism pertain to the same context and refer to the same problem, making concessions to paradox to which Śaṅkara strongly objected. *Advaita*, *Viśiṣṭādvaita* and *Dvaita* (doctrines of non-duality, specialized non-duality and duality within the absolutist philosophy of India known as *Vedānta*) all have the notion of *Brahman* or the Absolute as their central notion, but differ merely in their methodological and epistemological approach.

In the West dualism is expressed in a different philosophical form. Kant's *a priori* reality and contrast between the phenomenal and the thing-in-itself have been variously worked upon by later idealists. Humanistic and pragmatic thinkers have found extreme academic abstraction repugnant to them in various degrees. The history of philosophy of post-Kantian idealism reveals through Herbart, Schliermacher, Fichte, Schelling and others, a large variety of degrees of duality as between those who made concessions to paradox or relativism. Some used dialectics partially, and some with a historical bias. Some were optimists and others pessimists. The Will that they glorified was the *Will to live* or the *Will to power*. Pure idealism was absolutist in content, but expressed itself in various levels or degrees of compromise with the relative.

Post-Hegelians, like post-Kantians, reveal the same variety based on the concessions made to necessity culminating in that final stage where dialectics, instead of supporting the spiritual factor, openly claimed to be materialist in Karl Marx. In all these cases what should be of particular interest to us here is to notice that dialectics comes to its own again in the history of thought, and that all dialectical approach necessarily has the notion of the Absolute, whether positive or negative, implicit in it, whether the Will, or the Superman, or Historic Necessity is given the central place in the particular school of thought concerned.

The Terms of the Paradox have to be Bridged

The *Upaniṣads* refer to the Absolute as the bridge between the immanent and the transcendent. The *Bhagavad Gītā* (VII.7) compares the Absolute to a string of correlation of value-factors. Elsewhere (X.33) it compares the Absolute to the duplicative inflexion (*dvandva samāsa*) which brings two terms on an equal status conjointly together. A whole chapter — the fifteenth — in the *Bhagavad Gītā* is an effort to explain unitively the nature of the Absolute.

Śaṅkara himself refers in his commentary on the *Gauḍapāda Kārikā* of the *Māṇḍukya Upaniṣad* to the subtle nature of the paradox involved in resolving the nature of the Absolute. The *Sāṁkhya Kārikā* which has duality as its basis between Nature (*Prakṛti*) and Spirit (*Puruṣa*) which are its dual prime categories may be said to mark the extreme position of dualism between the positive and negative aspects of the Absolute.

Both orthodox and heterodox schools in India have made attempts to bring the two notions together and reconcile one with the other. There is something very suggestive though elusive in the *Upaniṣads* that encourages all of them to feel that such a unitive Absolute is possible. Through Nāgārjuna, Asaṅga and Vasubandhu of the heterodox Indian schools, to the vast variety of Vaiṣṇavites, we have all the possible valid positions represented. Vallabha, Nimbārka and Caitanya in the North and the three great Vedāntins of the South have their numerous followers who give rise to all varieties and degrees of dualism as between the Absolute and the Relative.

A galaxy of adorable entities, a whole pantheon of Gods, as a result, have emerged into view, all of which has to be brought under the aegis of the unitive Absolute scientifically and dialetically conceived. A fresh start has to be made here, in which the idea of the Absolute as the Adorable will not suffer by any negative stigma, but will act positively as a leaven in human affairs all the more effectively under the norm of all norms in the correctly formulated Science of the Absolute.

The Zig-zag Course of Indian Logic and Thought

The so-called logic of Indian philosophical thought consists, as it were, of a staircase of three flights. The first consists of the twin systems of thought known as the *Nyāya-Vaiśeṣika*. This flight may be called the level of existent reality where mechanistic logic is still valid. The degree of duality here is very marked, and the difference is sometimes called *dvandva* (dual pairs of opposites). Heat-cold, pleasure-pain are the contemplative factors involved here as the *Bhagavad Gītā* cites (II.14).

In the next flight represented by the *Sāṁkhya-Yoga* twin systems, thought becomes more theoretical and formal. Existent aspects of contemplative reality give place to subsistent ones and mechanistic aspects of reasoning have no function any more because of the mental, meaning or sound content of the material of reason involved here.

In the third flight of thought the twin schools are the *Purva* and *Uttara Mīmāṁsās* (earlier and later critiques of philosophy) which have a still higher contemplative status. Here logical methods go beyond all the varieties and modes of reasoning found in mathematics or grammar. Although contemplation even at the primary levels of the previous flight has to be unitive, here the unitive character of the reasoning becomes more pronounced so that the problems of unity or duality may be resolved. While *dvandva* (double contradictory pairs of opposites in a relative context) was the problem of the previous zone or level of reasoning, *dvaita* (duality) is the problem to be confronted here by the contemplative. The difference in the former case of *dvandva* lay in the horizontal plane of space. Here however, the *advaitic* (non-dual) unity is to be sought in the vertical axis, so to say, of time or duration.

Unitive contemplation comprises both these modalities of reasoning before it attains its full maturity or term, when the thought-system comes to the twin philosophies of Indian thought known as the two *mīmāṁsās* (critiques) of which the *uttara* (later one) is the *Vedānta* of Bādarāyaṇa. Śaṅkara started by commenting on this highest development of Indian thought in the *Brahma-sūtras*, but he resorted to his own brand of logic in which the *a priori* based on a hearkening back to the authority of the *Upaniṣads* played a large part. The other teachers (Rāmānuja and Madhva) who contributed to the same development of thought, admitted dualism of different kinds and degrees for resolving the paradox between the Absolute and the Relative. The orthodoxy of all the three teachers was what kept their thought short of attaining the white heat of a final non-dual or dialectical reasoning.

Symbolic Logic in the West Cannot be Expected to Resolve the Paradox

The gap found in Western philosophy as between the rationalists and the vitalists or the pragmatists and the idealists represents the same element of paradox, duality or principle of difference as in Indian thought. Bertrand Russel may be taken to be the representative sceptic here who states that the element of probability (*p*) which contributes to the vagueness of our concept of Absolute Knowledge can never be eliminated:

> The supposed absolute concept 'knowledge' should be replaced by the concept 'knowledge with degree of certainty *p*', where *p* will be measured by mathematical probability when this can be ascertained'
>
> (*Human Knowledge*, p. 517, Allen and Unwin, London, 1948).

This element of probability which is hiding the clarity of the notion of absolute knowledge is no other than the element of paradox involved in the notions of the Absolute and the Relative. The unitive Absolute is one which should have no vestige of duality attached to its notion.

In recent years symbolic or mathematical logic has developed a calculus as applied to propositions, functions or sets (classes or types) of entities which naturally might be expected one day to solve the paradoxical vagueness attached to the unitive notion of the Absolute, which is the blind alley towards which modern sceptical thought is at present heading. However, in the light of the following paragraph which we take from an article by Alonzo Church in the *Dictionary of Philosophy* (p. 181, Runes, Jaico, Bombay, 1957), even this hope of more perfected logic ever coming to grips with this knot of a paradox involved in the unitive notion of the Absolute seems to be receding more and more rather than coming within the reach of even this new kind of ratiocinative thought. He says (italics ours):

> Besides the Zermelo set theory and the functional calculus theory (theory of types) there is a third method of obtaining at system adequate for mathematics and at the same time — it is hoped — consistent, proposed by Quine in his book cited below [*Mathematical Logic*, New York, 1940] — *The last word on these matters has almost certainly not been said.*

One of the avowed aims of symbolic logic is to explain paradox. We have seen above how Russell left the nature of Absolute Knowledge with a paradox. Solving the paradox with a unitive notion of the Absolute is what would help us to arrive at a concept of the Absolute which would lend itself to be adored as the ultimate basis of all reality. From a perusal of the italicized statement of Church above, it would become evident that even this new logical approach is far from bringing human thought any nearer to the solution of the paradox persisting between two aspects of the Absolute. Pure dialectics known in the days of the *Upaniṣads* and of Parmenides has therefore to be relied on to come to the rescue in order to yield the central neutral notion of the Adorable Absolute as a supreme Value in human life.

Pure Dialectics Has to Come to the Rescue

Paradox is what we are faced with in this matter of arriving at a unitive notion of the Absolute as the Adorable. The existent, the subsistent and the value levels which belong to the Self within and to the phenomenal world without, have to be contemplatively understood as the non-dual Absolute. This is our central problem here. Keeping this in mind, if we should look for a philosophical way out, we find that two books, widely different in their origin, have stated the paradox correctly in dialectical terms, and boldly suggested a way out. One of them is the *Bhagavad Gītā* which claims to be a textbook on the Science of the Absolute. In Chapter II, 16 we see the dialectics involved stated as follows:

> For the non-existent there is no being;
> No non-existence could apply to what exists;
> The culmination of both these
> Has been seen by seers of Truth.

This challenge which suggests a hope of cutting the knot of the master paradox in respect of the Absolute finds its equal in the philosophy of Parmenides whose position is summed-up as follows:

> Come now, I will tell the — and do thou hearken to my saying and carry it away — the only two ways of search that can be thought of. The first, namely that *It is,* and that it is impossible for it not to be, is the way of conviction, for truth is its companion. The other, namely, that *It is not*, and that it must needs not be — that, I tell thee, is a path that none can learn of at all. For thou canst not know what is not — that is impossible — nor utter it; for it is the *same thing* that can be *thought* and that can *be.*
>
> (Frags. 4 and 5, Parmenides, quoted by J. Burnet, *Early Greek Philosophy*, p. 173, London, 1930).

If we should turn to the heterodox schools of the Indian nationalist tradition we have the instance of Nāgārjuna who teaches the same paradox under various twin concepts (e.g., "no production nor destruction; no annihilation nor persistence; no unity nor plurality; no coming in nor going out." — the famous "Eight Noes") pertaining to the same problem of the Relative and the Absolute, concluding in the following verses from the *Mādhyamika Kārikā* (*Teachings of the Compassionate Bhuddha*, pp. 174-75 Mentor, 1955):

> There is no difference at all
> Between *Nirvāṇa* and *Saṁsāra*[1]
> There is no difference at all
> Between *Saṁsāra* and *Nirvāṇa.*
>
> What makes the limit of *Nirvāṇa*
> Is also then the limit of *Saṁsāra.*
> Between the two we cannot find
> The slightest shade of difference.
>
> [Insoluble are antinomic] views
> Regarding what exists beyond *Nirvāṇa*,
> Regarding what the end of this world is,
> Regarding its beginning.
>
> Since everything is relative, [we do not know]
> What is finite and what is infinite,
> What means finite and infinite at once,

What means negation of both issues.

What is identity, and what is difference?
What is eternity, what noneternity,
What means eternity and noneternity together,
What means negation of both issues ?

Bliss consists in the cessation of all thought,
In the quiescence of all plurality.
No [separate] reality was preached at all,
Nowhere and none by Buddha!

(*Mādhyamika Kārikā*, XXV, 19-24)

The Absolute is Adorable and Merciful

From the theological angle God or Deity even as the Most High Absolute is not only the Adorable but the All-Merciful. Absolute knowledge, free from subjective or objective prejudices can be appraised by consciousness in man as in two mirrors facing each other. Both can be images or reflections of the other. It is in reference to the Self that the sub-divisions of knowledge could be enumerated. The Self has its own counterpart in the phenomenal where the same gradations of reality could be discovered. Between the Self, and the Self, thus brought together with an equal status, a constant dialogue goes on.

When the voice of the Absolute is thus heard and when man wishes to respond, the mood of exaltation results. The prose version of the Absolute then receives poetic embellishment. The Absolute of poetry is not inferior to that of prose. Alternately matter-of-fact and exalted, the notion of the Absolute glows subjectively within, and shines in radiance outside, in terms of Self-consciousness. It is terms of knowledge that is pure that this unity is best established. What Śaṅkara saw in terms of prose Rāmānuja preferred to view more poetically with more of the element of adoration. The cosmological version is only a dialectical counterpart of the psychological. It is in terms of Self-knowledge that the final synthesis of the Absolute is to be attained. Intellect and feeling would be seen to participate in an equal measure in this unitive notion. (The subtle synthesis referred to in this paragraph is effected most successfully in the fifteen verses on Knowledge (*Arivu*) written by Nārāyaṇa Guru).

Rāmānuja's attitude which represents the culmination of the tendency to think of the Absolute as the Adorable can be gleaned from the following quotation from *L'Absolue selon le Vedānta* by O. Lacombe (Geuthner, Paris, 1937):

> The consciousness that the Most High has of His generous fecundity is interior to His personal consciousness, but after the manner of an intimate resonance and without constituting a distinct personality in respect of Himself, it concretizes itself as the immanent term of an eternal dialogue, God entering with Himself into the subject of His creation in which He wishes to spread His glory. This polorization of the divine life by *śakti*, His creative capacity, is called Śrī by the Vaiṣṇavites.
>
> (p. 322 - translated)

Conclusion

The true contemplative or *yogī* is one who has no contempt for any aspect of the Absolute as long as it falls within the natural range of notions or entities natural to human nature within or nature without. He is one versatile in equating inner and outer aspects in terms of a central Absolute with which he remains ever tuned, harmonized or identified. There is a dynamism of an open kind of spirituality which ever seeks the sameness of inner and outer factors in life.

As a scientist he is neither orthodox nor heterodox in his attitude. He avoids fixations whether at the higher or lower levels of reality which are both made possible for him through ascending or descending dialectical contemplation. A full ripe fruit for a hungry man can loom large in the consciousness and take the place of the Absolute with him for a moment. Plenitude can be appreciated at the level of the ontological *Śrī* or at the teleological level of the Supreme Absolute or *Para-Brahman*. The amplitude between the extremes can be filled with *vyūhas* or hypostatic entities of various spiritual or theological schools. All of them can be understood as valid and given their respective places in the One Religion of Humanity which would be a corollary of a proper Science of the Absolute. Trinity and unity could refer to doctrines that could be accepted by the same man without inconsistency. Vasudeva, Saṅkarṣaṇa, Pradyumna and Aniruddha — the four *vyūhas* (hypostatic divinities) of the Indian Bhāgavata religion, could then take their places in a vertical scale of unitive contemplative values. A cosmology and a psychology consistent with a Science of the Absolute could be outlined, in which all possible divinities, galaxies of angels or holy presences could be given their legitimate places to co-exist without hurting or displacing each other.

Thus in the name of the One Absolute as the norm of a Science of sciences, the unity of all spirituality could be effected. When even the varieties of holiness found among men could be fitted into a scientific scheme, the edge would be rubbed off from the possible hatred of one group of Absolutists against another. To the extent that such a science becomes generally and positively understood, human peace and understanding can be expected.

Reference

1. Buddhist terms for the Absolute and the Relative.

PART II

The Unitive Approach to Religion and Theology

8

Science and Religion Unitively Approached

RELIGION is a whole-hearted relationship binding man with his fellow-men or with some unseen value-factor. Because of having a religion or being religious a man behaves differently or feels differently from another unaffected by it. He may conform to group patterns of behaviour or live apart in isolated contemplation. If we may refer to him as the 'subject' of religion or faith, the other or second pole of the relational situation, which consists of whatever is dear to him religiously, could be referred to as the 'object-matter' of his faith.

Religion is thus a bipolar relation between these aspects of the Self and the non-Self respectively. When we approach the question of religion in this bipolar fashion, wherein a man and his faith are treated as dialectical counterparts, we are in reality approaching the subject unitively. Such an approach, further, would be consistent with the non-dual or Absolutist way of thinking in which the Absolute, with its theological, cosmological or psychological implications, takes its place as the central normative notion as proper to a scientific approach.

A non-unitive or unilateral approach to such a question as a man's faith would end in sterile or meaningless sophistry. Like speaking of food without the hunger that refers to it, or of a medicine without the patient concerned, it would be purposeless to treat of a religion as right or wrong in itself. A man and his religion have to be compatible before it can satisfy him. All religion is for some sort of satisfaction of the individual or of the group concerned. From sartorial or dietetic satisfactions to those that are aesthetic, moral or spiritual, the subjective appetites, aptitudes or tastes belong to the same pole, although referring to different grades of value common to humans as the second pole.

A man and his faith may be said to condition each other reciprocally in the same subtle way as when we say that "the dress declares the man". It is in this sense that the *Bhagavad Gītā* lays down the law of bipolarity implicit in all religion in the following words:

> According to the truth-quality (*sattva*) of each man, O Bharata, his faith comes to be: the man consists of his faith; that which his faith is, he is even that. (XVII.3)

Some sort of satisfaction of happiness is the goal implicit in all the religions of the world, wherever or whatever they might be otherwise. Happiness can thus be spoken of as the common value-factor which constitutes the object-matter of all religions. As a correct philosophical or scientific approach to this important subject which concerns the unity and solidarity of mankind would require the discrediting of private or partial truths conceived in closed or static terms, this unitive approach would also be the only correct one to adopt here as in the case of the question of 'caste'.

The Two Dimensions of Religion

Axiology, a modern term for the science concerned with human preferences or values, admits of two distinct dimensions under which they can broadly be classified.

Our definition of religion at the beginning of this essay was conceived on the basis of this possibility. Man is socially related to his fellow man when, through common belief or pattern of behaviour, he happens to belong to the same religious body or fraternity. Through orthodoxy or fanaticism such a relation can be exaggerated or magnified mentally so as to make it a matter of life and death as between believers and non-believers. Crusades and inquisitions implying martyrdoms or genocides have proved time and again in history the world over that, like caste, race or even rank politics, religion can express itself in the horizontal plane of values.

When two persons desire possession of the same object they tend to repel each other, while two concepts having the same value can bring the men accepting it closer together. The former may be characterized as a spatial, earthy or horizontal dimension of value. The latter, being based on a non-empirical abstraction of which only superior men are capable, may be referred to as the purer, unseen or idealistic dimension of height or depth. While the former tends to be ontological in its interest, the latter works, as it were, from a distance, and could be called teleological. Time or pure duration enters as an ingredient into this dimension of depth which is of the essence of true religious feeling where it exists.

These two dimensions, the horizontal and the vertical, are two important axes of reference which we have clearly to keep in mind, since we are approaching the question of religion and the theory or theology that goes with each, in what we have called the unitive manner. This approach further implies that the notion of the Absolute lies neutrally as the central principle of correlation as a scientific norm for our discussion. The vertical and horizontal aspects of religion meet in the central normative factor called the neutral Absolute.

Whether a religion calls itself ethical and atheistic as in the case of Buddhism or stresses surrender to a personal God-man or Man-god or to both as in the case of most other religions such as Christianity, the two axiological dimensions enter into the make-up of each in different combinations and proportions, depending upon historical and other circumstances of the origin and growth of each. When we know that such differences are only incidental and not fundamental to the faith as such, we come to recognize the underlying unity of all religions without which it would have been impossible even to compare one religion with another.

Just as the Perfect Human Form can admit of difference as between male and female, brother and sister, father and son and the various types possible among men and women, so differences between religions are only incidental and should be treated as mere individual variations of the one Religion of Mankind.

The Lost Dimension of Religion

Religion and Science have been considered to refer to two mutually exclusive domains of reality, truth or value. Science is usually known as something that 'works' pragmatically and visibly in the logico-empirical world of experimental or *a posteriori* verities. Although scientists employ symbolic forms of thinking, they want to find something that they can touch, see or objectively experience. There is duality of ends and means in science, which could be said to belong to the world of practical reason.

When the world of symbols is relied upon, with no such duality, for its own sake, in a more idealistic attitude, admitting *a priori* reasoning to its full and proper share, and giving only a second place to direct sense experience, we arrive at values that may not seem to work the same way as in science, but which contribute equally, if not more, to securing human happiness. This is what is meant by the saying, "Man does not live by bread alone".

The science of human values is common to both religion and science. The inner disciplines of both could be conceived as the same. After the invention of the telescope the onward march of science made man look outward into space at the expense of more really theological or psychological factors. What was removed by distance or time became discredited and thus a certain dimension which could be referred to as the depth aspect of the personality of man, became lost.

In America, at present at the forefront of pragmatically, empirically or technologically developed countries, the *Saturday Evening Post* of June 14, 1958, has a very significant and revealing article on this very subject, under the title *The Lost Dimension of Religion*. Coming from the non-oriental side of world opinion which is free from the charges of easy solipsism or sentimentalism often attributed to Asian thinkers, and more especially as the writer of that article, Prof. Paul Tillich of Harvard University employs the same frame of reference and adopts almost the same terminology as we have done for correlating our thoughts, not only in respect of religion but with regard to a varied range of subjects hitherto, we have been drawn to it here. Prof. Tillich puts it as follows:

> The decisive element in the predicament of Western man in our period is his loss of the dimension of depth. (p. 29).
>
> He further goes on to explain:
>
> The loss of the dimension of depth is caused by the relation of man to his world and to himself in our period, the period in which nature is being subjected scientifically and technically to the control of man. In this period life in the dimension of depth is replaced by life in the horizontal dimension. The driving forces of the industrial society of which we are part, go ahead horizontally and not vertically. (p.76).

Neutral Absolute at the Core of Conflicting Values

The Vertical is the world of pure symbols while the horizontal refers to practical values of action. A reference to particular objective values is implied in the horizontal. In the vertical, values exist for their own sake. The duality of ends and means remains unresolved in the horizontal. The distinction between the two as between the perceptual and the actual, the unitive and the dualistic, is perhaps the subtlest of philosophical differences that a man is called upon to recognize.

What we have referred to as the horizontal world is what the *Bhagavad Gītā* refers to as the *kṣetra* or 'field'; while what would correspond to our vertical is what the *Gītā* designates under the category of the *kṣetrajña*, 'field-perceiver'. Symbol exists for its own sake in the vertical and what is called 'fact' recedes into the background, while in the horizontal world, facts, actualities and things, gain primacy over ideas.

The capital error that has again and again been made from the most ancient times in the history of thought, and more particularly in religious thought, has been to think of symbols as facts and facts as having a symbolic value. To keep these domains of thought each in its proper place, as belonging either to the domain of Caesar or of God, and not to both at once, has been the most difficult lesson for the common man to learn from the teachers of mankind who appeared among them from time to time.

When Śrī Rāmakṛṣṇa said that shaking a calendar predicting rain on a certain day would not make water come out of it, this was a humorous reference to this tendency to mix up the perceptual and the actual, especially in religious matters. The *Gītā* also refers to this single problem as the most central in the whole range of wisdom when it goes to the extent of categorically stating:

> Understand Me as the *kṣetrajña* (Field-Perceiver) also in all fields (*kṣetra*); that wisdom which refers to the field and its perceiver is what constitutes wisdom (itself) according to Me.
> (XIII.2)

When we remember that Kṛṣṇa (whose utterance this is) speaks throughout the text in the first person as a representative of the Absolute, it becomes clear that this distinction between the vertical and the horizontal aspects of religion is all-important to the author Vyāsa in the unitive understanding of religious values in the context of the Absolute.

The Law of Reciprocity and Compensation

When the two axes of values have been clearly visualized philosophically in the context of any religion that has been the consolation of people for any length of time, it will be found that a subtle law of reciprocity and compensation is implicit between the two domains, the one of Caesar, the other of God. There will be seen also within it an element of paradox or contradiction. It is by virtue of this subtle relation that we arrive at dicta such as "one cannot serve two masters" or that "the rich man cannot enter the kingdom of God". While loving a neighbour pertains to the horizontal the love of God would refer to the vertical. A natural harmony has to be established between these two aspects. A tree that grows tall will to that extent lose in its girth.

When titled up, one scale of a balance brings the other down. What is gained in the horizontal side of religious life will likewise be lost to the vertical. As you cannot eat a cake and have it also, so to have gain in this and in the next worlds takes all the wisdom a man is capable of. What is only permissive vertically becomes obligatory horizontally. Similarly, stressing the side of works spoils the side of grace. *Jñāna* (wisdom) and *karma* (action) in the context of Indian philosophy and religion, have to be balanced through subtle dialectics which is called *yoga*. The obligatory and the free aspects of religion have always to be treated separately so that the logic of the one may not vitiate the logic of the other. The promiscuous mixing-up of the two worlds is referred to by Śaṅkara as the evil of *jñāna-karma-samuccaya* (the recommendation together of wisdom and works), which is always to be avoided in scientific religion. The conditioning of one type of thought by the other which is called *adhyāsa* by which what is meant to be symbolic is treated as actual and *vice-versa*, has been the fecund cause of monstrous errors in the matter of religion and theology in both the East and the West even from the most ancient of times.

Prof. Tillich, whom we have cited above, has put his finger on this very principle of contradiction, paradox, compensation or ambivalent reciprocity. This writer who has to his credit other works called *Dynamics of Faith* and *Systematic Theology*, recognizes the ironical circumstance which brought discredit on religion by its own hands, when he goes on further to say:

> The first step toward the non-religion of the Western world was made by religion itself. When it defended its great symbols not as symbols but as literal stories, it had already lost the battle. In doing so the theologians (and today many religious laymen) helped to transfer the powerful expressions of the dimension of depth into objects or happenings in the horizontal plane. There

the symbols lose their power and meaning and become an easy prey to physical, biological and historical attack. (p. 76)

The Failure of Scientific Orthodoxy

Empirico-logical pragmatism as applied to some utility in life or to what gives physical advantage over others or over nature, was the cult of the scientist who called the age of belief as dark while naming his own age that of reason. The physical tangibility and rigidity of matter as understood at the dawn of the physical sciences, when inertia and uniform motion were understood mechanistically and deterministically, made it the rival branch to all that referred to what was flexible or indeterminate. Thus were produced two camps of rival orthodoxies, one strictly exclusive of the other. God and dogma were ruled out by the scientist, and he preferred to claim the title of materialist and was ashamed of being called 'spiritual'.

In recent years, however, this proud position has become more and more untenable. In a sense it can be said that the scientist has begun to have a religious attitude in certain matters. His orthodoxy regarding the uniform nature of natural laws is now on the verge of an impending defeat. The Quantum Theory has brought in an element of indeterminism and introduced whim or fancy into what once admitted of no imagination or intuitive guessing. Matter itself has become, like the notion of God of theology, a concept that admits of the greatest mystery.

New scientists in the field of particle physics may be said to have become heterodox in the sense that they have had to abandon fundamentally their original position and begun to resemble religious believers in something vague, mysterious and unknown. Such a mutual interchange of orthodoxies as between the positive scientist and the negatively theological or dogmatic religious man calls for a general revision of the position of both in more unitive terms.

It is encouraging to note that in recent years some interest has awakened among scientists themselves for a fresh integration of all exact knowledge now divided into the rival domains of the humanities and the sciences. Schroedinger and Niels Bohr among many others, have attempted in their recent writings a fresh approach to the integration of the sciences and of all exact knowledge. With the contribution of advanced modern thinkers like Bertrand Russell it is legitimate to feel that the rival orthodoxies will be understood soon and fitted into a larger episteomology and methodology, with a scheme of human values proper to all exact thinking, by which, instead of competitive claims of each branch, they could be treated as complementing one another.

The normative principle of the Absolute, admitting of a cosmology, theology or psychology compatible with it, when given its legitimate central place, in the middle or neutral ground between the rival disciplines of the humanities and the sciences, may be expected soon to effect a new synthesis. The microcosm reached through scientific analysis and the macrocosm of supreme synthesis could then be related as two poles of a dialectical situation for which the normative notion of the Absolute itself would supply the principle of correlation.

The Return to Animism and a New Absolutism

Of all the nicknames that one set of believers flung at another, it was considered very degrading to call one an 'animist'. The word animism itself referring as it does to the doctrine of the reality of souls, had nothing fundamentally disreputable about it. On the contrary, together with hylozoism, once discredited in textbooks of modern Western philosophy, and monadology, which still holds the field as a respectable metaphysical theory, it is becoming harder and harder to laugh at the fundamental assumptions of the animistic position in belief.

This is becoming increasingly evident especially in the light of the revelations of modern particle physics. Animism used to be a favourite nickname in the mouths of missionaries and anthropologists as they travelled away from their own homes and from locally prevailing forms of faith, to condemn anything that looked strange to them in the religious life of so-called 'primitive' peoples.

Trinitarians and Unitarians likewise discredited each other within the theological formations of the civilized West itself. What was respectable theological belief for the Mussalman was not good enough for the Christian, and *vice-versa*, although both belonged to the prophetic type of religion, fundamentally monotheistic and iconoclastic. Spirituality that was earthy was repugnant to prophetic religions generally, and according to both these religious growths, to mix earth and heaven was a gross mistake.

The ritual of the Eucharist, baptisms with fire or water, respecting the church or mosque as a holy or sacred place and, above all, the doctrine of consubstantialism of the Father, Son and the Holy Ghost, however, remained questionable in the context of strict monotheism.

Orthodoxy always required that what was adopted as one's own was justified somehow, while the same or similar doctrines in another outside religious practice or belief was considered defective.

The name Pantheist applied to Spinoza and Pessimist applied to Schopenhauer, like many other similar terms like Pluralist, Nominalist, Optimist, Dualist, Idealist, Humanist or Personalist, have become easy nicknames for condemning rival closed or static formations in religious life.

Religions have now all to be understood unitively as belonging to the same context of the Absolute as the central Norm of all religions

A method by which all forms of theology can be strung together, ranging from the extreme limit of animism as understood in modern science, and reaching through pluralism where horizontal and vertical values intersect in common human life, to the most high concept of the hypostatic monotheistic idea of God or the Absolute, can now be developed on unitive, universal and scientific lines. Scientific method need not necessarily limit itself within the bounds of the empirico-logical or pragmatic world of *a posteriori* reason, but can include regions where the *a priori* is also admitted as legitimate to science. When this task is understood in its proper epistemological and methodological setting, the modern tendency of science to discard absolute laws in nature in favour of relativism can also be expected to be effectively counteracted.

The Ever-Deepening Mystery of Matter

Being ashamed of being called spiritual and therefore non-scientific, the modern man gave up religion. He preferred to call himself a materialist, thinking that here he stood on firmer ground. As soon as it became evident that the greatest triumph of the scientist consisted at best in giving man urban amenities and weapons of destruction for man's hatred of man, there began a set-back in the enthusiasm for technological and scientific progress. With the deepening mystery in respect of the nature of matter and the behaviour of the particles that constitute it, the scientist himself is now beginning to resemble the sentimental and dogmatic religious believer.

The following extracts from a recent article[1] by Dr. Oppenheimer, some time director of the laboratory at Los Alamos of U.S.A. where the first atomic bombs were made, will help us to appraise the present position in regard to the future of materialism of every kind, and more especially of that variety of materialism called the dialectical which enjoys much vogue at present.

Stating that matter consists of various grades of particles depending on mass, charge, electrical properties, the time they take to disintegrate and decay, and generalizing that all particles that have an electric charge have a mate oppositely charged but otherwise identical, Dr. Oppenheimer goes on to say:

> Matter as we know it consists of impermanent objects — a view which is quite unlike the ancient concept of immutable objects with attractions or forces between them. Our new atomic menagerie of thirty particles consists of the electron and the proton and the neutron and their electrically opposite counterparts or anti-particles. Additionally we know of nine other groups. Three are weightless . . . Three groups, a pair, a triplet and a quadruplet called mesons . . . Three groups of hyperons, a pair, a quadruplet and a sextuplet.
>
> Mesons and hyperons generally live less than a millionth of a second . . . the more energy, the shorter the life of the decaying particle . . .
>
> . . . only last year, we learned to our great astonishment that these same forces [producing spontaneous disintegration] discriminate sharply between left-handed and right-handed configurations of their products of decay . . . Most students of particle physics were delighted when the suggestion that this might be the case turned out to be right and two young Chinese physicists — Tsung Dao Lee of Columbia University and Chen Ning Yang of the Princeton Institute of Advanced Study — were awarded the 1957 Nobel Prize for their contribution to this theory.

The above extracts are sufficient to show that matter is at least as full of fickleness and change as the mind of man. Although Newtonian absolutism has been discarded by physicists of this modern group, a fresh return to absolutist notions is indicated in such statements as this (from the same article):

> The conservation of charge and the conservation of nucleon

number appear to be absolute physical laws. In no physical forces do they alter; no forces exist to promote their alteration.

Hypostatic Trends in Materialism

Both the telescope and microscope have contributed to the expansion of the deepening of the mystery of matter. The notion of the cosmos is a resultant of synthesis and the notion of the atom may be said to depend on analysis. The microcosm and the macrocosm approached through analysis and synthesis respectively, have contributed from both sides to the wonders of the physical world.

In the light of modern discoveries there are two sets of matter, one set ontological as given to the microscope and other apparatus, and the other set teleological as seen through the telescope and allied apparatus. The matter of the astrophysicist is said to act from great distances from outer space, such as the centre of the sun or the distant galactic regions of the universe. The Indian Vedic worship of the Sun as the source of all life and the mysterious universe "beyond darkness" sometimes mentioned in the *Upaniṣads*, have thus become more than mere myths in the light of modern scientific theories and discoveries. Cosmic rays that mysteriously 'create' matter hereunder, functioning as "the galactic super-accelerators of outer space" as Dr. Oppenheimer calls them, have begun to resemble the hypostatic entities of theology. He writes:

> In these discoveries the key role was played by cosmic rays, the products of the galactic super-accelerators of outer space. When these rays strike matter, they produce particles present neither in the rays nor in ordinary matter . . . .

In this statement, read together with a later statement in which he refers to some mysteriously strange and comparatively slow processes originating in the vast interior of the sun, we have what corresponds nearest to God as the creator of the world known to man from antiquity. The relevant part reads as follows:

> To one such slow change almost prohibited by a selection rule — an occasional collision in the vast interior of the sun in which two protons form a deuteron and a positive electron — we owe most of the heat and light reaching the earth.

As far as the common layman is concerned, he can hardly choose here between the esoteric language of the theologian and the highly specialized one of the scientific expert. Myth and fact resemble each other so much that as far as he is concerned, one is as good as the other. Apprenticeship or some sort of discipleship is implied in both scientific and theological disciplines. Dr. Oppenheimer himself admits:

> All of us in our years of learning, many if not most of us throughout our lives need some apprenticeship in the specialized traditions which will make us better able to understand one another and clearer as to the extent we do not. This will not be easy. To me it seems necessary for the coherence of our culture and for our future as a free civilization.

Synthetic Science and Analytic Theology

Science has succeeded in making a lump of earth sufficiently mysterious or spiritual. Theology has likewise now the task of taking up the challenge from the other pole of reality to discard its contempt of something that is "of earth, earthy". The word will be ready for great discoveries when the *a priori* religious tendency of reasoning is able to meet the *a posteriori* of science. The empiricogical preserve of science could then have no closed frontier as against the cosmology and psychology revealed to intuitive imagination through myth, parable or fable.

If we were to make a complete inventory of the problems, methods and uses of the vast field of wisdom now covered departmentally by science, philosophy and religion, and arrange them in columns accordingly, it would be seen that between the compartmentalized branches that convention keeps apart and watertight at present, there is much duplication, overlapping and common purpose. Pure and practical reason, analysis and synthesis, induction and deduction, the *a priori* and the *a posteriori* movements, meet and mix in the conquest of ignorance which is the over-all purpose of both science and philosophy. Religion, shorn of too sentimental myth and its horizontal hidebound aspects can be looked upon as serving the same purpose. In this sense, when free of its contempt for matter and its excessive love of the hypostatic at the expense of the hierophantic, the teleological at the expense of the ontological, religion could still serve the cause of wisdom as nobly as its two other sisters born out of the love of truth.

The modern West may also be treated as representing an attitude which would profit greatly by the wisdom of the East. The Meeting of

East and West which was once thought of by people of Kipling's generation as next to impossible, and which is the title of a significant book by F.S.C. Northrop, is not as distant as some may think.

There is interesting evidence also of a fresh approach to religion in the West revealed by titles such as *Exploratory Studies on Empiric Approaches to Religion* coming from Waterville, Vermont, U.S.A., as we see from the title of a new periodical from the issue of January 1958, from which we extract the following random citation:

> Even a Soviet physicist concurs with the American. The power of the scientific method to elicit concurrence of men generally, whatever their previous cultural heritage, is a good omen for a scientific approach to religion and morals. Perhaps a scientific theology could unite such strange bedfellows as Christians, Mohammedans, Jews, Hindus, Buddhists and Communists, just as a scientific approach to the laws of physics can unite them regarding the interpretation of physical phenomena. (Quoted from R.E. Birhoe, Program Director of the Institute of Religion, in the editorial in the 19th issue of *Religious Inquiry*, edited by Dr. J.H. Shrader, Jan. 1958).[2]

A Larger Frame of Reference Needed

A methodological frame of reference which would accommodate at its core all worthwhile human values from urban amenities to the common happiness of mankind, has now to be supplied to effect the marriage of the *a priori* and the *a posteriori* findings of human progress.

If the East deserves leadership in the former domain, the West deserves to keep its faith in the regularity of the laws of nature which its logico-empirical methods have brought it to rely upon in regulating its free and critical ways of life. Closed and static esotericisms must give place to openly formulated dynamic approaches which would make life better or happier for all. The positive direction implied here is common both at the level of welfare or utilities as at the purer levels of aesthetic, moral or spiritual happiness.

If atom-smashing has the bomb as its by-product, it represents only a bypath and blind alley into which human genius and effort have unconsciously strayed by the bribery of national rivalries. It does not deserve to be called an item in progress, but rather one against it.

In reality human progress lies in a vertical golden mean of slow emancipation from necessity through vertical ascent into the domain of freedom and truth. It is true that this ascent at a certain level has to by-pass the horizontal axis of values which is the ground of rivalry and conflict. It would be misdirection and the prostitution of human intelligence to use the findings of science, such as the advantages of atomic power, for the gain of power over another human group. The collective consciousness of man must awake to the extent at least of desisting from such undignified misuse of human intelligence. It requires faith to step in if such a dire contingency as atomic warfare is to be averted.

Passing beyond this point of intersection of the horizontal and vertical sets of values, progress must employ *a priori* reason to ascend still higher to the conquest of values which do not refer to the earth but to those regions which the language of modern science would still insist on referring to as the regions of outer space where the mysterious super-accelerators creating new matter on earth may be said to reside.

Already there are signs of the rapproachment of East and West when we read of the almost juvenile intuitive genius that two young Chinese physicists have brought to bear on the problems of particle physics. The discovery, simple as it seems in itself, is likely to be the forerunner of many more which may be expected soon to give us an altogether new picture of the universe. Shortly stated, the scientists Yang and Lee have dealt a death blow to the Parity Theory as between an ordinary particle of matter and its twin counterpart when both are radioactive. The present disproof of parity between them has revealed that they can emit energy at two opposite poles. The repercussions of this disproof of parity are strikingly summed-up in popular language by the science editor of *Time* magazine of January 28, 1957:

> The new, better theories may create new ideas about the universe. Matter and space as science now knows them may have a right-handed twist, like the screw with a right-hand thread. Matter in other galaxies may be left-handed, or perhaps left-handed matter can be created or assembled on earth and prove to have different and startling properties.

The radioactivity of particles in other galaxies can have a different polarity with reference to a vertical axis common to it and its counterpart on earth. Thus it would not be wrong for us to think of two distinct kinds of particles, some naturally found in outer space or the galaxies and some that are normally found on earth. They have a right-handed and a left-handed spin with reference to a vertical axis that joins them. Those particles which respect the law of parity may be said to be those endowed with the quality of what physicists have distinguished as the quality of 'strangeness' lying in the horizontal plane which contribute their changeless stability to the firmness of the earth when we call it 'terra firma'.

The microcosm of physics and the macrocosm easily taken for granted by the theologian, have to be fitted into a larger vertical-horizontal frame of reference, before they can make meaning any more, as the natural environment of man.

Vertical Exclusion and Horizontal Explosion

Neither science nor religion are purposeless. They should be understood in the light of some human goal or value factor. Science is not without its own cultus which refers to some such value factor if not necessarily for acceptance then at least for denial. To admit of an arbitrary god outside law of any kind is what the scientist would be most ashamed of as a true follower of his profession. To admit too easily a private god who is a law unto himself is the tendency natural to a theological believer. Thus there is an exclusiveness on both sides which it is hard to abolish. Even Dr. Oppenheimer whom we have quoted more than once here, concerned as he seems on one hand about such matters as "the coherence of our culture and for our future as a free civilization" and in the matter of achieving through particle research "new concepts of natural harmony and order", reveals an orthodoxy which becomes patently evident when he says:

> In particle physics we may have to accept an arbitrary complicated and not a very orderly set of facts, without seeing behind them the harmony in terms of which they might be understood. It is the special faith and dedication of our profession that we will not lightly concede such a defeat.

The fear of the atom-smasher is that an arbitrary god subject to no laws himself might hold way over humanity and tend to disintegrate his relations with the physical world. The fear of the theologian is that science might upset his pet ideas of God. The two rival orthodoxies are affiliated to closed and static and mutually exclusive values in life. The atom-smasher serves power politics and his exclusiveness might end in an explosion if humans do not beware. The exclusiveness of the religious man is like cold war freezing within each man encouraged by a selfish orthodoxy. It may be said to express itself vertically, while the exclusiveness of the atom-smasher works horizontally and overtly.

Both can be equally disastrous to the individual or for humanity. The possibility of an explosion outside is at least as great a danger or evil as the interior exclusion that can divide humans into rival camps in the name of religion or theology. If we could place the Absolute Self of man as a normative principle at the core of the rival situation that has arisen with regard to both these orthodoxies, and also think of Human Happiness as the collective goal of mankind, the unitive approach to one religion for humanity would become an accomplished fact.

God as a Vertical Axis

God is not a thing. He is not usually to be touched or to be seen. He is mostly treated as if outside the empirico-logical world. If religion is to be conceived as a dimension of depth, God being the essential content of religion should also be capable of being conceived likewise.

A personalized god is a favourite symbol found in most theologies, as representing some unseen human value to be attained, reached or grasped. If humans could be taught to separate the symbol from the verity symbolized and, conversely, to differentiate between the symbol as such and its objectified content, the tension of exclusiveness or explosiveness in the human situation could be eased. Man could then live in greater individual happiness and collective security.

In reality God is a generic term covering many symbolic grades or points in a vertical scale of human values. This vertical scale has its ascending and descending limbs and all theological notions of the concept of God could be arranged on the vertical scale if the word God has ever been applied to any worthwhile human value for the true man or group of men at any time or in any clime. The verity symbolized by the word God is in reality a vertical correlating principle with its positive and negative limbs. The horizontal plane of actual values of everyday life intersects this vertical polarized scale of ambivalent values. On this vertical scale there is room for every conceivable god known to man, whether hierophantic or hypostatic.

The God with the capital *G* of monotheistic or prophetic religions is an abstraction symbolizing an aspect of absolute reality in positive terms. The idolatrous presences of the animistic theologies are each a presence here and now in nature, like the living atoms (or whatever is prior to matter as its direct cause) in the same context of absolute reality.

The ascending and descending dialectical limbs of this vertical axis could symbolize all gods from the alpha of the atom to the omega of the infinite as represented by a Zeus or a Jehovah. The prius of the atom could also be spoken of symbolically or mythologically as Pluto, Demeter or Ceres. A scientific theology could refer to all possible gods or to God by thinking of a vertical axis of value correlating all values that a man could relate himself to whole-heartedly.

Thus we return to the starting point of this essay where we described religion as a whole-hearted relationship. The horizontal corollary of the axiomatic verity of a God conceived as a vertical axis of correlation of all worthwhile values in human life consists in recognizing in fellow man one's equal as dear to one as one's own self. As man is a measure of all things and Self-knowledge is the core of all wisdom, this corollary expresses itself in actual human relations as a love of one's neighbour. Here the 'neighbour' should be understood as anyone outside one's own house. All humanity is comprised by the term. As a crow will naturally call a fellow member of its species when, by good luck, it finds some food for itself, the principle of sharing the goods of life with one's fellow men is the applied aspect of this corollary in the most practical domain of human relations. *Mutatis mutandis* this same corollary must be applied to all fellow creatures who love to live happily themselves. Equating himself with the objective aspect of his own environment of values, religion amounts to a whole or integrated way of life in which the Absolute is the most central normative principle.

References

1. *Saturday Evening Post,* July 5, 1958.

2. The writings of William E. Hocking, *The Coming World Civilization;* Trueblood D. Eltons, *Philosophy of Religion*; Edmond W. Sinnot, *Matter, Mind and Man;* and Winston L. King, *Introduction to Religion* are recent works (reviewed in *Religious Inquiry* above) which point at the scientific approach to religion.

9

The Lord's Prayer for Man

ALL prayer has a double reference — to life hereunder and to the reality that is beyond. It is an attempt to equate oneself with the mystery, truth or wonder of the Unknown or the Absolute. In the most famous of universal or common prayers meant for humanity as a whole,[1] this subtle alternating reference to the here-and-now values and the values belonging to the distant reaches of the mind find full interplay.

"Thy will be done on earth, as it is in heaven", is a very good example of the dialectically conceived structure of the best type of prayer extant in the world today. The two sides involved are always dialectical counterparts whether they are philosophically, psychologically, cosmologically or eschatologically conceived. Prayer is thus capable of being looked upon as an absolutist attitude or point of view in which the person — or better, the group of persons — who prays equates himself unitively or dialectically with the Absolute or God who is prayed to, "Thy kingdom come". The kingdom of God is meant to be within each, and oneself and his Father in heaven are to be understood as the same in principle. Prayer is a form of meditation upon the Absolute or the Most High for Man as well as God at once. God has to get a correct notion about the devotee by the prayer, and *vice-versa*. When both the parties get merged or dissolved in the high value of the Absolute, differencelessly, then prayer may be said to have best succeeded. All prayer thus comes to have a high educative value.

The Best Prayer Asks for Nothing

"Give us this day our daily bread" is a very significant phrase inserted into the Lord's Prayer that Jesus himself gave full assent to. Bread touches a human necessity of a here-and-now order. This reference to food, so pointedly put, effectively falsifies the charge often made in modern times that religion only refers to far-away or life-after-death values at the expense of the ontological or immediatley real values.

Necessity with a capital letter is given its full share of recognition in the Lord's Prayer, and if it is put in the form of a request for food, that is only to be taken as incidental to a prayerful rhetoric. It should not be construed by the critic to mean that God is not himself aware of the needs of man. The request should rather refer to the devotee himself on whose side a certain initiative should be present in placing his case squarely before God without that form of absent-minded piety that can only raise its fatigued eyes to heaven, forgetful of the reality below, where absolutist values can reside with equal validity.

Prayer Establishes a Unitive Relation

Prayer establishes a unitive relation between the one who prays and the one who hears the prayer. There is a *rapport* and a *rapprochement* between the two counterparts involved, and it is when this condition is fulfilled properly that prayer may be said to be most effective. The prayer and its answer are simultaneously implied one in the other.

The Limits and Content of Prayer

The instincts of self-preservation and fear of the unknown may be side to mark the starting-point and the outer terminal limit respectively of the attitude of prayer in the common man. Justly he feels insecure in this spacious universe of possibilities good or bad, into which his life is cast. Whether primitive or civilized, the fear is but legitimate and self-preservation is only the counterpart of the same fear. Primitive man may have had to fear snakes or tigers before, while now the fear has shifted its ground into the domain of road accidents or man-made weapons of destruction which have become more and more fearful with the march of 'progress'.

To fear is nothing illegitimate or superstitious as long as human life is insecure, which happens to be more true in modern times than in times of antiquity or primitiveness. Prayerfulness for man is therefore always in order, always natural and legitimate. It is an attitude of the spirit in which it swings in its desire for security and peace between the poles of the self-preservation instinct *within* and the fear of the unknown *without*. In its amplitude it covers life values ranging from food here and now to freedom or happiness in the contingent aspect of life that is beyond.

Food is the first rung of the ladder of values reaching from the necessary to the contingent. The whole gamut of values in life may, without superstition or error, be referred to, as in the antique scripture, as a golden ladder reaching from earth to heaven, the latter representing those higher contingent values which are as important as food or other necessities. A scientifically correct prayer should make reference to all unitive values which normally enter the life of man in a certain graded order. While it fingers the successive strings in the harp of life-values or interests true prayer stimulates in the self an ineffable sense of peace or happy contentment. The wonder of the Absolute sustains the interest all through with its reliance on something that passes understanding.

All prayer thus comes to produce in the person who prays a sense of the *numinous* which, when analysed philosophically, may be said to be of the very stuff and substance of the Absolute or its equivalent in common parlance, the Most High God. God and Happiness thus become equated.

Prayer Implies a Bipolar Relation

Prayer is a bridge between heaven and earth values while it is also a bipolar relation between two aspects of the Absolute. Glorification, thankfulness, gratitude, abundant sense of enduring security, generosity that spreads evenly over all parts of the globe, all-inclusiveness of sympathy or kindliness, irrespective of subject or object — these are features common to all the best prayers.

Often we find that subject and object are interchangeable. God's attributes could apply as well to man. A correct human touch would only add and not detract from the status of Godhood. An angry or punishing God is needed for certain types of people, while God's kindness is meant to induce the same attitude in certain persons who pray. In Islam the prayer is conceived without indirectness or a third factor coming in, in a strict bipolar sense. The idol or the interceding priest do not complicate or compromise the prayer or spoil its direct appeal. The Most High God who is the Generous and the Merciful One is able to induce the same attitude in the true believer by the very bipolarity and directness of the call to Allah by the pure Islamic supplicant. The rhetoric of prayer has also to recognize this directness. The heaping of indirect epithets is inferior in style to those where God and Goodness are identified.

Conditions of Correct Prayer Fulfilled in Varied Forms

Prayer can have various forms without violating the possible forms of correct prayer. It is supposed by some modern theologians that only a monotheistically conceived prayer is correct. This view, however, does not make allowance for the verity, which is dialectical, of the Absolute being the meeting-place of all possible contradictions. God is *One* and *Many* at the same time. He is both *big* as well as *small, near* as well as *far, within* us and *without.* Pluralism and unity meet in a conceptual unitive nominalism in the correct dialectics as it applies to the Absolute, which the Most High is supposed to represent in every prayer. The sources or the wombs of God are *everywhere* and *nowhere* at the same time as the *Upaniṣads* would declare. Even the *Bhagavad Gītā* refers to this when it states:

> Others too sacrificing through the sacrifice of Wisdom, worship Me as the One and what is many, different and every-where facing.

The philosophical justification of this will take us to the pre-Socratic thinkers of ancient times such as Parmenides and Zeno referred to by Plato in his *Republic* where even the One and the Many are reconciled and understood unitively. Whether a prayer is conceived monotheistically or even when gods belong to a pantheon, hierarchically arranged, there cannot be any valid objection to a good prayer which fulfils the strict scientific requirements of prayer. This only requires that it should be contemplatively and dialectically conceived and that it should give primacy to the notion of the Absolute under whose aegis all other value notions of the deity could be comprehended inclusively. As the gold coin could include all small change, the Absolute would cover all possible deities. The vast variety of human prayer which has ever consoled or helped man, viewed in this light, could all be considered valid or good. If, however, the dialectics of prayer is consciously followed in any prayer, that would be the best kind.

Unitive Prayer is a *Darśana*

Indian Vedāntic philosophy has what is called the *darśana-śāstra* which is a scientific method in which a central concept of absolutist status is treated methodically and exactly as a vision of Truth. A diamond can have many facets. Truth or the central Absolute Value implied in all life may be approached from many angles, points of view, or through its many facets. Each such facet of Truth when studied within its own frame of reference or as it lives and moves within its four walls, constitutes a *darśana* or a vision. Thus we have the *Yoga-darśana* in which dialectical personal contemplative discipline is studied, and there is also the *darśana* in which action (*karma*) is the central concept chosen for correct contemplative dialectical treatment. Whichever may be the central value factor selected for a particular *darśana* or vision of Truth, the method and the implied theory of knowledge would be the same. Prayer itself is thus capable of being treated as a vision of Truth in which the prayerful attitude of the self when equated to the non-self, attains a status of the Wonder of the Absolute, with fear and self-preservation as its two poles. A global sense of peace that passeth understanding characterizes the emotion or passion of prayer.

Dualistic and Non-Dualistic Prayers

The point of view of prayer must necessarily admit of a differential as between the one who prays and the one prayed to. Prayer must use the dual differential principle as at least its starting spring-board. The supplication that might sound object or undignified in certain prayers is to be justified only on the score that it is what could supply the elasticity of the board from which devotees could dive properly into the mystery of the Unknown.

After thus taking off from firm ground, true prayer can make the spirit soar or sink or even do both in the most symmetrically conceived prayers. Sinking ontologically into existence is as important as soaring hypostatically into the higher worlds of the intelligibles. Whether prayer is a peroration, a sublime song or hymn rising or sinking into the scale of values that come within the range of contemplative life, whether a state of exaltation, submission or surrender is implicit therein, the core of correct prayer spells the formula of non-dual unity as expressed by the great sayings of the *Vedānta* such as "That Art Thou" (*tat tvam asi*). God and Man become interchangeable in this sense, and then prayer fulfils its noblest purpose as far as the aspiration of the soul of the intelligent man is concerned. If we are to use the Buddhistic terminology which is wrongly understood to be atheistic and prayerless: The dewdrop slips into the shining sea.

The Solipsist Principle Implicit in All Prayer

Food has to correspond to hunger; so too prayer has to correspond to ability or need involved. A superior prayer grafted on to an inferior mind spoils the case for both the prayer and the man. The law of "to each according to his need and from each according to his ability" applies here also. A prayer could be conceived as a high philosophical vision, but if it does not touch the heart of the devotee it fails to be valuable to that extent. Gold could have a high value, but a hungry man would give away his gold to get his bread. Sublime prayers need not thus be superior to simple ones as long as the component parts as in a good meal, are found in both.

This law of solipsist compensation makes all correct prayers have the same constant value. A child eats less food but gets a unit of satisfaction, and surfeit of food is a meaningless absurdity. True prayer has thus to be composed by a master mind in such a way as to square with the needs and aspirations of the devotee or the common man as a representative member of the human race. The Most High God and the God of the Here and the Now have to be praised or supplicated through epithets that help us to appraise the Absolute affectively and intellectually at once. Cosmology, psychology, philosophy and eschatology have to be cleverly woven into the fabric of a true prayer.

The Law of Reciprocity in Prayer

In the Lord's Prayer of Christianity there is a very intriguing phrase which we ought to notice before understanding fully the dialectical implications of prayer. "Forgive us our trespasses (debts) as we also have forgiven those who trespass against us (our debtors)", like the other biblical saying: "all things whatsoever ye would that men should do to you, do ye even so to them", is a corollary of this law of reciprocity, involved in our correct relationship to the Absolute. Unilateralism would not work here. Prayer, like the quality of mercy of Shakespeare is a double blessing. "It blesseth him that gives and him that takes". A killer cannot pray for his life to be saved by God, as Guru Nārāyaṇa puts the verity (*Jīvakāruṇya Pañcakam*). "We do pray for mercy; and that same prayer doth teach us all to render the deeds of mercy" is another Shakespearean dictum with the same law implied therein.

Correctly conceived prayers in which the Absolute Principle is given full primacy in whatever variety of rhetoric written, or with whatever human value implicit in them, have the same status as prayers. Prayer knows no distinction of publican or pharisee, master or slave, priest or sinner, as long as normative and unitive human values enter therein, always under the aegis of the Absolute.

Reference

1. THE LORD'S PRAYER

Our Father who art in heaven,
Hallowed be the name.
Thy kingdom come,
Thy will be done,

On earth as it is in heaven.
Give us this day our daily bread;
And forgive as our trespasses (debts)

As we also have forgiven those who
Trespass against us (our debtors);
And lead us not into temptation,
But deliver us from evil.

Jesus Christ (Matthew vi. 9)

10

The Lost Idiom of the *Bible*

THE *Bible* has become more or less a closed book to moderns. Its subtle parables, enigmatic sayings, the paradoxes with which it abounds, its figures of speech and even its highly suggestive style, not to speak of its turns of expression, have lost their ancient flavour to the matter-of-fact and mechanistic tastes of moderns. The living waters of the Biblical message are beginning to taste queer at least to a half of our own generation.

Instead of relying, as they did in older times, on the thoughts and sayings derived from the Bible, even the pulpit sermons of a sunday have begun to borrow many analogies and examples from the sporting field or from the banalities of everyday life as reflected in mass produced magazines and newspapers. It would seem that in certain ultra-modern circles Jesus himself has to be presented in a streamlined setting to be acceptable.

The appetites of children pampered by artificially enriched foods or flavours both in respect of physical as well as mental nourishment, can hardly be expected to turn with relish from comic strips and crime stories available in large profusion with Sunday morning breakfasts to the sad historical anecdotes of the Old Testament. The hated hours of the Sunday school, if any, come side by side with the time for cow-boy or bandit games with revolvers in either pocket.

God must hurry up to answer prayers if faith in such methods is to continue. Pious works must have quick results in the manner of slot machines. The modern man is impatient with anything that does not 'work' as in the familiar world of gadgets.

Two Categories of Thought

The truth is that the Bible belongs to literature of a perennial and contemplative order. The modern man's idioms on the other hand are derived mainly from physics and mechanics. The spectacular success of the machine has invaded the subconscious of the present generation. Contemplative modes of thought and expression have receded to the background.

It is true that the admission of biology to a respected position among the sciences has done something to break the rigidity of the mechanistic pattern of thinking that was most in vogue at the end of the last century. Vitalism has displaced rationalism to some extent. A biological organism had necessarily to be thought of in terms of life duration or functioning. Thus a new time dimension had to be added to our notion of the physical world. From this notion of organic duration to that of the process of evolution, whether conceived with a mechanistic bias as with Darwin or more 'creatively' as in the case of Bergson, the transition was only normal. Some sort of belief in 'evolution' whether treated as a 'theory', 'hypothesis', or even loosely as a 'fact proven beyond dispute', may be said to be at the bottom of the modern man's pattern of thought.

Crossroads

Taking a backward glance we could say that the Bible derived its idiom from Socratic or even pre-Socratic literature known to the Mediterranean world which itself was the melting pot of more ancient tongues whose confusion was heard at the time of building of the Tower of Babel. Neo-Platonism had much in common with the thought patterns found in the *Bible*. As theology passed through the Dark Ages and emerged into the Age of Reason, these patterns became effete. The stunning blow of the age of mechanistic modernism all but killed it outright. The shock was relieved by the living vitalism of Bergson. We stand today at the threshold of an era in which this generation still views the whole of the Biblical mode of thought with great mistrust. To choose between the creative process as in the first chapter of *Genesis* and the same viewed in the light of evolution represents the crossroads at which we may be said to be still lingering at the present time.

Mistrust in the more ancient patterns of thought was marked very distinctly by the emergence of the UNESCO. Educational and cultural interests were thought insufficient to give a finalised character and name to this organization which is the characteristic child born of the last world conflict. The letter 'S' for science had to be deliberately inserted as an afterthought between the 'E' for education and 'C' for culture at the instance of some influential sponsors of the organization when it was being formed. Later developments made it sufficiently clear that these sponsors had in mind 'the fact of evolution' as something that corresponded to what might be called the *credo* of the modern man when science was thus given a position at the very core of even the name of an organization which could legitimately be treated as the official outcome of the 'spiritual' or 'mental' aspirations of the modern post-war generation.

Wisdom-reasoning

It would be safe to assert that the language of *Genesis* which reads: "And God said, Let there be light and there was light. And God saw the light, and *it was* good: and God divided the light from the darkness. And God called the light Day, and the darkness he called Night . . ." is poles apart from the thermodynamical picture of a universe that is presented to us by the scientists. We cannot blame altogether the young people of our generation if they refuse to be enthusiastic for both these forms of expression in one and the same breath.

In spite of being so different, however, they need not be considered as mutually exclusive versions of reality. They are still reconcilable in the light of a certain unitive approach in which Human Values are given their legitimate primacy. This way of wisdom was a way of higher reasoning known to the ancients and is not altogether unknown even at the present-day in certain so-called recessive parts of the world. This way is akin to the intuition which is able to see the middle ground between two reciprocal propositions which seem mutually exclusive of each other. Zeno and Parmenides were ancient exponents of this way of reasoning. Plato referred to it as the 'hymn of dialectic' and Plotinus paid homage to it referring to it as the 'eye of the soul of man'.

The great kings of literature, irrespective of the time or clime in which they lived, have been master dialecticians in their own varied ways. In fact their works may be said to have derived their very greatness from the secret element of dialectics contained in them. The works of a Kālidāsa, a Dante, a Shakespeare or a Milton, not to speak of the great Vyāsa, author of the *Bhagavad Gītā*, that scientific text-book of dialectics (which is none other than what it refers to as *Yoga*), breathe the full flavour of the idiom proper to the science of dialectical reasoning.

The *Bible* itself would not have come to be considered 'The Book' if it were not permeated from beginning to end with that particular dialectical idiom which makes it a treasured book of mankind for all time . . . The generation of moderns needs badly to re-learn this lost idiom of the *Bible* if the interest in this treasure of contemplative wisdom writing is still to continue amidst us.

11

Allāh the Absolute

THE Status given to God in the *Qurān* by Mohammed is what gives Islam its one excellence among the latest revaluations of religious life in the world.

In Islam God is not to be mixed up with a demiurge, a holy presence, or even a *deva* or an *īśvara*. He represents the Most High. He is not to be confused with other gods or deities, ancestral or heavenly. His unity is to be beyond suspicion. His supremely absolute status is not to be compromised, He is the high Ruler of all worlds and His law cannot and should not be transgressed. Man's multiple relativistic interests here should not be allowed to colour or vitiate God's high purity and aloofness. God is not merely good, but Goodness itself. There should be no watering-down of the intense or fervent content of the reality of God by loose analogy, comparison, substitution or transferred holiness through any indirect representation by imagery or impotent symbolism. He is unique and only comparable with His own High Self. Literary, philosophical or theological indirectness in the approach to God are to be discredited. The messenger of God, his apostle or prophet, should not be encouraged to shine with any glory which truly belongs to God alone, as that might confuse or confound the supreme Goodness or Value of God in the eyes of the common man. Such is the zeal of the simplest member of the Islamic fraternity with which he safeguards the absolute status of the One God that knows no second. "None but the Most High" is thus the true watchword of Islam.

Enigmatic Epithets

Although thus the most exacting God and One always to be obeyed and feared, stern in His decrees and inexorable, the most favourite and oft-repeated epithets applied to Him are that He is *Ar-Rahman*, *Ar-Rahim* — The Beneficent and the Merciful.

To fear God and yet consider Him loving is a double-edged challenge presented by Islam. Neither the lukewarm 'believer' in something indirectly and conventionally accepted as God, nor the disbeliever can by-pass in a lazy indifferent mood this challenge which Islam poses before him. Those who are not with God are against Him. Such is the firm position that the religion of Mohammed offers for one to accept or reject. All cant and double-talk are ruled out by the *Qurān* in such final terms that some have mistaken the zeal for fanaticism.

God's will must prevail one hundred per cent and yet there should be no obligation, compulsion or coercion in religious matters as the *Qurān* clearly lays down (34. 256). There is thus a major enigma in Islam which is that in Islam there is the meeting of two factors — Freedom and imperative Necessity. The God of Islam is at once the highest and only hope and the categorical and imperative necessary factor for happiness or salvation.

Challenge and Recognition

Khatija, the first wife of Mohammed, first saw through this secret enigma that her husband taught her with love. His cousin Ali responded to the message with characteristic enthusiasm and fervour. Aisha, his younger accomplished wife, responded also to the verity thus revealed, though in a less clear way. But the Arab tribesmen and various kinsmen of Mohammed mistrusted and disadopted him, and thus the tearful growth of Islam began to trace its keen note through the pages of its long and troubled history. Humanity has still to travel in order to see through the challenge that Mohammed has placed before it.

Understood in the same strict sense that Mohammed himself intended, the absolute status and value of God to be recognized by humanity, the open, dynamic and scientific verity that the God of Islam represents, remains unquestionable. Presented in its pristine purity, it is a revealed or *a priori* verity that each must accept whole-heartedly in the interest of the humanity which is dear to every member. Then let Allāh be praised as He ought to be; let Him be understood as evermore He should be. Such is our fervent prayer.

12

Temple Exoterics

REALITY is not always self-evident. Conversely, all that glitters is not gold. That which hides as reality behind appearance thus gives room for what is known to the lay thinker as esoterics. This kind of knowledge has flourished in many lands in the various epochs of human history. Logic, reason, systematized philosophy and higher intuition have made attempts to dive into this hidden treasure so as to be able to formulate esoteric secrets in terms of exoteric doctrine.

Such attempts at the rationalization of esoterics have produced good, bad and indifferent results. When the process has had a steady and lasting record, a precious streak of wisdom has been left behind sometimes, on the river-beds, so to say, on which ancient civilizations have traced their course. The Cabalistic, the Tantric, the Hermetic, the Theosophical, the Rosicrucian or the Masonic are just some names applied to such streaks of precious wisdom-deposits found alongside with much dross which the course of civilizations have left in different contexts.

The common human intelligence which is behind such traces of subtle wisdom, springs from the same stratum of human life where the myth-making tendency also resides. Through proverbs and fables much common sense attains to universal validity instead of just remaining vague, dull or useless to mankind. These often enshirne wisdom values which should not be treated light-heartedly.

Iconographic Esoterics

In the context of idol worship in South Indian temples, under the general title of *Āgama* or *Tantra Śāstra*, the present writer has been familiar with a very interesting streak of exotericized wisdom of this kind deposited through very ancient times.

In considering the methods of installing idols of the familiar South

Indian gods in temples and in the very elaborate formalities of their daily worship, as laid down in various books, and in examining the various ramifications, gradation and precedence to be given to the vast hierarchy of gods and goddesses, we are able to discover implicitly or explicitly much mystical or contemplative doctrine or philosophy of great value to humanity. Academic philosophy could hardly be expected to retain such wisdom and pass it on from one generation to the next without losing its essential flavour or interest to the mass of contemporary human beings.

One has only to glance at the long list of books pertaining to the *Āgamas* are the *Tantra Śāstras* to be convinced of their vast variety and quantity with many ramifications. The South Indian section of the Tantric tradition comprises such schools as the *Prājāpatya* (based on Vedic cosmology), the *Vaikhānasa* (based on austere practices of the Viṣṇu tradition), and the *Pāśupata* (based on the tradition of Śiva) with its secondary branches such as the *Gāṇapatya* (giving primacy to Gaṇapati the first-born of Śiva). The *Mahārṇava* and the *Tantra Samuccaya* are prevailing text-books used in the extreme south of India. Any attempt, however, to follow up these books with any degree of understanding or fidelity by the modern man would be sure to land such a novice into such a maze of injunctions and counter-injunctions having such a close mesh of elaborate detail in acts to perform that it would be likely to leave him confounded. However, the saving feature is that in and through these ramifications the critically-minded seeker would still be able to discover a streak of precious unitive and universal doctrine, forming the simple base of the technique and theory of an otherwise very elaborate temple esoterics.

Microcosm and Macrocosm

One of the basic ideas underlying idolatry or temple worship is that there is a presence invoked which represents the Cosmic Principle. Psychic factors meet the physically cosmological elements, bringing together unitively the dual aspects of Spirit and Nature. The sacred presence has always a lower half or negative side which is represented as evil to be rejected. On the top of this is the positive, the good or the bright which prevails in glory. The dark side of *māyā* or ignorance is transcended by light or wisdom which is masculine or positive. The female principle is sometimes given a higher status as the Ganges in the crown of Śiva's locks. At other times she is a co-partner. In one rare case, that of the androgynous Śiva (*Ardhanārīśvara*) the male and female principles meet bilaterally in the same central presence which is neutral and represents the Absolute.

Cosmological, psychological, theological, ethical and eschatological factors are brought together and meet in elaborately devised images and are further enriched with the help of the uttered formula and the attendant formalities of the ritual and ceremony. The many hands and heads on Indian images are meant to represent varied aspects of the doctrine synthetically brought together and juxtaposed.

Images thus speak an esoteric language of their own, containing and revealing valuable mystical doctrines to the connoisseur. The tendency of hypostatizing is made to meet that of hierophantizing, and there is an implicit ascending and descending dialectics in the secret language of temple esoterics which we can but refer to here in passing. In short the image represents the microcosm and the macrocosm at once, not in the usual sense but in a sense in keeping with the contemplative perennial wisdom tradition of the soil of India.

Equating Self and Non-Self

Another fundamental principle of temple esoterics is the equating or the equalization of the worshipper and the worshipped. Philosophically this is an attempt to bring together the self and the non-self into one unitive or absolute notion of the Self that is Most High (the *Puruṣottama* or the Paramount Spirit of the *Bhagavad Gītā,* XV.19).

Indian temple idolatry consists of the ringing of bells, waving of lights, burning incense, sprinkling water, the offering of flowers to the image, besides dressing and decorating it and washing it with ablutions of rose-water, milk, oil, honey, tender-coconut-water, lemon juice, etc. Jewels are put on the image also, with the mutterings of *mantras* (incantations).

By all this ritual, the attempt is made to equate the worshipper with the worshipped. The worshipper places himself mentally in the position of the worshipped so that through the sympathetic sense of identity the suggestion of a higher personal value is mutually induced. Eyes meet eyes, and feet and hands come together through subtle and delicately devised symbolic acts. Before being laid at the foot of the image a flower is thought of as corresponding to the dialectically conceived corresponding counterpart of the worshipper. Finger gestures (*mudrās*), postures, beckoning calls, exorcising signals and sounds, the invoking, pleasing or placating of the various secondary deities and the scattering of evil forces that range in all directions of the compass, as well as above and below, are some of the component parts of temple, ritualism, all of which have esoteric doctrines or meaning to reveal to the critical student.

The Vertical Axis

When any temple is to be erected according to the tenets of temple esoterics, the expert who is called upon to do so first visualizes a vertical axis which links together all the elements of the earth and sky in a series conceived from base to zenith. Man or the spirit principle dominates them all. The main subtle principle to remember, however, is that there should be no duality between matter and spirit. Matter merges into spirit and *vice-versa*, and the fecundity potency of the lower merges with the fearful awe-inspiring factors of the thunder and lightning of the higher spheres.

The *Śiva-liṅgam* (the phallic symbol representing the virile principle of Śiva) is both an ontological and teleological presence or entity. The glory of fire surrounds it and the round stone is sometimes imagined by the worshippers as a *jyotir-liṅgam* (a pillar of light) reaching from earth to heaven as in the biblical story. The two poles of this pillar of light represent within their range a scale of values which can be ascended or descended; but at the different levels of existence or formal subsistence always revealing unity. It represents the golden ladder of Jacob's dream upon which winged angels could go up or come down. A mystical doctrine is enshrined here which knows no limitations of the East or the West. An ancient language of perennial wisdom is implied.

The Six Value Nodes (*Ṣaḍ-ādhāra*)

In Indian temple esoterics, however, this vertical axis is further divided into six centres or plexuses, each representing a value-node in the contemplative spiritual discipline known to *yoga*. These centres are found in the worshipped and in the worshipper at once. Three of them below the navel are negative, or represent *Śakti*, and those above represent the positive aspect of the Absolute known as the *Śiva* principle by which was burnt the three cities with a flame from heaven.

The temple itself, with its *arudtha* or spire, its *garbha-gṛha* or seat of the golden germ of the Absolute and its *prakāra* or surrounding enclosure, octagonal, square or circular, is supposed to enshrine *prāṇa*, the life principle, or *ātma*, the Self itself, in its living process of growth and becoming, touching the elements and the highest God above. Even the three bends to be found in most of the images of Śiva, Pārvatī or Viṣṇu are representations of the psycho-physical value centres of the highest range or level, or the positive factors in the spiritual contemplative path of the temple votary. The intelligent votary is expected to keep these centres or value nodes in his mind while offering his worship through the laudatory description from head to foot of the worshipped image. A process of mentally sympathetic suggestive equating is implied here also.

During times of festivals the ceremonies usually commence with the placation of the outer principles and the *dikpālaks* (guardians of the directions), the elementals, and above all the head of all living beings (*gaṇas*) who is the elephant headed God, Gaṇapati (lit., 'Leader of the series' of troops or species), the first-born of Śiva himself. In the Viṣṇu context there is a regular science of precedence among the holy attributes or presence of the Absolute. The *tulasī* plant (*ocimum sanctum*, the sacred basil) is treated as the Mother and consort of the Absolute and is tended ceremoniously in every Vaiṣṇava home, especially by women and children. Going around such presences is also an important basic feature of temple worship, for which there is often a walled-in courtyard. The correct *pradakṣiṇā*, as such circumambulation of sacred presences is called, has always to be in a clockwise manner, and never in reverse.

The labyrinthine ramblings into the forests of temple esoterics is almost without possible end. We shall travel no further into it for the present. All that we wish to point out here is that the subject is of growing interest even to the scientifically minded modern man. Students of Freud and Jung find temple esoterics of absorbing interest. The academic philosopher has much to gain and nothing to loose by taking some interest in this subject. If one day the doctrines could be gathered, graded and arranged critically, that would be a stride forward in the direction of a more intimate understanding between peoples and in the formulation of a universal *lingua mystica* common to all humanity, so as to promote a solidarity and peace of mankind.

13

The Androgynous God of South India

ŚIVA as the Most High God (*Maheśa*) holds supreme sway in the context of Indian spirituality to the present-day. He is Lord of Himālayan Heights (*Kailāśapati*) and in holy Benares on the banks of the Ganges, he reigns as the Lord of the Universe (*Viśvanātha*). Śiva is primarily a god of the South (*Tennād*) as mentioned in ancient Tamil writiṇgs, and the same view finds confirmation in the title of the God Facing (or of) the South (*Dakṣiṇāmūrti*) which is applied to him in his aspect of Wisdom Teacher or Guru. He is here the prototype of all Gurus who taught by mere silence by the *via negativa* (the negative way) or the *nivṛtti-mārga.* He is the Dancer too, called the *Tāṇḍava* which, according to scholars, implies that he transcends the here-and-now aspects of life values and reaches to higher values beyond.

Śiva and Dionysos

Some scholars have been struck by the resemblance of this prehistoric God of India to Bacchus and Dionysos of the ancient Greek world. The trident, the tiger or panther, the sacred twig, the frenzy that characterize him, his strange apparitions and exits whether in mid-ocean or forest, and above all his love of intoxicating drink and unconventional affairs with love-excited women, are features common to both Dionysos and to Śiva. The mad Crescent-Moon-Wearer (*Candramauli*) with snakes and skull garland has thus much in common with the hero of the Dionysiac mysteries. Even names like Ivan and Iacchus from which some derive the name John itself, could be traced to Dionysos who later became the patron saint of France and particulary of Paris, as St. Denis.

As a household word of India, Śiva thus comes to have a common human origin and basis. He is essentially a product of peasant devotion. Although as the Burner of the Three Cities (*Tripurāntaka-mūrti*) he is referred to as having descended flame in hand from above, the three cities (*tripura*) being graded in a vertical series consisting of three metals, noble, ordinary and base, Siva has a purely ontological significance and here-and-now existence.

A People's God

Hypostatic or teleological significance or value is foreign to this 'hempen homespun' God, a creation of the peasant mind. He, as a people's God, comes down to us from prehistoric times. As hunter and husband of the daughter of the Himālayas, he has a native touch. As father of Gaṇeśa the elephant-headed mouse-vehicled God and more still as the Lord of Beasts (*Paśupati*) he is to be meditated upon as the *yogī* sitting under a tree with all beasts around him. The virile bull is his symbol and the round *Śiva-Liṅgam* (phallic sign) often consisting of a simple cylindrical stone with or without a pedestal is a much misunderstood object of worship from ancient times to the present-day.

The empire under the extensive sway of Śiva is the extensive region covered by the Indus Valley civilization once reaching from the banks of the great rivers of antiquity, the Nile, Tigris and Euphrates, and the Indus and Ganges and far south to the Kāverī and reaching furthest south to Cape Comorin (*Kanyākumārī* : Virgin Maiden Goddess). From South India this Śiva empire has spread into Greater India and South-East Asia generally.

The *Liṅgam*

Besides being worshipped, anointed, bathed in rose-water, coconut milk, lemon-juice, honey or milk in thousands of temples, and decorated and propitiated with flowers, ringing of bells, burning of incense and waving of camphor lights day after day, this simple stone or metal phallic symbol is seen to have undergone dialectical revaluation and elaboration from one epoch to another. As a result we have the Pillar of Light (*Jyotir-liṅgam*) whose depths Viṣṇu could not unearth when incarnated as a boar and whose heights Brahmā could not soar up to as an incarnated swan, as legend depicts.

Another form of dialectical revaluation and elaboration has resulted in the bronze masterpiece of the Dancing Śiva of Chidambaram which has attracted the attention of art critics and scholars, both Eastern and Western, for some decades past. This Dancing Śiva model is unique in that the common man has been able to arrive at a notion of the High Absolute in here-and-now ontological terms in a spirit very much akin to that of the 'existentialist' and the 'dialectical materialist' of modern times. God is seen to dance in ecstatic joy discarding the recumbent evil in man and rising over him into the glory of the Platonic world of the intelligibles. Between the prostrate form at his feet and the crescent moon in his hair, all legitimate human values find graded representation in the Dancing Śiva form. The stone or metal image speaks sermons innumerable to the peasant votary who is no mere idolator. He still understands something of this stone language.

Here we shall focus our attention on one aspect only which is perhaps the most intriguing of them all. Śiva is the Half-Woman Half-Man God (*Ardha-nāri-īśvara*).

Release from Sex-sin

Sex and sin are often considered interchangeable terms. This is because of its mechanistic unilateral treatment. Man's better half is woman as the idiom goes. So called sex 'perversions' like transvestism and homosexuality which have been looked upon with a guilty conscience by those affected by them and in some countries as crimes by the police who are rarely good psychologists, have to be re-examined in the light of the androgynous (i.e., uniting the characters of male and female) nature of the Universal or Absolute Human Spirit that is neither male nor female. It unitively transcends both sexes and could be called androgynous if any stigma attached to this term in the Greek context could be carefully eliminated.

Man has no psyche apart from the feminine aspect and a mere 'he' man or 'she' woman are to be looked upon as abnormalities, freaks or aberrations. Perfect beauty is revealed in the symmetrical middle that the half-woman half-man God represents.

The opening verse of a Tamil classic touchingly begins by referring delicately and subtly to this ancient God as *Thodudaya Cheviyan* (one who has a woman's ear ornament in one of his ears). The thrill that the transvestist whether male or female might get on meditating on this androgynous God not only liberates him or her from any guilt complex but contains an element of a corrective and contemplative mysticism of the true *Yogī*.

It is said of the saint Ramakrishna that he used to dress in women's clothes for days together and behaved like a woman. He would have been branded a perverted criminal and outcasted in the West but, under a spiritual atmosphere which admitted of a middle-sexed and middle-eyed god Śiva, his sainthood had full scope to express itself and attain to its full height.

In these days when male and female sex life in the West, and more particularly in America, is being voluminously studied and statistically scrutinized, the voice of this ancient androgynous God of South India might have a consoling message to both 'perverts' and 'non-perverts' in sex. The former might gain normality and the latter release from the repression that sex-sin based religion or civilization consciously or unconsciously imposes on free born men and women.

The abstract notion of the Absolute is nowhere given name, description or form with such elaborateness by the mind of the common man as in this concept of an androgynous Śiva surviving from prehistoric times and still kept alive by millions of votaries within his vast Asian empire.

14

The Philosophy of the Divine Family of Śiva

THIS chapter is intended to throw some light on a subject which for both the modern man to whom legendary gods may be without intelligible meaning, and for large numbers of the fellows of Narayana Gurukula in South India and South-East Asia generally whose sympathetic understanding in such matters is highly valued and sought after. The scholar has to meet the peasant in the task of evolving a common language wherein man can share his highest ideas with his brother without reserve, and across the barriers of time, clime and culture.

The One Absolute has been conceived, not only as the Most High God or *Puruṣottama*, but also under the names of various divine personalities, presences or entities. Such divinities have belonged either to the formal world of ideas or have been actualities worshipped in sanctified places such as temples. Each tabernacle is dedicated to one or other of such presences or divinities. Based on the values that human nature places on such factors, life is filled with activities.

Sometimes instead of a single divinity, the demiurge or *Īśvara* is placed on a single pedestal or niche, and we have divine families, angelic hierarchies or numinous galaxies of graded importance filling the various sacred spots which human nature seeks and provides for the godly hosts who fill earth or sky.

The worlds of holy activity have many ramifications or knotted networks of value-action links which sometimes range hypostatically upwards and at other times bend hierophantically down to the lower reaches of common human life-interests.

Myth and Philosophy

Whether good, evil or indifferent, these entities which claim various degrees of holiness, thickly populate the spiritual consciousness of man. They thrive now as strongly as ever before, in spite of man's vaunted modernism. Their place in human affairs increases in importance as 'progress' takes forward strides. The old wine is put into ever newer bottles. New gods emerge when the debris gets filled with discarded ones which the slow moving flux of time rejects or leaves behind on its glacier-bed.

In a few cases such integrated groups of divine factors get formulation according to an implied subtle dialectics. The myth-making instinct in man works hand in hand with the search into the mystery of the unknowable Absolute. We then have the case of holy families as in the Christian Trinity where the three Persons together are meant to throw light on the notion of the Absolute. Such integrated groups constitute a challenge, generation after generation. Their subtle wisdom prevails millenia beyond their initial presentation. They come to live perennially in the imagination of the masses with more than a merely religious creed implicit in them.

In some of them, philosophy and religion meet inseparably. Through them myth lends support to the perennial philosophy. What was but closed or static becomes open and dynamic. By them, the *lingua mystica* gets enriched and much sustained human interest and scholarship grows around them. Thus it was with the Olympian, the Dionysian, the Hermetic and the Kabalistic mysteries which have engaged the attention of scholars for long periods in the West. And in India we have the Vasudeva cult with its holy family.

The Śiva Family

The Holy Family of Śiva as known in the spiritual life of the teeming millions of South-East Asia offers to the modern wisdom-seeker much interesting and challenging material. A precious streak of contemplative content is found here which could be the fertile basis for the discussion and clarification of many esoteric doctrines. We have referred to this in one chapter appeared previously as 'Temple Exoterics'.

The Divine Family of Śiva consists mainly of the Father who is Śiva himself, an ancient hunter lost in mystic frenzy and dance reaching out from the limitations of the here and now to the freedom and radiance of the Absolute. His feminine counterpart is daughter of the mountain (*parvata*) and hence is called Pārvatī. No earthly love was involved in their union and the Indian Eros (Kāma) was burnt to ashes before they were united. They had two strange children, the first-born being heavy and elephant-headed and known as Gaṇeśa, the second-born, on the other hand, being so light and luminous that he rode the peacock in his glory and is known as Subrahmaṇya.

Between the ponderous Gaṇeśa and the buoyant Subrahmaṇya there is a dialectical interplay of contemplative value-factors which the votary or the hierophant has to understand through the myth associated with the two gods. Stone images, ritual, legend and fable interlace in this fine antique fabric woven by the popular mind. New flourishes and ornamental touches are added to the antique pattern from time to time by wise men who see through the outer motifs and can discern its inner contemplative and timeless content. Temple esoterics thus transmits wisdom values from one generation to another.

In such a task of transmiting common-sense wisdom not only scholars or wise men but all men, women and children, not excluding grannies, have their full share. The claim of the human species as a wisdom-seeking animal is thus kept justified through the ages.

Śiva Legend and Wisdom

The highest member of the Divine Family, Śiva, is strangely the least conventional, conformist or respectable of them all. Like Bacchus, the intoxication of drink is part and parcel of his make-up. Frenzy, ecstasy, even sheer madness are meant to be compliments to his character. His potent middle eye spits fire and burns all dross away. No poison can pass his blue neck which can absorb and nullify all evil. Eternal time plays about him in the form of snakes big or small, single or many-headed, as the nature of the dialectical tradition or value involved requires.

His feminine counterpart can be seated beside him or better still be one half of his own person as in the Half-Woman-God (*Ardhanārīśvara*) which is a very popular representation in stone language expressing the androgynous Śiva Principle of the Absolute. All goodness sometimes flows as a celestial river (the Ganges) from the matted crowning locks of this ancient hunter. Beyond the reaches of the highest peaks of the Himālaya his matted crown is adorned by the sun and the crescent moon which are his highest and brightest ornaments. The gods of the Olympic regions of hypostatic values reside here.

Destruction, which follows the wake of the forward process of Time's becoming is often depicted as a garland of skulls round the neck of Śiva and the ashes with which his whole body is covered as he dances in the burial ground, gives the final touch of austerity or severity to the contemplative image of the Absolute which the Śiva imagery is meant to evoke in the votary.

Between the simple *Liṅgam*, the phallic symbol, virile masculine principle representing the urge and necessity of imperative becoming, implied in the living notion of the Absolute, and the figure of the Dancing Śiva standing in his glory on the recumbent or crouching form of an evil spirit which represents the background merely of contemplative values, we have the interplay of ascending and descending contemplative or dialectical movements. The searching inner eye brings to its vision many pearls of price and leavening potent factors of power. These potent value-factors may be attributed to the worshipper or the worshipped. Subject and object have an interchangeability which is one of the first secrets of the *lingua mystica* which we should note here at the very start of this review of the divine members of the Śiva family.

The Pārvatī Set of Values

The second member of the Śiva Family is Pārvatī. As a daughter of the Mountain Himālaya her origins are rooted in the earth. In her, however, the earthy element has nothing inert or gross about it, but, as stated already, is a potent and fecund value-principle from which all goodness emanates.

She is also in a state of ecstasy or dance; only her dance is not the transcendental one known as *tāṇḍava*, but is *lāsya*, a radiance which shines dim or bright, here and now. Her horizontal expression could be the whole visible universe, but the principle which runs vertically through the different levels of her personality which cover the five elements (*bhūtas*) and the three modalities (*guṇas*) of nature, knows no difference between the relative and the Absolute. All vestige of duality is abolished in her when conceived as the pure representative of the Absolute. Thus her status can soar above that of Śiva when the latter is conceived as a God who is worshipped as a mere member of the Indian pantheon. Viṣṇu and Brahma have then only an inferior status to her.

When each god is given primacy as the Absolute, the others who come into the picture incidentally at least recede and fade into the relativist background. This may be said to be the second of the secrets of the *lingua mystica* which we have touched upon so far. In the androgynous representation of Śiva divided bilaterally into male and female, the left being the female, we have the same scheme as in *Genesis* where Eve is created out of the left rib of Adam. A vertical series of values ranging from the most earthy to the most celestial, and a horizontal division of the plus and minus aspects of the Absolute are implied in the *lingua mystica* of Indian and especially of South Indian, iconography.

Secrets of Stone Language

Every icon worshipped as representing the Absolute is taken to be locally fixed by the eight principal points of the compass. When fixing the idol one has to relate it three-dimensionally to space at the meeting of these eight directions. "Binding the eight directions" (*aṣṭa-bandha*) and basing it on "the six nodes or levels of contemplative value" (*ṣaḍ-ādhāra*) are two other of the secrets of stone language understood in temple exoterics to which we have made allusion in chapter 12.

The implicit dialectics still more subtle and elaborate when we pass on to the two sons of the Divine Family of Śiva. The two sons themselves could be treated as counterparts and there is a delicate interplay of spiritual values as we enter into the esoterics of what each of them represents. Besides what is evident in the muscular and cerebral dispartity of types, the brothers could be compared and contrasted in many other respects also.

Gaṇeśa

Gaṇapati or Gaṇeśa, the elder is the continuator of the tradition of the father Śiva, who was known as Paśupati, "Lord of all Beasts" that ever came forth. Gaṇapati means "Lord of *Gaṇas* or ranks of beings" and is a slightly revised representation of the same principle.

The rat or mouse is portrayed as the vehicle of this elephant-headed deity, and taking the elephant to represent the alpha or the biggest of animals that entered human life and the field mouse as coming up in the rear as the omega, we have in between all animals appearing in nature. The Elephant-Headed God thus comes to represent all beings anterior to man's emergence. The vertical series of living beings when contemplated upon telescopically and collectively together gives us a depth of vision which is retrospective and precedes the fully prospective contemplative vision which it is the share of the younger brother to supply to the situation.

When treated globally both sons of Śiva together are meant to yield the full notion of the Absolute in terms of a contemplative human Value. The foundation for the knowledge of the revalued Absolute is thus laid by the elder of the two sons of the Śiva family. Kumāra (another name of Subrahmaṇya), meaning the younger, represents the glorious superstructure of contemplative values.

Subrahmaṇya

The younger brother has many significant names and attributes. Traditions about him abound in Ṣouth India and his supremacy spreads over the vast area of Greater India which includes the islands of the Indian Ocean and the Pacific where temples dedicated to him thrive to the present-day. At Tiruchendūr on the extreme South and at Palni further north and in Tiruttani on the way to Bombay and at all intermediate places, there are thousands of shrines where daily offerings are made to Subrahmaṇya. The varied epithets and apellations by which he is known all give us a sufficiently interesting idea of what he represents.

In the first place his insignia is the cock. He is therefore called *Kukkuṭa-dhvaja*, "One of the Cock-Flag". However, he rides on the peacock, which is a glorified cock, perhaps pointing to the fact that a certain prehistoric deity which had the cock insignia or emblem became revalued in historic times into a more glorified God who rode the peacock instead. The legend indicates also that a prehistoric demon divided himself up into these two aspects of the cock and the peacock when he was vanquished by the War-God (one of the names of Subrahmaṇya), the former serving as emblem and the latter as his *vāhana* or vehicle.

An element of immaculateness of conception is associated with the birth of this War-God. The central eye of Śiva emitted fire which fell into the marshes of the Gangetic valley where six infant forms were produced from the six sparks that thus fell. These had the six *Kārthika* (Pleiades) mother for nurses. The six male infants got fused into one body with six distinct heads and twelve shoulders by the loving embrace of Pārvatī who became their foster-mother. This combination probably represents the five senses and the mind which were sometimes called gods or *devas* in Vedic literature. They were all derivatives of the principle of light and were therefore celestial in status.

Guru-Aspect

The War-God has the epithet *Śaktidhara* which points to his lance-shaped weapon, a revalued form of trident which his father Śiva wielded. Potency and power were lodged in this weapon.

On the Palni Hills in South India where millions of pilgrims gather year after year, the War-God is represented as a recluse in loin-cloth and ashes. He received the status of Guru to his own father Śiva. Brahma (masculine deity) himself was once punished by him for not repeating the lesson on the principles of the Absolute when questioned by the Guru Subrahmaṇya. Agastya, a *ṛṣi* (seer) or *muni* (silent recluse) of the Āryan context who came to the South, recognized the Guru status of Subrahmaṇya, and the Vedic Gods were merely the camp followers of Subrahmaṇya thus known as Skanda, the General of the Gods of heaven. He was also referred to as the mature fruit of all wisdom. The secret of the mystic syllable AUṀ was supposed to be held by him.

Āryan-Dravidian Fusion

Somewhat in contradiction with this picture of Subrahmaṇya or Skanda as an ascetic and celibate there is the rather intriguing legend in which he is known to have wedded two wives, one called Devayāṇī, daughter of Indra (Vedic chief deity), and the other called Vallī, a dark girl from Tiruttani who was the daughter of a nomadic tribesman or hunter, said to be of the Kurava tribe. Evidently the fair Devayāṇī represented Āryan culture and the dark Vallī represented the ancient culture of the South, which was the heritage of the common man, who was often the humblest of individuals living an open air life in nature.

Mythology had its way of expressing the fact that the God Subrahmaṇya represented the blending of the Āryan and non-Āryan cultures and that he represented the Most High principle of the Absolute above the world of the luminaries or the intelligibles. Both poles of the Absolute found in him a dialectically revalued synthesis. He was neither this nor that, here or in the hereafter. He touched both heaven and earth at once. Born of fire, and thus named Agnija, he was of a scarlet hue and his six eyes at the middle of the six bright foreheads, each as radiant as the moon, represented the Absolute as far as popular imagination could visualize it through the help of myth, legend or traditional lore.

There is a strange blending and intermixture of earthy and celestial factors in this deity who is perhaps one of the most popular gods of South India even to the present-day. His popularity is not on the wane either, but is rather one which is growing and gathering momentum.

15

The Spiritual Role of the Sikhs

MID-SEPTEMBER 1960 to mid-October of the same year was a comparatively uneventful period. Between a visit to the West Coast of India to the Gurukula at Varkala, and preparations for a trip to North India, I spent my days in relative unconcern about things and happening.

The autumnal evenings had their charms which have not been missed by the poets especially of the West. The exuberance of springtide contrasts most strikingly in northern latitudes with the mellowed note of melancholy that attends the sense of autumnal months. Less strikingly contrasted in warmer climes, where one long summer spreads more evenly underneath all the seasons, the message that autumn still brings is unmistakable.

The cycle of the seasons has always its charm to the poet or the contemplative whether understood or felt in inner or outer sense of beauty. Beauty is in reality neither inside nor outside. It belongs to the Absolute. It borrows from the nothingness of the Absolute whatever tinge or tint of colour or joy it could be supposed to have. Neither the colours of the spectrum nor the blue of the sky are strictly 'out there' as we tend to think. They are present within and without psychophysically.

Meditation

The Indian festival of lights, Dīpāvalī, which falls roughly in mid-October, is the limit for the peasants to begin to think of the freshness or frost of the winter months. The conditions are favourable for introspection just as the dusk or the twilight hours are when daytime imperceptibly passes into night. The outer darkness may be said to reflect the inner light and both together glow with a dull grey that is neither black nor white.

When the mind dwells neutrally between the points of the positive and the negative, man is said to meditate in the best sense of the term.

Meditation is not *upāsanā* (worship) nor *dhyāna* (concentration) which have both some positive content, but becomes rightly established when the mind is poised correctly between outer and inner factors.

It was in this sense that during this autumnal month I introspected or meditated and became fully interested in myself without selfishness. I sometimes let my thoughts or memories flow backwards in the stream of life playing like breezes on "the silken sail of infancy" and at other times I carried myself forward into the future, eliminating actual content as much as possible. With curtains undrawn at dusk I gazed out or closed my eyes alternately, trying to think, as far as possible, of the nothingness which was really of the essence of the Absolute.

Yoga Can be Only One

The various kinds of *yogas* that people write learned treatises about, belong together to one unitive state of mind that participates neutrally in the notion of the Absolute that is nothing and something at the same time. The favourite scene at which I looked, or the imaginations and memories that were allowed to have their goings and comings within me did not efface the Absolute but brought this high central human value sometimes near, sometimes far, but all the time present.

When we remember that *each* chapter of the *Gītā* has a different type of *yoga* implied in it, and also understand that modern textbooks of *yoga* do not go sufficiently to the root of what *yoga* implies in the more finalized context of *Vedānta*, but tend to compartmentalize it into special arbitary branches, the truth of the *Gītā* injunction that the *yogī* should *think of nothing* (VI.25) not even recommending an *iṣṭa devatā* (a preferred personal deity) as many spiritual instructors often do, would become understandable as part of its unique way of wisdom.

Even the distinction between the *yoga* of wisdom (or *jñāna yoga*) and the *yoga* of action (*karma yoga*) becomes a matter of no great importance in the correct light of contemplative spirituality if the unitive approach to the subject is once grasped.

By whatever label, known to experts on the subject, there can be only one *yoga* — that which contemplates the Self in the Absolute as one supreme human Value. This Value is neither inside nor outside but sits neutrally between both, as the common ground of all dualistic thought or feeling. If there are two kinds of *yoga*, to that extent each is deficient, though it must be conceded that textbook *yogas* can be many.

Guru Formation of the Sikhs

My forthcoming visit to the city of Amritsar where I was invited to preside on October 16 at one of the week-end sittings of the All India Vedanta Conference, naturally turned my thoughts on other kinds of socio-religious units that exist in India, and which with their linguistic or other problems, form at present a fecund field for irritating the central administration of this country.

I was already thinking of the Golden Temple and the pure, sacred or holy waters of the lakes generally attached to the Golden temples, not only in Amritsar but in other places where the *Granth Saheb* (Holy Scripture) of the ten Gurus of the Sikh religion is kept and honoured by uninterrupted reading by Sikhs who are meant to be *Śiṣyas* or disciples of the Guru line.

Being myself head of the Gurukula movement newly started on revalued and restated terms at the extreme foot of mother India, removed a thousand miles and more from this Guru group formation that took place in the north-west in the fifteenth century, I was interested to renew my acquaintance with Sikhism.

The hierarchy of ten personal Gurus succeeding one another in vertical line from 1469 to 1708 founded by Guru Nanak and terminating with Guru Gobind Rai Singh represents a chain of events in group life which has its valuable lessons to teach the most advanced sociologists and even politicians of the present-day.

Indian Behaviour Patterns, Dynamic and Static

Patterns of behaviour and ideologies persist through generations with a strange and innate tenacity and coherence according to laws as invisible and inexorable as the law of gravitation itself. Gravitation is operative in the physical world while atavistic group behaviour patterns persist through pure time with mental forces no less real than what makes an apple fall.

Physics might call for advanced mathematics but the laws of spiritual life pertaining to group behaviour need a kind of advanced mathematics beyond the infinitesimal calculus of a Newton or a Leibnitz or both, the first chapters of which are only being touched upon by a Frege and Cantor of modern times. It lies beyond the domain of paradoxes of modern symbolic logic and pertains to the unitive way of higher reasoning yet little understood by modern thinkers.

Patterns of behaviour have persisted and traced themselves on the Ganges of Indian Life for thousands of years and constitute what makes India interesting still to the modern research scholar and keeps it a veritable museum of rare instances of subtle scientific phenomena or facts. The enigmas of Indian group life have scared invaders and puzzled or confused the zeal of prophets. Out of the debris of the past which contains many a fossil or rock of the most ancient strata of human history, the latest and the most interesting phenomenon in group life is the socio-religious expression called Sikhism.

What we distinguish as the prophetic and the animistic or pantheistic aspects of religious expression are beautifully blended, revalued and restated in Sikhism without violating the best in either the way of the *Upaniṣads* on the one hand, or the contribution of the outlook of Islam on the other hand, in the full spiritual climate of which Sikhism may be said to have had its development.

Even today intelligent Sikhs are often heard to distinguish themselves and assert the uniqueness of their religion, by saying that they are *neither* Hindu nor Muslims. A better way of saying the same, more correctly, would be that they represent *both* Hinduism and Islam when at their best. The dialectical difference implicit is all-important.

The miniature sociological phenomenon represented by the way of life of the Todas of the Nilgiris of South India has been recently scrutinized by us elsewhere. The Todas, as we have seen, belong to the past more than to the present or the future. In them is represented a pattern of life and behaviour that is getting fast overlaid by fresh deposits of ever-renewed and revalued patterns. The history of religions and social units is nothing other than the history of groups of people who hold on to some dear human value, and persist in doing so in spite of the adverse winds blowing their sandstorms against it. All religions are thus dialectical revaluations. The stronger the adverse circumstance, the firmer is the foothold that the religious pattern gets in the hearts and minds of the believers. This is how religions persist through time when empires fall.

The Sikh Pattern of Behaviour

The Sikh is recognized by his dress, habits or faith in the first instance as different on the one side from the followers of Mohammed beyond the borders of Hindustan or India, and those in the second instance who belong more properly to the great Gangetic plain and are known as Hindus.

The Land of Five Rivers (*Panch Ab* — Punjab) has a personality of its own. Great rivers of the world, whether the Nile, Danube, Volga or Yangtse Kiang and Hwang Ho, have each a group of people clinging to their waters as a hierophantic value, cultivating a group behaviour unique to themselves and to the soil that is theirs.

If anyone should give articles of faith which further regularize the coherence of the group as it were from above, where hypostatic values reside, the resulting socio-religious phenomenon becomes a real socio-logical factor which cannot be killed out any more. A great French sociologist recognized this invulnerable element when he said that there were 'social things' (*choses sociales*) which had as real a status as any physical entity such as a bit of rock.

Religious groups become real and invulnerable in a certain psycho-physical sense and this is one of the secrets that the way of higher reasoning has still to teach humanity. The slightest error or miscalcula-tion here has been the cause of genocidal disasters all over in human history. Till man can learn the secret of human integration and group behaviour, events such as the wholesale beheading of the Sikhs which took place around the year 1726 (and which did not exterminate the Sikhs as it was meant to do by the rulers who promoted it) cannot be seen to be foolish.

Such events in Sikh history, instead of abolishing Sikhism, have even contributed to close the ranks of the Sikhs and made them drive deeper roots underground, making the organic socialized entity survive stronger onslaughts against it in more recent years. The virility of the group has reasserted itself characteristically time and again in the course of its history, and at the time of writing these lines about them, the voice of the Sikhs is again being raised higher and shriller everyday in the name of a politico-religious personality of its own with some trivial linguistic issue as the nominal bone of contention.

The result in actual terms cannot be anticipated at present, but it is certain that the integrated personality which reveals itself as a hungry lion now and as a dove of perce and fellowship to all mankind at another time, is not one to be appeased or won over statically for all time. Sikhism is as alive today as it has ever been before. Unlike the Todas, with the Sikhs one can feel definitely that they are still a live-wire religiously socially, economically and even politically viewed.

Amritsar, the Northern City of Dream

My thoughts were now getting more and more filled with what this wonderful religion which derived its motive from the relation between a *Guru* and *Śiṣya* (Master and Disciple), in the purest of contexts known to the Indian soil, could mean at present, especially with the prospect of actually going to Amritsar, the city founded by Guru Ramdas, the fourth of the line of Sikh Gurus, in 1574.

The name Amritsar could be paraphrased as "The City of the Immortal Lake". The Ganges is the sacred river of the Hindus. Likewise, the Golden Temple of Amritsar with its marble steps and pavemented quadrangle, is today the Mecca of the Sikhs who adore the Book containing the Wisdom of the Gurus with all the embellishments and veneration that marble, gold, and the silent offerings from a never-ending stream of pilgrims daily could bring to the sacred spot.

Guru Arjun, the son of Guru Ramdas, completed the sacred tank of clear water in which pilgrims could bathe without being permitted to fish or to use soap. No caste is observed here and the only obligation is that one should take off shoes and wear something on the head. The closing tendencies found in the Hindu way of life in the name of caste or clan have been completely overcome in the Sikh way of life. The Sikh is thus a *Śiṣya* or Disciple who follows a line of Gurus who combined the prophetic and the apocalyptic in religion with what is based on the recognition of hierophanies and holy presences in equal proportion.

Values and Guru Loyalties

These two sets of values have been referred to as twin binding forces of religion in the *Bhagavad Gītā* (XV. 2). They arise from the double-sided aspects of value relationships that the human mind is capable of in the domain of spirituality or religion, one referring to the hypostatic values in the world of the intelligibles and the other pertaining to existential presences here in a more ontological sense.

All religions based on the idea of holiness have these two ambivalent or polarized factors which bind the followers to patterns of behaviour or to items or articles of faith. The dividing line between the Hindu and the Sikh is where hierophantic values gain primacy over the hypostatic ones. Translating high doctrine into liveable terms of daily common fellowship, avoiding separatist orthodoxies and the exaggerations that attend them, whether in its higher or more ordinary aspects, is what gives to Sikhism its charm and attraction.

Just as there can be no fire without some smoke implied in it, no religion can be conceived as so pure that it is without taint at all. Anything that touches the earth must participate of dust. Making due allowance for this limitation it is possible to assert confidently that Sikhism represents as clean a religion as could be possible anywhere. Judged further in the light of the chequered political history of India at a time when the best heritage of the country stood in danger of being overturned, the credit for preserving to this day some of the best aspects of what is called Indian culture or spirituality may be said to go to two groups of Indians, the Maharashtras and the Sikhs, both of whom gave primacy to Guruhood and developed their religion round this central value. Sikhs and Maharashtras have had common Guru loyalties at certain epochs in their history and have been facing Afghan invasions together side by side to keep the integrity of India about the year 1758.

First Aquaintance with Sikhism

It is nearly 28 years ago that I first made direct contact with a Sikh. I had heard of the Akalis who came to the Vaikom Satyagraha in Travancore (now Kerala) to offer volunteers and a free kitchen to help in the struggle against casteism in that part of the country more than thirty years ago. The subtle wire-pulling contrivances of Sanātanī Hindus had made even Mahatma Gandhi to refuse help on grounds that were not clear from the Mahatma's pronouncements which I remember to have carefully scrutinized at that time. Whatever that might be, it was when I was sitting next to an actual Sikh when returning by bus from Simla in the summer of the year 1938 to Ambala Cantonment that I first made direct contact with Sikhism.

The Sikh is to be distinguished by the five signs named with the initial letter K (*keśa*, uncut hair ; *kaṅga*, a comb ; *kachha*, a pair of shorts; *karā*, steel bangle; and *kṛpāṇā*, a short sword). He is not necessarily a vegetarian, but unlike a Hindu who would get a sheep or a goat first killed by a Mohammedan before eating it, the Sikhs kill and eat without any sin-absolving intercession to save their conscience. If Moslems shave their head, the Sikh will never touch a razor. Persecuted by the extreme orthodoxies of both Hindus and Moslems from either side, their own orthodoxy had to find some sort of *via media*, some items of which might not stand the light of critical scrutiny, but, as necessity sometimes known no law, circumstances that involved their very survival had to shape the faith and conduct of these brave and generous people. Thus true to themselves, they cannot be charged with falsehood or evil.

The twin clauses which occupy the fourth and fifth positions in the very first formula for meditation in the *Jap Jī* by Guru Nanak himself, contains the reference to two high human values *abhaya* (fearlessness) and *nirvair* (non-hateful or generosity of attitude) which could be virtues only in days of difficulty or danger, which were in reality the most important factors that we have to remember in connection with the history and growth of the religion of the Sikhs.

Abhaya (fearlessness) as we know, is a value that finds place even in the *Bhagavad Gītā*. There, Chapter XVI begins by giving prime importance to the personal value, and as for generosity, in the very second verse *akrodha* (angerlessness) is given due place.

If we should further scrutinize the doctrinal aspects of Sikhism, we find that the very first value they stress is the unitive approach and the second refers to *Auṁ-kāra* (the syllable *Auṁ*) which is treated as synonymous with the Absolute in the same way as understood in *Upaniṣads* such as the *Māṇḍūkya*. Although we read in Sikh history that Sanātanī Hindus and even the Ārya Samājists have been against them at different epochs for various socio-politically complicated reasons, Sikhism may still be looked upon, even today, as representing a clear and filtered essence of what is most precious in the Upaniṣadic way of life when rid of much extraneous dross that adhered to it as accretions due to special historic circumstances.

If the intelligent Sikh of the present-day could only be taught to say "I accept the best in the Hindu and in Islam" instead of adopting as his basis the doubly negative formula or rejecting this or that item in either of the religions between which Providence has cast their lot, we would be seeing the emergence of a new spiritual impetus of great significance in the history of India that is still to be written. An open dynamism will then accrue in favour of this interesting integration that has taken place in the soil of the Five Rivers due to rare historic circumstances. Static closing tendencies have to be countered by translating double negation dialectically in terms of the oneness of the AUṀ of the very first part of the *Jap Jī* of Guru Nanak.

On the 9th October was to be celebrated by the Gurukula the 106th birthday anniversary of Guru Nārāyaṇa who may be said to correspond to Guru Nanak in our own particular hierarchy. Between the Himālaya and Kanyākumārī (Cape Comorin) in the extreme south of Mother India, there is a dialectical inter-relationship. Guru Nārāyaṇa and Guru Nanak, like the Maharashtra Gurus such as Tukārām and Rāmdās belong to an India that is not visible to many modern Indians who are carried away by political or so-called "progressive considerations" in which more problems are born each day than can be resolved. Fossilized or effete forms of religion, however valuable as curiosities or fossils cannot be expected to deliver the goods that alone can sustain human life.

With these thoughts it was that, while waiting for the projected trip to the very cradle of the Sikh religion, I was tempted in my leisurely and meditative hours to take up and read a precise account of Sikhism by Principal Tejh Singh. I went through the small and clearly written volume with all due attention. I am able to assert that I could not find one detail in all that I read therein on which I could base an adverse criticism against Sikhism. When I consider that I am temperamentally one who enjoys pulling things to pieces wherever possible by hypercritical observations, the very fact that I could not do any such thing with the religion of the Sikhs is perhaps as high a compliment to this religious expression that I can possibly pay.

Anything Better than Something Worse

One can go to a man who is five and a half feet tall and say to him that he could have been full six feet in stature. Conversely one can easily console oneself saying that something is not worse than it actually happens to be. Judging other religions has these two kinds of pitfalls, neither of which can be considered as implying the right attitude. It is true the Sikhs could be better than they are in such items as non-killing, but that would not be fair. The preference that I have expressed for the religion of the Sikhs does not have its reason in any extraneous norms applied to it. My duty has always been to examine each religion in the light of a science which takes into account the Absolute as the normative regulative Value in human life.

In the light of a science of the Absolute which has a strict methodology and an epistemology of its own, it is my task to examine various socio-religious formations so as to fit them correctly into a scheme without trying to judge them from any preferential angle at all.

Just as solving a mathematical problem does not admit of any personal preferences, religions must be capable of being comparatively studied in the light of a science of sciences, wherein all significant values in human life can be fitted without favour to anyone without fear of hurting anyone's feelings. If in my remarks above, and in speaking of the Todas, I have lavished praise, it should not therefore be construed that I personally like the Sikhs or the Todas. I would prefer readers to think that I like them because they accord with the norms of human existence, subsistence or value in the science of the Absolute.

PART III

Guruhood

16

The Glory of Guruhood

A GURU is a man of renunciation. He is one who has banished himself and loves to live in utter loneliness outside the pale of society. Not to be dictated to by any society but to try and tell society something good for it, is the difficult role that Gurus are expected to play. Otherwise society will drift its own way without any standards or *norms* which might lead social units to become stagnant and steeped more and more in the bog of relativism. It is the Guru's influence that can act as a leaven to raise the moral and spiritual standards in any society and mix in fresh water and clean out the stagnation that is otherwise to be expected.

A long line of Gurus has been known on the soil of India, from the most ancient times. They should not be mixed up with pontiffs or dignitaries of institutionalized religions but should be seen as free representatives of the Wisdom heritage of the common man. This Wisdom heritage tends to become out-moded time and again in the history of peoples. When such a deterioration of standards in life takes place, it is the Gurus who enter the scene and by a dialectical revaluation of the Wisdom situation, together with its language and idioms, bring fresh life for the thoughts to be retained once again for use and contained, as it were, like old wine in new bottles. Thus the role of Gurus is a delicate yet a significant and glorious one.

The Model Gurus of Indian Tradition

From the time of Bṛhaspati and Dakṣiṇāmūrti we have had ancient models of Guruhood in India. They were free individuals who lived sometimes in dry-leaf-huts in the forests or in out-of-the-way places, far from the madding influences of the crowd and its ignoble strivings. The *Yogī* meditating under a tree with wild and domesticated beasts standing around him, has been an ideogram known in the Mohen-jo-Daro seals. The same picture is retained later in the famous hymn to *Dakṣiṇāmūrti* written by Śaṅkarācārya in which the ideogram is seen repeated after thousands of years. Translated it reads:[1]

> A picture-marvel, under yon banyan tree behold !
> Old are the pupils and the teacher he is young withal:
> In utter silence the teaching goes on
> And yet the pupils with full-banished doubt remain !

This picture has nothing in common with what a religious dignitary might represent. The tree under which the Guru chooses to live, is to ensure his utter independence and freedom from those obligatory aspect of religious life into whose harsh aspects a Guru would never wish to dip his hands to stain them with anything not perfectly just. The Inquisition and the bloodshed that has drenched the soil repeatedly in the history of religions is not a chapter that could be associated with Guruhood. The burning at the stake of a man of science or the sin of having an innocent maid consumed in fire lit in a market place, or, enviously hacking to death a beautiful woman philosopher have fortunately never tainted the glory of Guruhood as it has been preserved in forest hermitages by men of utter renunciation.

The Gurus have always stood for kindness to all life, and it accrues to the credit of one disciple of a Guru at least, that an emperor once laid down his sword when engaged in actual warfare in the name of non-hurting of fellow man. Living on roots or fruits that involve no hurt even to vegetable life, wearing the barks of trees only, and observing the everlasting vow of not hurting even an ant, such is the dedicated model of Guruhood and its glory.

Godly Men and Fully Human Divinities

Further, a Guru's glory consists in that he is ever free from any relativistic affiliations or commitments, whether in the name of his own or other religions, races or nations. He speaks in the name of all of them and refuses to add to any of the flames of separation or fanaticism. Exclusiveness is a word unknown to all model Gurus and, although orthodoxy can sometimes becomes so harsh as to connive at such ideas as cutting out the tongue or filling with molten lead the ears of a low-born in the name of so-called caste in India itself, references that blemish the pages of some of the most respected of canonical writings of even the most tolerant of peoples otherwise found within any religious groups, amends are soon made by the Gurus who come after them, in the same spiritual lineage, so as to raise their reputation above all taint of relativistic attitudes within the Wisdom they represent. Untainted by anything mundane or what sets one man against another, Gurus generally may be said to have remained above the dust clouds of relativistic dispute and to have represented God on earth. They could be called godly Men or fully human Divinities. Whether put one way or the other, one and the same truth in respect of the normal and neutral Guruhood, is revealed by either statement.

Guru Model not Confined to India

It is true that Gurus have always been recognized and respected normally in India; but this should not mean that the geographical limits of India alone can produce this type of Wisdom that makes for Guruhood. Mystics and contemplatives, whose qualities have conformed to the correct requirements of Gurus or Wisdom teachers, have lived and died unknown in the farthest corners of the globe. They have all been representatives of the Absolutist way of life and of thinking in one way or another. The local vernaculars that they spoke and the background to which each belonged might have irradiated its particular tint to each one of them. This is inevitable, as when we find a colourlessly transparent crystal placed on a piece of crimson satin looking red without itself having the colour intrinsically. Gurus cannot totally avoid their own particular contexts but in spite of this limitation they shine in their own white and crystalline radiance for all time without any limitations either of clime or period. They belong to the context of contemplative Wisdom, mysticism or perennial philosophy and thus make a world fraternity knowing no frontiers. Christian, Sufi or Tao Gurus, not to speak of pre-Socratic ones, belonged to the same fraternity. In India, Kapila, Kaṇāda and Gautama have risen to the stature of Gurus in their own times, whether they are at present considered orthodox or not. Both the sceptic and the believer can join hands in the true light of Absolutist Wisdom that Guruhood has always represented irrespective of any possible Bṛhaspati or Dakṣiṇāmūrti archetype.

We Need Reaffirmation of the Glory of Guruhood

Humanity stands today in need of the message of Guruhood revalued and restated in a form to fit the prevailing scientific climate and idiom of our times. A scientist in Russia can understand what a fellow scientist discovers in a different part of the world. The same cannot be said to be true in the domain of religion or nationhood. These form closed areas and the language of one group is treated distrustfully by another even when strictly speaking they might be using synonymous expressions. In content 'democracy' cannot be so different from 'communism' but the political and closed colouration of these words in actual use in journals would make us believe that the fundamental content of these expressions are diametrically opposed. This is due to subtle Babelization involved here of which no journalist however clever, can abolish the evil. Guru-wisdom alone fully absolutist in import and content, can rub off the edge that hurts as between these groups, who consider themselves rivals when they really stand for one and the same human value precious to each and all of us at once. The secret of Guru-wisdom consists in that it can transcend paradoxes and solve conflicts.

Let us sing again the glory of true Guruhood and let each one of us, inspired by its high value help to spread the glad tidings of the re-discovery of its glory for the good of mankind everywhere !

Reference

1. *citram vaṭatarormūle vṛddhā śiṣyā gurur yuvā gurostu maunam vyākhyānam śiṣyāstu chinnasamśayaḥ.*

17

A Guru Tradition Above Time and Clime

WISDOM is not mere reason prevailing at a given moment at a given place. That would be only a cross-section view of truth. Wisdom is more like a great river which silently flows through time. Neutral or absolute wisdom has been compared to the ocean, changeless and ever-filling. Teachers have arisen from time to time in every clime as spokesmen of wisdom. They have flourished in various ways, intensively or extensively, according to the seed or the soil of the wisdom they represented. Such teachers have been called Gurus in India and have been held in esteem and have been honoured in different ways in different world contexts. Their teachings have influenced generations through myth or legend, theologies or mysticism, religion or philosophy. Whatever form they may have taken they have always had a perennial content and message for humanity.

Three Wise Men of the East

The three wise men of the East who were present at Christ's nativity were guided by a star representing human aspiration or hope. They must have represented those fully awake to wisdom-values in human life, ready to recognize the dialectical revaluation which was going to be inaugurated in the name of Christ.

There have been three wisdom teachers in South India who were at once seekers and spokesmen for wisdom in their particular contexts. We could find equally well, three wise men belonging to the context of Chinese, Persian or Russian thought. If we could brush aside historical consideration and refuse to let ourselves be confused by anything local that might have conditioned or coloured their message, it would be possible for us to see clearly the truth of what the Guru Nārāyaṇa wrote as an *envoi* to his poem called *Scriptures of Mercy*.[1]

High scripture's meaning, antique, rare,
Or meaning as by Guru taught,
And what a silent sage conveys,
And wisdom's elaborations of every sort
Together they all belong,
One in essence, in substance the same.

Modernism is not without its Gurus or wise men either. What commands respect now-a-days is what is called science. Although etymologically, science and wisdom are interchangeable terms, it is no longer usual to think so. The physicist is the most respected of the scientists. Truth is confined by them to matters calculable or measurable while to be a metaphysician is at once a discredit in the eyes of the modern man.

There have recently emerged however, three philosophers of science who have willingly or unwillingly stepped beyond the strict limits of logico-empirical science and landed themselves on the true terrain of metaphysics, without themselves admitting it or perhaps realizing it fully. Eddington, Whitehead and Russell are three of the leading thinkers of this scientific age. We shall focus attention on them for a while here so as to fit them and understand them in the schematic frame of reference we have developed in the previous article.

From the comparatively antique South Indian context we shall focus our attention likewise on three Gurus of the wisdom tradition of India — Śaṅkara, Rāmānuja and Madhva who have been respectively labelled 'non-dualist' (*Advaitin*), 'specifically non-dualist' (*Viśiṣṭa-advaitin*) and 'dualist' (*Dvaitin*). The effective use of the frame of reference would become evident only if we can employ its schematic language to compare, interpret, or better understand divergent schools of wisdom.

The three Gurus we have selected are generally representative of the Vedāntic tradition as a whole as it prevails to this day in India. In the same way the three mathematical scientific philosophers of the West may for our purpose be considered representative of the latest expression of the modern wisdom of the West. Between the two sets of three each which we shall study here, may be included, in principle, all intermediate grades and varieties of wisdom teachers on the general world context, whose number or variety would make it impossible for us to discuss all within the span of one short essay. Without attempting the impossible, it is our aim to briefly review the teachings of these philosophers or Gurus (if we may call them so), and thus see how they can be understood unitively and universally as exponents in their own ways of the Wisdom of the Absolute. In this matter we have to take special care that the labels applied to their teachings as being theological or scientific or anything else should not mislead us. We here make bold to suggest in advance that the content of all theology, philosophy or wisdom worth such high names is always bound to be the normative notion of the Absolute, or at least some aspect of the Absolute.

The Absolute as the Common Content of Duality or Paradox

The problem of wisdom in the Eastern context is between degrees of duality or non-duality. Nowhere have the subtle capacities of the human intellect been more profusely lavished than around this central problem of wisdom as understood between such Gurus as Śaṅkara, Rāmānuja and Madhva.

In the Western philosophical or scientific scene, the same central problem has taken the form of solving the paradox. From the Cartesian duality as between the mind and the body, which may be said to be a paradox also, outmoded through psycho-physical parallelism or interaction, the tendency of modern philosophers is to stress the unity underlying the duality, paradox or conflict, not only as concerns mind and matter, but generally in the various sciences. Bergson's *elan vital*, like the concept of the Neutral Monism of Russell, the 'Subjective Selectivism' of an Eddington or the 'Organism' suggested in the writings of Whitehead as the content of truth, whether conceived in terms of being or becoming, all presuppose at present a unitive content for all philosophy or wisdom.

Although the method adopted is mathematical or logical, empirical or *a priori*, the content of philosophy does not change. It can be said to concern a notion of the Absolute, as something subject to 'creative' becoming or 'selective' and subjective understanding. It could also be conceived statically or dynamically, negatively, positively or neutrally with different degrees of duality or the principle of paradox implicit in it. The terms of the paradox, say '*p*' or '*q*', could be thought of under all the possible varieties of the propositional calculus, such as known to symbolic logic and as represented by signs beginning with *pq* and ranging through intermediate varieties of conjunction or disjunction (each with its sub-divisions of inclusive or exclusive disjunction) to the last of the series represented by *p/q* or total disjunction.

Under whatever garb, modern or ancient, Eastern or Western, the problem might present itself to us, we have first to be able to see that they all refer to the central normative notion of the Absolute, without which all wisdom research or philosophic adventure would be like a ship without a captain on the high seas. This does not mean that a theological, anthropomorphic God is necessary to postulate for all wisdom. It means only that even as a mere mathematical sign the content of wisdom must be kept in mind.

The Rapprochement of Eastern and Western Tradition

Eastern philosophy has often been discredited on account of its tendency to be *a priori*, 'solipsist', 'sentimental' or 'uncritical' as against Western philosophy which has claimed to have an objective empirico-logical, positive or critical status. Its great glory is that 'it works', while 'escapists' who succumb to natural forces in undignified servility have a theological dogmatism which is not philosophical at all. J.E. Erdman can be quoted as an example of this prevailing attitude. At the beginning of his introduction to his large volume *A History of Philosophy* he writes:

> The task of apprehending its own nature in thought can only tempt the human mind, and indeed it is only then equal to it when it is conscious of its own intrinsic dignity — and as in the East except among the Jews, this point is not reached, we must not be induced to talk of a pre-Hellenic philosophy or worse still of pre-Hellenic systems.

Even a person otherwise sympathetic to Indian thought such as Romain Rolland, speaks of the *libre critique* of the Occident as contrasted with the lack of such in Oriental thought. Such a contrast between the East and the West is only given to superficial thought and lack of equal familiarity as between the two wisdom-growths. It is true that from the time that discoveries were made in the name of science, a positive attitude to knowledge has progressively gained ground in the history of Western thought at the expense of what is generally referred to as humanistic studies.

The ground gained in recent history has, however, come to be lost again within the last few decades after the discovery of quantum mechanics and the indeterminism associated with the Einsteinian relativist view of the world. If we should pick on Bertrand Russell as representing the latest and finalized expression of the positivist attitude in philosophy, we have unmistakable signs now of his accepting the limitations of the empirical approach. Although he remains as thorough-going a sceptic as he ever was, in one of his later works, *Human Knowledge, Its Scope and Limits*, at the conclusion of his last chapter, he wrote:

> Indeed such inadequacies as we have seemed to find in empiricism have been discovered by strict adherence to a doctrine by which empiricist philosophy has been inspired: that all human knowledge is uncertain, inexact and partial. To this doctrine we have not found any limitation whatsoever.[2]

When Russell refers to a *doctrine* that *inspires* the empiricist to which he dogmatically asserts he has found "no limitation whatsoever", he either is merely a cocksure Englishman or speaks a language of a rank believer rather than of a sceptic which he proclaims himself always to be. At a later date, contributing his article to the *Encyclopedia of Unified Science* he is however, seen again to water down his dogmatism somewhat when he hesitatingly admits, "The old view that measurement is of the essence of science would therefore seem to be erroneous".[3]

This read with his categorical admission in his chapter on the limits of empiricism, quoted above, that "Empiricism as a theory of knowledge has proved inadequate" (p. 527) gives us from himself a picture of a philosopher who was a thorough-going sceptic before, but whose attitude was undergoing drastic change in a later stage. As one fully alive to the findings of modern thinkers, his 'conversion' if we may say so, could be taken as representing the change which is coming over the whole of the Western world at the present time.

Thus there is to be expected a *rapprochement* between the philosophical attitudes of the East and the West. Such a process could be accelerated from the Eastern side if some of the logistic, semantic or syntactical methods are employed in a correctly re-stated Science of the Absolute having its roots in the Eastern Guru tradition such as the *Vedānta*. The union of Eastern and Western philosophy could be expected to become an accomplished fact, more because of the changing outlook in the West rather than in the traditional attitude of the East. Further confirmation of this tendency of the West can be gathered from the positions of Eddington and Whitehead, the two others of the Guru trio of the West whom we shall presently pass on to examine.

The 'Subjective Selectivism' of Eddington

Eddington by employing his own sedenion algebra, has succeeded in showing the most astounding fact that "reason alone can give us more accurate knowledge of the Universe than crude experiment", and that actual measurement of time or space with a chronometer or measuring rod of any kind could be dispensed with in arriving at important results as an 'experimentalist' himself could arrive at, by their cruder laboratory or other methods.

This is a most revolutionary revelation of modern times, from whose surprise and wonder Western scientists are still to awake fully. While admitting the astonishing nature of Eddington's findings, the dazed hesitancy to appraise him correctly is reflected in the following concluding extracts from an article by Dr. Burniston Brown, Reader in Physics of the University of London:

> Eddington's astonishing calculations seem to revive the ancient idea that reason alone can give us more accurate knowledge of the Universe than crude experiment, but for *the reason I have given*, I think this is an illusion. What Eddington's work should do is to warn us very forcibly of the hypothetical character of a great deal of modern atomic physics and astronomy.[4]

The reason said to be given by the writer here is contained in the following words of the previous paragraph in the same article:

> Eddington's reduction of the mathematical theories of physics to sedenion algebra is a tremendous intellectual achievement, but *I don't think* there is any fundamental difference between it and the simple geometrical example that we have considered . . . There is no guarantee whatever that new experimental discoveries will not upset these theories. So our *conclusion must be I think* that ordinary scientific method still remains the only way of arriving at true statements about Nature.[5]

If we should read this hesitant paragraph side by side with such sentences as:

> This work which is an intellectual feat of the first magnitude is summarized and expounded in his last book called *Fundamental Theory* which he was unfortunately, not able to finish before his death . . . The philosophy which Eddington adopted is called Subjective Selectivism but it is *difficult to be quite sure* what exactly he meant by this.[6]

and read between the lines, one cannot miss noting how there is a diehard conservatism even in the domain of science which has its own brand of orthodoxy. All that we want to glean from the above is the very evident fact that something that discredits experimental science has been stated by a first-rate scientist himself, and that this places the accent again on the inner rather than the outer world of values or realities. In ,this way the West is on the brink of a new sentimentalism which might prove to be as bad if not worse than the subjectivism for which Eastern thought has so far been blamed.

Whitehead, a Platonist with a Bergsonian Background

Whitehead is another leader of modern mathematico-scientific thought, whom we have to estimate in order to relate him to our scheme of wisdom-correlation. To get started in so doing, we shall rely again on an estimate of him by one of his admirers. We quote the following about him from L.L. White:

> His attempt at a synthesis centred on one philosophical idea, that of the creative passage of nature, the time-process which somehow transcends apparent separation of individual entities and carries the whole on to new forms of existence. But Whitehead expressed himself in very difficult metaphysical language, and those who do not believe that philosophical truth need be obscure — and I do not — must ask why this was so. Perhaps it is because Whitehead stood precisely at the climax of a great intellectual transition from the world of permanence represented by Plato — the doctrine of unchanging personal immortality and conservation principle — to the new world of process, the world of Bergson, historical transformation and changing relationships which concern contemporary science — such relationships as the one-way process of the second law of thermodynamics. Whitehead saw the truth of the new attitude, but he could not renounce the old foundations; hence the obscurity and occasional confusion as when he called the atom an organism.[7]

Although we do not see eye to eye with the writer above, we are able to concede that Whitehead as a philosopher speaks both for 'being' and 'becoming' at once. Here it is possible to see that his essentially dialectical approach to wisdom as a river rather than as a cross-section view of truth, makes him a puzzle to the modern mind, such as that of Mr. White.

It is possible also that Whitehead himself was not aware of the dialectical role he was playing. 'Being' could be thought of unitively side by side with 'becoming' and reality conceived both dynamically or statically, creatively or selectively according to the particular aspect to the Absolute that a philosopher might wish to elaborate. There is no violation of epistemology or methodology in so doing. The eternal process could be contained in terms of consciousness in the pure eternal present. It is not impossible to think of a continuous process of a dialectical revaluation of Plato, through neo-Platonic thought, reaching to the philosophy of flux and becoming of Bergson, when all is understood to be based on the subtle dialectics of Parmenides and Zeno (whose paradox is by-passed or solved) of pre-Socratic times. This dialectical method has been brought up to our own times by Hegel and Karl Marx though only in some of its partial aspects. Whitehead's philosophy thus could be easily fitted into the frame of reference we have suggested, consisting of a time-space continuum with the possibility of an 'organism' or 'monad' conceived at its core of the eternal present. The obscurity attributed to his philosophy by those who ignore the unitive dialectical approach, can thus be explained and excused.

Complementary Aspects Represented by the Three Philosophers

If we now try to fit the three Western philosophers we have chosen into the frame we have evolved, it would, in the first place, be easy to see how Eddington, as a "Subjective Selectivist" as he himself named his philosophy, really represents the neutral vertical aspect of the Absolute. The series of constants which he arrived at through sedenion algebra may be looked upon as various points in the vertical axis which refer to the plus and minus sides of reality at once, so that one could be verified in reference to the other. As with a mirror reflection, there is a correspondence between the two sides, which enables him to verify or correct the plus result of an experiment with the minus result of his sedenion algebraic calculations or *vice-versa.* His reference to an expanding universe shows that he also thinks in terms of 'being' and 'becoming' at once. In Eddington we have the case of a man who started as a pragmatic experimental scientist, being suddenly converted into an enthusiast for pure subjectivism, through mathematics. He could now be included as a contemplative philosopher and his interest in the Absolute consisting of what pertains to its vertical aspect, according to the scheme we have developed.

Whitehead and Russell were complementary to each other. They were both mathematical philosophers who were capable of employing thought on publicly valid lines for the discovery of truth. This did not deter them, although they were the joint authors of the *Principia Mathematica* (vast volumes) from the one tending towards scepticism as an ideal, and the other to a form of Platonized monadology in the light of Bergson's creative evolutionism, as a believer, L.L. White's estimate of the two philosophers underlines for us the contrast we have referred to in a couple who otherwise could be considered intellectual twins:

> As mathematicians Whitehead and Russell were in full agreement . . . but they differed in personal temperament . . . Whitehead was more deeply marked by the traditional Platonic outlook and also had a rich sense of the role of the religious, aesthetic and moral elements of human experience.

And speaking of Russell the same writer continues:

> Something of the iconoclasm of Voltaire and the scepticism of Descartes were combined in the profoundly original and logical mind of the young Russell.[8]

If Russell could be called a realist, Whitehead could be called an idealist. These terms however, as used in the course of philosophical thought have been applied to various names so that their conations stand at present much compromised and confused. The best way for us therefore would be to rely on our schematic language and say that Russell used verticalized mathematical methods of thinking to arrive at the point where the horizontal axis intersected the vertical, while Whitehead was capable of soaring higher through hypothetical constructions, also mathematically conceived, into the world of Platonic ideas. Russell was more of a hesitant Aristotelian while Whitehead was a confirmed Platonist.

If we could put together the whole truth as separately envisaged in the philosophies of the three together, we could thus reconstruct for our purposes, the whole picture of the notion of the Absolute which is neither positive nor negative only, nor attached to horizontal or vertical values only, but is to be globally understood unitively as a normative principle for all philosophical discussion. When such a scheme is properly visualized by the modern mind, the much respected place that Eddington would have to be given, in the discovery of this normative principle would become better understood. In passing, it would be advantageous to notice that some sort of wisdom or Guru-tradition operates even in the scientific West, especially when we see that, in spite of their common methods, Whitehead and Russell responded to different philosophical backgrounds if not traditions.

The Seat of Philosophical Paradox or Duality

We have already stated how the terms duality of the *Vedānta* context and paradox as the problem of modern philosophers like Russell, really refer to aspects of the same Absolute.

The principle underlying the possibility of paradoxes is also to be carefully examined before its solution or its transcendence can be properly understood. Paradox can be stated pragmatically, semantically, or logistically. It is usual in formal logistic to refer to it as existing between the terms *p* and *q* which could be juxtaposed conjunctively or disjunctively. Dilemma is also essentially of the same stuff of paradox where instead of opposition together there is possibility of an alternation or choice between two points of view. 'If', 'either-or', 'when', 'only if', 'if them', 'not', 'if and only if' are expressions indicating various alternating or mutually exclusive types of the principle of paradox as evidenced in life problems. Between a newly-wed couple and their post-divorce relations various degrees of conjunction, or disjunction, inclusive or exclusive, as the case may be, in their possible relations, can be thought of. Degrees of duality, similarity, permit of varieties, as known to the Indian *Tarka Śāstra* under what are known as the *abhāvas*. The alternative relation is found employed dialectically in the *Bhagavad Gītā*, Chapter II. 26. ("Or again, if you should hold This to be constantly-ever-born or as constantly-ever-dying").

Transcending paradox has been one of the central problems of the philosophy of Russell. The importance of solving paradox occupies a very prominent place with him. This can be understood from the following extract from the article under "Paradoxes, logical" by Alonzo Church in Runes, *Dictionary of Philosophy*:

> Russell's solution of the paradoxes is embodied in what is now known as the *ramified theory of types*, published by him in 1908, and afterwards made the basis of *Principia Mathematica*. Because of its complication, and because of the necessity for the much-disputed *axiom of reducibility*, this has now been

> largely abandoned in favour of other solutions.
>
> Another solution — which has recently been widely adopted — is the *simple theory of types* . . . This was proposed as a modification of the ramified theory of types of Chwistek in 1921 and Ramsey in 1926, and adopted by Carnap in 1929.[9]

Our familiarity with mathematical logistic being still poor we can only suggest that a solution to paradoxes of this kind might be found along the lines of Pierce's law, stated in the following formula:

$$[[P \supset q] \supset P] \supset P.$$

corresponding to what is intended by our vertical axis.

Another fruitful line of investigation beyond paradox is suggested by the Max Planck constant, *h* and other similar constants, the former implying the "uncertainty principle" between position and momentum in quantum mechanics.

For our part, at present, it would suffice for the purposes of the present discussion to note that a solution for the duality implicit in paradox has not yet been finally reached by Western thinkers. We shall not venture any further on this point at present.

Does Eastern Vedānta Fare any Better?

If we should now turn to the Gurus of the East for a solution, we see that on the South Indian soil polemical battles are still being fought as between the non-dualists (*advaitins*), the pure dualists (*dvaitins*) and the qualified non-dualists (*viśiṣṭa-advaitins*) as the followers of Śaṅkara, Madhva and Rāmānuja are called. That the fires of controversy have not yet died down is sufficiently reflected in the following extracts from *The Life and Teachings of Śrī Madhvācāriar*, by C.M. Padmanabhachar (Madras 1909):

> Śrī Madhva condemned the system of Śrī Śaṅkara with all the vehemence of which he was capable, as he considered *Advaita* to be totally destructive and subversive of the very spirit and essence of theism. (p. 240)
>
> Coming after Śrī Śaṅkara the school of Śrī Rāmānuja shows leaning towards *Advaita* in some respects as its name imports. The theory is generally known as *Viśiṣṭādvaita*. It is said to be *Advaita* though with a difference. *Para-Brahman* in this school is often described as the *material* and *efficient* cause of the

> world. It is difficult to see how God can be the material cause, in any school of Dualism. In this and some other respects Śrī Madhva differs from Śrī Rāmānuja. With regard to the individual souls for example Śrī Vaiṣṇavas hold them capable of infinite knowledge and bliss and say that when the final release occurs, all the released souls enjoy bliss in an equal measure of perfection, equal to God himself. Sad Vaiṣṇavas (i.e., Madhvas) do not grant this. To them the idea of *jīvātmās* ever reaching a footing of equality with God in point of bliss or any other respect is repugnant. (p. 259)

Again bringing out the difference between Śaṅkara and Rāmānuja he continues:

> While Advaitins maintain the unreality of the universe, by reason of Māyā (illusion) Viśiṣṭādvaitins took up a position of diametrical opposition and maintained that there was no such thing as illusion in the world at all in matters mundane or divine. They held that even the silver in the mother-of-pearl and the snake in the rope (*two common illustrations of mistake-making used by Śaṅkara*) are realities and not illusory. Śrī Madhva occupies a position of the golden mean. With him the world is real and not illusory . . . He was not prepared to hold that when a rope is imagined to be a snake, that the snake exists in reality in the rope, and is not a mere figment of the imagination. (p. 260)

Coming from an orthodox Madhva follower of modern India, although academic poise is lacking in the style, and cross-references are omitted, in the above extracts, they give us enough insight into the nature of the controversy between the three schools.

We cannot enter here into a closer and more authentic scrutiny of the three positions as between duality and non-duality as represented by the three Gurus we have chosen. The monumental work of Dr. O. Lacombe of Paris University, *L'Absolu selon le Vedanta* (Geuthner, Paris, 1937) is recommended for the study of the subtle positions between Śaṅkara and Rāmānuja. We give here but one short quotation (translated) from this great work.

The distinction drawn by Lacombe between Śaṅkara and Rāmānuja with regard to the Self in relation to its attributes will make explicit the non-duality of the two kinds represented by these Gurus. While Śaṅkara would say the body and such effects are false appearances foisted on the Self, Rāmānuja would confer equal dignity to the Self and its attributes in an inclusive non-duality as having a common substantial basis. Lacombe paraphrases the position of Rāmānuja as follows:

> The soul is a person; it expresses itself in an 'I' which signifies its substantiality, inasmuch as, at the same time, it engenders its essential attributes, and with which it distinguishes itself, as when for example it says 'I know', inasmuch also as it is extrinsically qualified by its body and its subtle or gross organs, because it is with them in a real conjunction as between one substance and another substance. (p. 194). This is based on *Śrī Nivāsa Deepikā* of Rāmānuja school.

The body-mind duality is here retained as well as transcended by a unitive notion common to both, pertaining to the Absolute Self.

Unitive Understanding of the Three Gurus of *Vedānta*

As we have been able to do in the case of the three mathematical philosophers with reference to the paradox of the Absolute, we could now also try to understand unitively the three Gurus of the Vedāntic context, in the light of the schema of the normative notion of the Absolute which we have developed step by step in the present series of articles.

Eddington and Śaṅkara could be first bracketed together as both being subjectivists who tend to minimise the importance of the objective side of reality as such. The former with his selective subjectivism working with a mind introspectively fixed on fundamental principles, as against what is visible, could be called as *a priori solipsist* as much as Śaṅkara who has been blamed for calling the world and its human value-contents as mere nothing but appearance, or else as merely due to nescience or *māyā*.

Rāmānuja would resemble a Platonist because of his acceptance of the *viśeṣa* (the specific aspect) of the glory of the Absolute as a personalized or high human value. Like Whitehead, he stands for the vertical 'plus' aspect of the normative principle common to all philosophy or theology.

As for Madhva's pure duality, we can see that he instists on it more for methodological rather than for doctrinal reasons, because in point of his loyalty to the Upaniṣadic notion of the Absolute he is no whit less orthodox than the two other Gurus. Madhva's theology is based on the supreme position to be given to Viṣṇu as the highest representative of the Absolute. When this is done the positive pole becomes supplied and a graded hierarchy of values ranging from the highest Viṣṇu or Nārāyaṇa to the most hierophantic representation of it in the Tulasī plant (the Indian sacred basil, *Ocimum santcum*), considered the consort of Viṣṇu, in his divine hierarchy of graded values, called *tāratamya* (comparative gradation of holy values) bringing up the rear or representing the negative pole in the scale of absolute values, becomes understood.

Śaṅkara's interest in the Absolute may be said to be epistemological, Rāmānuja is more interested in methodology, and Madhva's interest is mainly axiological. All are loyal to the cryptic and mystical notion of *Brahman* (the Absolute) contained in the *Upaniṣads* and as arranged in critical sequence in the *Brahma Sūtras* (Absolutist Aphorisms) of Bādarāyaṇa or Vyāsa. Thus they remain true Vedāntins of the context of *Brahma-Vidyā* or the Wisdom of the Absolute.

Unitive Trends in the Modern West

The West on its parts is beginning to see clearly the limits of the empirical approach to wisdom. Eddington, Whitehead and Russell represent three movements or trends in modern thought. They are all hesitant still about recognizing the mystery that they are facing as consisting of the wonder or the enigma of the Absolute which is fundamental to wisdom itself. While Whitehead and Russell together have been partners in sharpening the instruments leading to the knowledge of the Absolute, they have not been bold enough to name it as such. Russell in particular seems to find particular satisfaction in remaining a confirmed sceptic in spite of his ability to see beyond the limits of empiricism and admit the inadequacy of the method by measurement of science. Eddington on his part retires more into himself in subjective selectivism as against the forward urge of the creativism as understood in the Bergsonian context. He resembles thus any Oriental contemplative who is at peace with himself with his eyes shut. He comes nearest to catching up with what is known as *Yoga* in the Indian wisdom context.

References

1. The full poem translated and explained, will be found in *The Word of the Guru,* by Nataraja Guru, pp. 355-72.
2. Allen & Unwin, p. 527, 1948.

3. Vol. I, p. 41 Univ. of Chicago Press, 1955.
4. *The Listener,* p. 466, March 16, 1950 (*italics ours).*
5. *Ibid. (italics ours).*
6. *Ibid.,* p. 465 *(italics ours).*
7. *The Listener,* p. 677, April 22, 1948.
8. *Ibid.*
9. Jaico, Bombay, 1957.

18

The Role of the Guru Today

In the domain of contemplative relationships Guruhood represents a high human value. It constitutes the Central notion round which the Science of the Absolute lives and moves.

The Guru is not necessarily a living person. Śaṅkara himself gives him a paradoxical status when he refers to him as "visible to Vedāntic doctrines yet invisible" (*Vivekacūḍāmaṇi*, verse 1). The high value that Guruhood represents requires the yogic or the dialectically contemplative eye to recognize and accept without distortion, one-sided exaggeration or confusion.

Although it thus belongs to a context of subtle dialectics which may be said to be beyond the reach of the common man, there is no notion which is so current a coin in the timeless India of the villages even today. The peasant grandmother teaches the child to touch the feet of the Guru and, although modernized sections in India feel uneasy when required to behave in this traditional style, a great deal of the ancient pattern of behaviour presists in India at the present-day. Neither is it likely to pass away.

Guru — A Suspect Word

The word 'Guru' which has been introduced into the West through cheap and sensational literature has, in most cases, a strange effect when mentioned in the company of critically minded intellectuals there. Something of the world of the hocus-pocus naturally lingers on in connection with it. Puerile or abject kowtowing subjugation as well as outer tyrannical power exacting obedience in all circumstances are imagined to be implied in the Guru-disciple relationship. Often it is even suspected that Guruhood is a veil hiding hypocrisy or more disreputable tendencies. Such a suspicion may not in all cases be unjustified. But just as all patriotism is not the "refuge of a scoundrel", as Dr. Johnson put it, so claims to Guru-wisdom need not all be suspect.

In the varied public and private domains through which humanity is constantly shaping its future, it gets into relativistic impasses again and again. And whether in a village or at the head of a world assembly, the presence of a Guru or Gurus can give quite a new and unexpected character to the situation. Matters which, when left to themselves, would have ended in greater confusion, become reoriented, so that new solutions are reached and many a tension eased. A pinch of absolutism when added to the situation, from above as it were, can change its whole complexion. It is the "one pearl of great price" and the "little leaven that leaveneth the whole lump". As the *Bhagavad Gītā* puts it: "Even a little of such a way of life saves from great fear". (II.40)

A Subtle Fire

Let us take the instance of the Guru Nārāyaṇa. He loved to move from village to village. Guruhood came to dwell on his features with a natural grace by its own innate right. He cleared the jungle that had overgrown round neglected temples, he wrote new and better prayers for the village boys and girls to repeat, he revalued and restated their economic, educational, social and religious outlook and tried to put order where chaos prevailed. He settled long-standing disputes and even interested himself in arranging marriages, avoiding ritualistic waste. He started weaving sheds for poor boys which normal authorities forgot or neglected.

While these miscellaneous items were being incidentally attended to, his overall status as a teacher of absolutist humanized Wisdom still remained very effectively operative. The heat of the ascending contemplative self-discipline (known as *tapas*) that he represented in his personality as a Guru warmed the whole atmosphere in and through the existing set-up, without any duality or disruption, just as a ball of iron can be raised to white heat without changing its molecular structure.

The Guru-role is thus a subtle fire that fulfils without destruction. The Guru puts old wine into new bottles without creating dissenting new groups. No branch of human life is too mean or too noble for it. Viewing all humanity unitively, with an equal eye, the Guru-role is both humble and proud at once. The friendship of a village cowherd led is as important to him as being the head of a world gathering. As the water of an expansive dam is one with the water of the well that was once on the same site, but now overcovered by the flood, so the unitive wisdom which the Guru represents counteracts all relativistic limitations and in and through them triumphs above all obstructions, bringing in a subtle factor to prevail in human affairs.

Guruhood Principle in Daily Life

As a matter of fact this same principle of Guruhood is already implicit in our daily human life. Why does a son when still young have to bend to the wishes of a father? Why should the wife be taken by a husband and guided through a public place? Why should a subject obey the ruler? Or, more philosophically, why should cause be related to effect, or a map be related to the land? When answered completely and consistently, it will be seen that all such questions imply the same theory implicit in the principle of Guruhood which we are examining here.

Whether we speak of the international personality of the United Nations Organization by virtue of which, in certain instances at least, the International Court of Justice supports the supra-national rights of the Secretary General of that body, or the right of a son on his father's death to see that his father is decently buried, we tacitly accept in a certain sense of Absolute Necessity notions that are forced on us. What we wish to point out here is that even now in both the larger and local problems which face man, whether as a simple individual or as a member of the human race, a science of the Absolute is being relied upon loosely and unconsciously. As part of such a science, the subtle principle of Guruhood is implied in all worthwhile human situations.

If we are to save ourselves from the impasse that faces humanity at present, the Guruhood of mankind, whether particularly or universally viewed, when understood with all these implications, must become once again an operative and living principle in human affairs.

Freedom and proper spiritual orientation to unitive wisdom are crying needs of the present-day. We must know the Truth that shall make us free. In this task which presses on us imperatively, the Gurus of mankind, whether contemporary or belonging to the long vertical line of Gurus who have lived at all times and in all climes, have a role to play which is neither new-fangled nor outmoded . . . As it was in the beginning, is now, and ever shall be, in a world without end . . . Let us bring such an attitude to bear on man's life, but more scientifically and positively than hitherto. Then many a closed door will be opened, many a hurdle will be crossed and many a conflict will be resolved.

PART IV

Integration of the Sciences

19

Science and Human Values

THE need for integrating the vast body of knowledge that men have been able to accumulate into a coherent whole is a subject that has begun to engage the serious attention of educators. Practical aspects of knowledge are now being stressed at the expense of the purer branches. Advanced studies now refer mostly to technological subjects. The universities turn out more and more experts or specialists. As a result, those aspects of higher knowledge which were covered by the term 'humanities' have been by-passed and left behind.

Except in a few places such as the College de France, the Institute for Advanced Studies of Princeton or perhaps also in the recently started Committee on Social Thought under the University of Chicago, attempts at any serious integration of courses seem inadequate and negligible.

There is however, at the present time, a growing feeling for a fresh synthesis of knowledge, so that the sterility of over-departmentalization and consequent lack of the human touch in education may be effectively stemmed. Specialization at least must not be for its own sake but must serve some tangible end to produce a better educated man.

Private Bodies Representing Integrated Education

Besides the UNESCO which may be looked upon as an expression of the desire for a revised impetus to culture and science on a world-wide scale, there are at present many private foundations both in the East and in the West standing for the same ideal. They adhere to varied programmes, some being overtly scientific and others relying more on esoteric cultural values. A particular cosmology or a tacit dogmatic theology can be seen to be implied in many of them. Even the theory of evolution itself is being treated by some of them as an article of faith. They often become thus open to the objection that they tend to be dogmatic, sentimental or religiously pre-disposed. They would fall short of the requirement that any modern attempt to integration of knowledge should be conceived on more positive or scientific lines.

No Common 'Intellectual Formation'

Although senior professors of universities who may be in charge of admission of students for the higher courses may be heard to refer to what they call 'intellectual formation' as a necessary pre-requisite for following a certain specialized course, this expression remains still a very vague one. What precisely the expression is intended to convey may not be clear even as between one professor of a certain department and another, who might belong to the same university. The expression as applied to inter-university standards generally becomes still more vague, because cultural backgrounds differ widely, not only between the universities of the Old and the New Worlds, but even between universities of the same continent or even country.

Eastern and Western cultural standards may be said still to lie poles apart. German universities have each an academic reputation and tradition all their own and certain universities specialize only in select branches. Even in England an Oxonian is expected to have a formation different from a graduate of Cambridge. In France, although the situation has been somewhat mitigated by the existence of the centuries-old foundation of the College de France, the 'intellectual formation' demanded by a certain professor even in the department of letters, may differ from the one required by another.

In India, which has no university tradition to call its own, but tries to graft oriental culture on to the stem of occidental classical academic tradition, the case for a preliminary intellectual formation for higher studies is in a sad state indeed. The influence, in itself not salubrious, of the non-idealistic and pragmatic tendency of the United States, that prevails in the cultural world, as in many other departments of life at the present-day, is tending further to lower standards in cultural education. Measurement is being given primacy, and everything that does not lend itself to a brass instrument experimentation or testing, is tending to be discredited.

This influence, which is itself enough to dampen intellectual and moral enthusiasm for culture, works hand in hand at the present-day with that other tendency to be noticed in India, which gives primacy to localized cultural values. Linguistic preferences in the name of a pseudo-nationalism which encourage parochial loyalties and closed orthodoxies of different shades, are being allowed to compromise more or less completely the cause for an open and universal outlook in favour of any integrated education worth the name. In this connection it has been interesting to note that a group of Indian university vice-chancellors have recently been touring the United States of America seeking a formula for integrated education. From the report of their impressions it would appear that nothing striking was discovered for adoption in India. In the United States themselves we find a dissatisfaction which is expressing itself in the form of sporadic instances of revolt by youth.

Unitive and Universal Approach Needed

Whether we are concerned with 'basic', or 'fundamental' education for the emancipation, social or cultural, of the masses of the world, or think in terms of higher cultural values of an idealistic non-utilitarian programme in education for the select few, it is highly necessary at the present time to visualize the scope and methods of integrated education more clearly than hitherto. We have to be able to think of common human values in the global context of one solid humanity.

There should no longer be cultural preserves or prerogatives which try to divide humanity into sheep or goats. The myth of the primitive or inferior man has to be abandoned. The orthodox and the heterodox, the conservative and the liberal, the rightist and the leftist, must be able to meet in the endeavour to preserve the best human heritage that belongs to all. A common cultural language which would enable these precious values to be referred to, irrespective of the linguistic or traditional barriers, has to be evolved. Such a mathematically precise language would pave the way for the formulation of a regular science. Values preserved through humanistic studies could then be effectively cultivated without the arbitrary and sentimental barriers that history or geography might interpose between people. An open, dynamic and positive scientific attitude must invade the closed, static and private preserves in which higher human values have hitherto remained enclosed.

In other words, the challenge involved here is to bring back the humanities and the human values involved therein, into line with the other scientific values which, for no just reason, have in recent years tended to be considered as if divorced or disjunct from the former.

Positive and Negative Sciences

In the days of Aristotle all wisdom disciplines were more unitively understood than at the present-day. The term 'science' covered equally the whole range of subjects, starting from physics and natural history (or rather natural philosophy), to metaphysics, ethics, economics and politics. The Doctrine of the Mean which was Aristotle's contribution to thought, was a subtle underlying unitive principle which strung together branches of knowledge that have now come to be considered as different or disjunct from one another.

From the time when writers like Mill began to arrange cultural or economic notions on a less idealistic and 'utilitarian' basis, the firm hand of classical unitive thinking based on such bold dicta as "It is in ourselves that we are thus or thus" and the singleness of human end or purpose in life, gave way to the hesitant and wavering attitude implied in such expressions as "not expecting more from life than it is capable of bestowing". Unitive values began to be confused with non-unitive ones. The right regulative or normative principle that related ends with means through deliberation, began to be compromised. Horizontal or "here-and-now" values of an ontological nature were stressed at the expense of idealistic, teleological or vertical ones. The intuitive understanding of the Doctrine of the Mean was lost forever and thus cultural enthusiasm began to flag.

If we could again think of science as including both moral and physical sciences, the task of finding a basis for integrated education could be more easily accomplished. Knowledge can direct its search outward from the seat of the mind or soul within us. The 'eye of the soul' to use Aristotle's expression, can look 'positively' and 'objectively' into the world of the 'knowables' or subjectively or introspectively into values or virtues within the personality of man.

The latter has been known as the negative way which, by the eye of the soul directed inwardly, can still conduct 'auto-experimentation' by comparing common human experience of the *a priori* order. While the positive sciences are *a posteriori* and actually objective, these negative sciences could still be 'objective' in discipline in a virtual or conceptual sense. The strictness of scientific exactitude in thinking need not necessarily suffer in the latter case. When proper terms have been fixed to refer to aspects of knowledge, the whole range of knowledge can be made to come under one science which could be called the Science of sciences. In fact this is what the Science of the Absolute (or *brahma-vidyā* as such is called in India) claims to be. 'Knowledge' (*jñānam*) and 'the knowable' (*jñeyam*) are here to be distinguished, the first as negative and the second as positive. An epistemology and methodology based on a correct contemplative scale of values is here implied.

Integration can be Attempted from Different Poles

Some recent attempts at integration of knowledge have proceeded from the variety of specialized analytic knowledge towards their synthesis. Thus there is the famous instance in which the top-ranking nuclear physicist Schroedinger makes a serious attempt to relate biology with chemistry and physics. In his booklet entitled *What is Life*? an attempt has been made to bridge the gap between inanimate and living matter. Later writers such as Andrew A. Cochran[1] have availed themselves of the quantum theory to establish a link between life and matter. Such attempts may be said to travel from the positive and overt aspects of reality towards the innate and subtle aspects, or from the positive pole to the negative.

Conflicting Scales of Values

Even while we speak in terms of poles we have to distinguish two sets of poles as belonging to two distinct aspects of values or interests in life.

Reality, it must be remembered, is to be studied for the human interest in it, rather than just for its own sake without reference to human interests or values. All attempts at integration are for man and not for knowledge itself. When we visualize the world of values correctly, we will be able to see a vertical series of values in which the positive pole is the world of pure reason or that of the Platonic Intelligibles. The negative pole of vertical values will be in the *prime means* to the *supreme end* of attaining to the world of the Intelligibles when understood unitively and synthetically. Thus there is a vertical world of pure values and a horizontal world of material values.

The building up of a cultural life in a person means the recognition of both these sets while the Doctrine of the Mean must constantly convert knowledge in favour of virtues. As we have elsewhere tried to develop, it is possible to bring Gold, Goodness and God to be comprised within the amplitude of a personal scale of values between the poles of which the life of man may be said to oscillate. The science of things taken in themselves, and considered without their fundamental value-import for man, is like the magnetic field secondary to the main current along which life flows. This latter may be said to be along the vertical axis of pure deliberative virtues by means of which man decides to affiliate himself to a good life. Actual physical life is of the nature merely of an epiphenomenon to the real life interests normal and legitimate to man as Man.

The Key to Integration Hidden in the Human Personality

It is a recognized fact tacitly understood already in the East as well as in the West that man himself is the subject of proper study. *Ātma-vidyā* (Self-knowledge) in India has been treated as the same as *Brahma-vidyā* (Wisdom of the Absolute). *Ānanda* (Happiness) as a Supreme End or Value in life, has also been treated as, in effect, the same as the Self or the Absolute. Thus the key for integration of knowledge of wisdom is to be found in the human personality itself where the subtlest aspects of wisdom find a natural home. The Self is the most precious of values for man and the *mahāvākyas* (Great Dicta) such as "Thou Art That" signify this supreme point of culmination of all integrated wisdom.

With such as the target before them, it is encouraging to note even physicists like Schroedinger have made some first efforts to bring these divergent aspects of human knowledge into integrated relationship. A contemplative Science of the Absolute conceived in terms of Self-knowledge could include the *Chief End* or the *Final Good* on the one hand and the negative or prime counterparts of the same in actual life within the range of an integrated Science of sciences, combining ontological and teleological values. Aristotle's Doctrine of the Mean could then be understood in terms of *sāmya* (sameness) which is the central doctrine of such Eastern texts as the *Bhagavad Gītā*.

When both are properly grasped without prejudice, culture would tend to be integrated and understood in unitive and universal terms.

Reference

1. Mr. Cochran writes a very interesting and well-documented article on *The Quantum Physical Basis of Life*, postulating a basic hylozoism with the 'wave' phenomena as the conscious aspect of matter, in the May 1957 issue of *Main Currents in Modern Thought* (Journal of the Foundation for Integrated Education, 246 East 46th Street, New York 17, N.Y.,U.S.A.). Mr. Cochran is attached to the U.S. Bureau of Mines.

20

Science and Certitude

KNOWLEDGE that has a certain degree of certitude is called science. In its original meaning the term science was not limited to what is now distinguished as the 'positive', 'objective' or 'experimental' sciences. When physics began its role as a science it set the model for forms of exact knowledge which began to be accumulated and put on shelves of their own in the department of the exact sciences. Physics soon gave way to chemistry, and then biology, which till then, had been called Natural Philosophy, was admitted into the realm of science.

Measurement of some sort enters into our notion of science. Experiment, observation and inference constituted the scientific method according to Bacon. Biological measurements however, were not as strict or rigid as measurements in other sciences such as physics or mechanics. Control experiments were conducted in biological laboratories which were accepted as normal to that branch, as giving that degree of certitude in knowledge which the nature of the subject-matter of biology, which was living organisms, permitted. Duration of life-cycles were measured with maximal and minimal probabilities instead of in terms of a rod of platinum preserved in a museum.

Thus the norms and standards were relaxed. When astronomy was included as a science the space-time factors involved were so great that all rigidity of Euclid and Newton had to be given up, and the physical world came to be recognized as an indeterminate entity which allowed much flexibility and fluidity in an ever changing flux of a universe.

Science and the mind

From the peripheral limits of the universe the onward march of exact thinking reached centrally into the study of the mind of man. Here laboratory experiments even of a 'control' kind became difficult. Proverbs and common sense adages were pressed into service by scientific writers to give precision or plausibility to their findings and conclusions. Later, normative methods through the statistical study of averages and probabilities began to be admitted and accepted as scientific and respectable. Questionnaires were invented where the degree of objectivity involved became further impaired. Questions were framed which often reflected the partialities and prejudices of those who framed them; and now much misleading evidence passes for scientific, when at best it represents the pet theories or fads already in the minds of the investigators.

Much ingenuity is thus being wasted at the altar of that idol which the scientist, like the old mathematician, still worships, called 'proof'. Many so-called proofs leave the man of common sense in a sounder position of certitude than the academic student.

Empiricism fails

The complete inadequacy of the empirical approach to knowledge or for certitude is now beginning to be accepted by leading thinkers like Bertrand Russell and leading scientists like Eddington.

After laboriously treating all aspects of "Human Knowledge — Its Scope and Limits", Russell, in the concluding section of his book, on its last page significantly admits that "empiricism as a theory of knowledge has proved inadequate, though less so than any other previous theory of knowledge." Eddington has striking paragraphs which bring to light the total absurdity of the physical world when viewed strictly according to the notions about the world that surrounds us held by present-day scientists.

A Revised Approach Imperative

If the empirical approach has failed in bringing us nearer to knowledge, it has not failed to bring us another form of certitude. This is the certitude that if science goes on influencing humanity as it has been doing during the past few centuries, the doom of humanity is not to be dismissed as totally remote or uncertain. The human being and his survival begins to loom large as a question claiming inclusion as a legitimate and all-important subject of study for all thinking men. Thus we are brought to the portals of a new science at the centre of which we place man himself.

Man has to be studied through man for man in what constitutes human nature itself and its highest value or goal.

Psychology, sociology, politics and economics, although claimed to be sciences in the modern world, cannot be counted as such because the very first pages or text-books on these subjects reveal that their very opening definitions vary according to the fancies of one professor or another. The methodological and epistemological premises of such sciences are neither strictly laid nor universally acceptable or understandable. Even the fact that these sciences depend on the interrelation of person with person or of person with object (value) is not so far recognized. The human being is still treated as a specimen in the museum to be studied *in situ* as it were, whether megascopically or microscopically, synthetically or analytically. The dialectical approach by which subject and object, cause and effect, mental and material, outer and inner, personal and impersonal factors are treated together, instead of disjunctly as at present, is deplorably absent to the present-day.

The Frustration of the 'Positivist'

For many centuries now the world has had before it such sayings as "Know Thyself" and "The proper study of mankind is man". Although they are generally accepted as very true and wise dicta, scientists have not paid any attention to them. The positivist thinker like Auguste Compte wanted to get rid of all dogmatism, theology and mythology from our modes of exact thinking. He hoped to discover laws in sociology and allied sciences and thus put away dogmatism forever. It is a sad reality however, that in spite of the ambitions of such positivists we are still no nearer to enunciating universal laws of human nature or relationships. Positivism seems to be like a horse with a rider in the dark at the brink of a precipice. It will not and cannot go any further. Positivism is really at an impasse and, unless it knows how to turn right about and follow another course based on a revised methodological and epistemological approach, generations will still find the horse facing the same situation in the dark.

Some Heterodox Scientists

However, there is still a ray of hope for the scientist. Some of them have been able to shed their orthodoxy and closed or special conditioning. We find examples of first-rate scientists such as Schroedinger and Dr. Alexis Carrell who seem to talk a new language, Schroedinger even using such Vedāntic dicta as "That Thou Art' in his writings in discussing the nature of life.

Human life as understood in living terms without the limitations of the dissection table has been dealt with by professionals of unquestionable standing like Carrell. Journals and personal correspondence are beginning to be focused more and more on the topic of how exact thinking has to progress along revised lines. Books like *The Reach of the Mind* by J.B. Rhine and 'experiments' which are 'para-psychological' are attracting much attention, not to mention the great interest in recent years in psycho-analysis and psychic research in general.

Reversion to Esoterics

As the present moment there is a strange symptom observable in the modern man in a reverse direction, especially in the West. There seems to be an exceptional revival of interest in primitive magic, secret doctrines or *siddhi* phenomena belonging to secluded and recessional traditional groups. The love of *yogī* literature is on the ascendant, especially in America. Literature which Easterners would consider hardly respectable is being put out which is voraciously consumed by the common reader in the West and, conversely, pseudo-scientific wonder-tales of space-time adventure are making inroads into the imaginative minds of Eastern men and women. It is time that we thought of a general epistemological and methodological frame of reference for human thinking which would be equally valid both for the East and the West. There should be a Science of sciences — in other words, a veritable Science of the Absolute in which the whole range of unitive human values would find their legitimate places is what has become imperatively necessary for safeguarding the future of the thinking of the human race as a whole. The lop-sided progression of present-day scientific thinking could then be balanced, so that humanity might progress normally, guided by its legitimate aspirations for the fulfilment of its highest natural values.

No Sacrifice of Certitude

Although it is evident that the empirical theory of knowledge has failed and that we are feverishly reaching out for methods that could be relied upon as the next best only, it is still important that the certitude which is the characteristic of any science should not be lost sight of. The methods which science evolved during its long years of progress while it groped in the dark for a clearer vision of reality need not all be discredited nor discarded in favour of less publicly valid methods. The scientific attitude could be continued in the same strictly open and critical manner into domains which may not be objective in the sense understood by scientists so far. Whether it is the mind of man acting on matter, or whether mind acts on mind itself, or even where matter acts on matter itself, the methods of arriving at certainty could be the same in principle. The laboratory experiment of the bell, jar, test-tube or crucible, the control methods of the biological laboratory and the normative methods of the statistical approach to certainty have all behind them a critical attitude of mind which could be kept alive even in the world of the study of the Self of Man. Mental experimentation could follow the same disciplinary outlines as laboratory experimentation. We could submit our findings to the same rigour of testing — not actually but my mental suppositions or by probings for probabilities or certainties.

As a matter of fact, as we travel from the domain of *a posteriori* knowledge to that of the *a priori*, degrees of certitude become possible even without orthodox experimentation or laboratory proof. The method of the *Mīmāṁsakas* (reflective investigators) of India correspond to such and have been as full of certitude as to be accepted as valid forms of reasoning for many generations of exact thinkers in India. In connection with *Brahma-Vidyā* or the Science of the Absolute, a whole system of exact thinking has developed in and through the six great systems of Indian philosophy. These, however, are gone into disuse but much of it could be salvaged for the service of the Science of the Self or the Absolute even now.

Without abandoning the critical method of overt public discipline which ought to characterize any science, it is possible to build up a body of knowledge which would enjoy at least the same degree of certitude that the physical sciences have had in the world of empirical events and facts. When this is accomplished, a global philosophy will emerge which will enrich and nourish science itself and give it a higher degree of certitude, and unviersal validity.

21

Mathematics and Mysticism

WHILE the mathematician may be described as a vertical positive type, the mystic is generally more negatively adjusted. Anti-social traits could brand both types as peculiar out-of-the-way people. How the pure mathematician tends to be a mystic and how the active mystic often has a generalized and mathematical notion of the supreme reality of theology are interesting and intriguing matters to which it would be worthwhile here to direct our attention.

God as a Mathematician

It has lately become the fashion to speak of God as a mathematician. Whether Jeans or Eddington was first responsible for the idea behind this slogan, it seems to have caught on wonderfully. The implicit correspondence here referred to is as striking as it is attractive to the modern mind.

God has been called the Great Architect or the Master Designer or the Creative Artist. We have ourselves reduced Him into terms of a vertical dimension. The anthropomorphic Zeus idea of a God has long been outmoded even as an idiom in the West. Even in the more sentimental climate of Eastern thought the *Bhagavad Gītā* refers to God both as the correlating thread of values and the machine behind the visible phenomenal world of necessary happenings (see *Gītā*, VII. 7 and XV. 6I). Kṛṣṇa, the Guru of the *Gītā*, refers to the latter God concept in the third person, suggesting its inferiority as a philosophical notion.

As humanity reads, hears or thinks for itself, the idea of God also changes to adapt itself to the prevailing idiom. The Guru Nārāyaṇa referred to God as the Great Captain of a steamship, while philosophically comparing him to the dimension of depth implied in phenomenal life.

The following paragraph from Sir James Jeans suffices for us here to point out that the role of God as a master mathematician is the latest of the similes applied to the concept of the Maker of all things:

> If, however, the more intricate concepts of pure mathematics have been transplanted from the workings of nature, they must have been buried very deep indeed in our subconscious minds. This very controversial possibility is one which cannot be entirely dismissed, but it is exceedingly hard to believe that such intricate concepts of a finite curved space and an expanding space can have entered into pure mathematics through any sort of unconscious or subconscious experience of the workings of the actual universe. In any event, it can hardly be disputed that nature and our conscious mathematical minds work according to the same laws. She does not model her behaviour, so to speak, on that forced on us by our whims and passions, or on that of our muscles and joints, but on that of our thinking minds. This remains true whether our minds impress their laws on nature, or she impresses her laws on us, and provides a sufficient justification for thinking of the universe as being of mathematical design. Lapsing back again into the crudely anthropomorphic language we have already used, we may say that we have already considered with disfavour the possibility of the universe having been planned by a biologist or an engineer; from the intrinsic evidence of His creation, the Great Architect of the Universe now begins to appear as a pure mathematician.[1]

Mathematics could thus be thought of as having a place in the mind of God and we could think conversely likewise that mysticism consists of knowing the same God through feelings rather than through thoughts.

The Content of Mysticism

The mystic is essentially a contemplative. Although it is usual to speak of an active and a contemplative mystic, just as we might speak of a pure or an applied mathematician, the true mystic is always one who lives in a world of imagination rather than of reality. An active mystic might engage himself in pious works for God or cultivate "the presence of God" in ways that reveal themselves in his outer behaviour, while the true mystic might resemble more the quietist who lives in silence and retirement.

The world referred to as the world of 'whims and passions' as also that belonging to the 'muscles and joints' in the above quotation from

Jeans, is one that is equally outside the life of both the mystic and the mathematician. The introversion implied in contemplative mysticism has been generally recognized. The world of the mystic resembles that of the subjective and selected world of a mathematician where only certain kinds of values or interests enter, while a great number of common human interests and connected activities are carefully excluded.

The mystic lives in a world of his own which, as we shall see presently is in all essential respects the same as the one in which the spirit of the methematician lives and moves. They are "of imagination all compact" as Shakespeare generalized inclusively in the cases of the lover, the madman and the poet. The resemblance of the pure mathematician to the poet or the mystic, however, needs some more explanation to be fully evident. The mystic feels a strange kinship with the life that is external to him, while the mathematical structure of reality or nature that the mathematician is capable of intuiting within himself establishes a similar bi-polar relation between himself and the Maker of all things here. Both become tuned to the same Absolute whether outside or inside, whether emotionally or intellectually, or both. Thus it is that mystics and mathematicians become strange bedfellows.

How Do Mathematicians Think?

From the day of the Pythagorean notion of the 'mystery of numbers' down to the day Eddington spoke of a 'sedenion' algebra the nature and content of mathematics has been the subject of much speculation.

Are mathematical judgements analytic or synthetic, *a priori* or *a posteriori*, subjective or objective, 'selective' or 'creative,' positive or negative? These are open questions, answered differently by different people. That mathematicians are 'queer folk' has been pointed out by both the parties concerned in such discussions. Whether experiments confirm the findings of mathematicians or whether mathematics deserves primacy of treatment in respect of scientific certitude seem matters not yet decided one way or the other.

The suggestion we make is that both could be equally true without scientific validity being affected one way or the other. Reality or truth as the Absolute has two sides which come together into a central unity without contradiction. How this way of thinking could be valid has been the subject of our inquiry in the pages of *VALUES* during the last few years. Unitive or dialectical thinking reveals the possibilities of such a notion of a neutral Absolute both transcendent and immanent at once.

We could therefore say that if God could be thought of as a mathematician, the mathematician may also be expected, in his thought at least, to resemble God. If we could think of this dual proposition without the anthropomorphic flourish which rhetoric might introduce, and imagine man's mathematics and God's creative thinking to be counterparts of the same unitive situation, belonging as they do both, to what we have tried to distinguish as the vertical aspect of reality, life or the Absolute, in the abstract as both transcendent and immanent, we shall have succeeded in equating the mystic and the mathematician with human and divine powers at one and the same time.

God as the designer of man thinks mathematically and man meditating on God as the mathematician is doing the same thing from another pole of the vertical axis which unites them both in a single dialectical situation. The best mathematicians when they are engaged with the fundamental problems of the universe are obliged to think like the Maker of all things, and the mystics on their part who contemplate God are another variety of subjectivists who are capable of fitting the notion of a unitive God into a picture of the universe which they can feel around them.

The kind of subjective selectivism represented by the modern physicist when he employs the symbolic language proper to his subject is a form of delving into the negative recesses of the self not different from the introspection of contemplative mystics. Only the style differs.

Mystery of the Language of Physics

Prof. George Temple put his finger correctly on the two extreme limiting points of the role of modern mathematical thought when he made the following statements:

> My answer to the question 'What is mathematics?' can be given in six words. I maintain that mathematics is the language of physics and that this conception of mathematics is the key to the contemporary organization of physical science.[2]

In his next broadcast published in *The Listener*, April 6, 1950, he amplified the above statement so drastically that he might be said to have, in effect, negated its import. He said:

> It would, however, be a profound mistake to think that the pure mathematician regards his work solely as conferring a certain formal polish and orderliness on physical mathematics. He does indeed recognize how much the applied mathematician has to learn from the pure mathematician, but the improvement of mathematics as the language of physics is by no means his main work. That work may be tentatively described as the creation of new languages unrestricted by any expectation that they may one day embody physical truth. Modern algebra may be broadly described as the systematic examination of all possible mathematical structures and linguistic situations . . . As for modern geometry, that is such an untrammelled flight of the imagination as to pass over the frontier of language into pure poetry.

Further the professor refers to mathematics as "this strangely esoteric science" and when we read such remarks from the lips of those who have full authority to speak on the subject, side by side with statements such as "There is no place in mathematics for passion or prejudice" and that "Mathematicians are queer folk" and that they live in "intellectual isolation" and that "no doubt these principles (of mathematical formulae embodying the basic principles of theoretical physics) have been *cogitated by induction* from a vast assembly of empirical facts" — all these remarks put together must give us now a clearer insight into the nature of mathematics than ever before. The professor also refers to a certain *dynamism in mathematical thought* which "carried on the mathematician from putting the question to devising the reply."[3]

Mathematics could therefore be thought of as qualitative operations in time which can predict what could be true by a kind of inductive cogitation from one set of abstract facts to another. It is a form of pure reason or intuition of a certain *thing-in-itself* without reference to anything that is outside the mind or itself. It refers to movements in consciousness lying along the vertical axis of the world of perceptual, not actual, values.

The Axis of Mathematical Dynamism

That there are two different levels in our consciousness where mathematical notions cluster themselves in the form of logical coherences or natural laws is an interesting feature which is coming more and more in evidence in modern thought. There is a subconscious or subliminal stratum in consciousness where mathematics resides in terms of feeling rather than as relations or entities of intelligent thinking. The latter has a level of its own and might give us useful notions in applied science holding the interest of the inventor. These two strata of mathematical thought react and combine under favourable conditions of the psyche. The following two paragraphs extracted from the writings of Henri Poincare enable us to distinguish the emotional and logical poles in which mathematical operations could take place in the psyche:

> For fifteen days I strove to prove that there could not be any functions like those I have since called Fuchsian functions. I was then very ignorant; everyday I seated myself at my work table, stayed an hour or two, tried a great number of combinations and reached no results. One evening, contrary to my custom, I drank black coffee and could not sleep. Ideas rose in crowds, I felt them collide until pairs interlocked, so to speak, making stable combination. By the next morning I had established the existence of a class of Fuchsian functions, those which come from the hypergeometric series; I had only to write out the results, which took but a few hours.[4]

The pairs that interlocked to give rise to the understanding of the functions in the above story of their discovery reveals the structure of mathematical thought which forms at two levels. The dynamism becomes more explicit in the following further explanation of Poincare:

> Now what are the mathematic entities to which we attribute the character of beauty and elegance and which are capable of developing in us a sort of aesthetic emotion. They are those whose elements are harmoniously disposed so that the mind without effort can embrace their totality while realising the details. This harmony is at once a satisfaction of our aesthetic needs and an aid to the mind, sustaining and guiding. And at the same time in putting under our eyes a well ordered whole, it makes us foresee a mathematical law. Now, as we have said above, the only mathematical facts worthy of fixing our attention and capable of being useful are those which can teach us a mathematical law . . . So that we reach the following conclusion. The useful combinations are precisely the most beautiful, I mean those best able to charm this special sensibility that all mathematicians know but of which the profane are so ignorant as often to be tempted to smile at its.[5]

Mathematics thus moves between two poles, one which appeals to the sentiments and the other which refers to formal logic. The purer the mathematics the more mystically aware of the global aesthetic pole of mathematics the mathematician will be. Invention or prediction implied in all discovery through mathematics is in the form of an interaction between the two poles, both of which belong to the order of abstractions of the mind. Interest is the vertical axis along which the two sets of mathematical entities whether known as emotions or facts, can interact. The mystical mood and the mood of the positive scientist have thus to co-exist and interact in any valuable human discovery, whether *a priori* or *a posteriori* or both, worth the name.

Quantitative and Qualitative Abstractions

When we count and pass from one-two-three to infinity there is something strange happening within us which we generally do not notice. Till three we really think quantitatively, but at the mention of infinity we stand face to face with something of quite another order. The quantitative infinities of numbers could be many, depending on the serial, cardinal or ordinal, which might be thought of. The Russell Paradox which he himself describes as follows could be overcome when we separate these two aspects of number, quantitative and qualitative, more correctly:

> Take the series of whole numbers from 1 onwards; how many of them are there? Clearly the number is not finite. Up to a thousand there are thousand numbers; up to a million a million. Whatever finite number you mention, there are evidently more numbers than that, because from one to the number in question there are just that number of numbers, and then there are others that are greater. The number of finite whole numbers must, therefore, be an infinite number. But now comes a curious fact. The number of even numbers must be the same as the number of all whole numbers. Consider the two rows:
>
> 1, 2, 3, 4, 5, 6 . . .
>
> 2, 4, 6, 8, 10, 12 . . .
>
> There is one entry in the lower row for everyone in the top row therefore the number of terms in the two rows must be the same, although the lower row consists of only half the terms in the top row. Leibnitz who noticed this thought it a contradiction, and

> concluded that though there are infinite collections there are no infinite numbers. Georg Cantor, on the contrary boldly denied that it is a contradiction. He was right. It was only an oddity.[6]

The Russell paradox as stated above is only a particular instance of subtler paradoxes mentioned by Zeno and Prof. McTaggart where pure or qualitative time is brought into contrast with space or motion. If we think of pure time as qualitative, space would be quantitative. The primacy of time over space as an abstraction, could be brought out by the following laws regulating the incidence of ordinary physical bodies:

(1) A given body could not be at two different places at the same time.

(2) Two different bodies cannot be at the same place at the same time.

(3) One body can be at the same place at two different times.[7]

The body and its location are horizontal aspects of reality, and only when the vertical aspect of time is introduced do we understand its reality more fundamentally. The paradox implied here has been analysed in a verse of the Guru Nārāyaṇa:

> The body and the like, one in another no being have;
> The converse therefore untrue becomes: as from day to day
> Unextinguished they prevail; assuming again their
> Existent form they keep ever becoming.[8]

The Primacy Due to Time Abstraction

In other words qualitative existence in time is of a different order from quantitative existence in space. Things cannot occupy the same space horizontally but could continue to exist in time as a vertical reality. Mathematical entities could be thus thought of vertically or horizontally. The horizontal admits of contradicton but the vertical does not. The Zeno and McTaggart paradoxes and that of Russell could attain to an intelligible status if this distinction of vertical and horizontal abstraction that mathematics is capable of, became better recognized. We could then see how to understand the Leibnitzian view as also those of Kant, Bergson or Descartes more unitively and intelligently.

The mystery of number which has persisted from Pythagoras to Eddington would be well on the way to being settled as understandable, non-understandable, or both, when our epistemological approach to abstract notions is better clarified. The vertical aspects should not be mixed up with the horizontal aspects with mathematical entities representing various values in consciousness. What Bertrand Russell dismisses as a mere *oddity* above is a deeper mystery to the truer philosopher like Leibnitz who sees in the oddity a contradiction which has to do with the enigma of life itself. His monadology in his answer where the vertical is given primacy over the horizontal realities of life. Russell prefers to remain a sceptic for its own sake and gives primacy to horizontal values, while Leibnitz as a truer philosopher tends to give primacy to the vertical. Reality can be viewed with equal validity, giving primacy to the one or the other of these axes of correlation.

It is up to each philosopher to say what he wants. Mathematical entities could be quantitative or qualitative abstractions and under each of these broad divisions there is a further possibility of degrees of abstraction. The difference between arithmetic and algebra already represents this possibility of abstraction; algebra being more general than the world of arithmetic which suits the quantitative aspect of reality better. The sedenion algebra of Eddington and the Fuchsian geometry of Poincare are more generalized forms of mathematics which can accommodate more particular cases than ever before. Topological geometry and projective geometry similarly represent the abstraction of flat Euclidean geometry which started with earth measurements. A football-like spherical space is going out of fashion in favour of something like the inside of a half-inflated tyre tube in cosmological imagery at present.

Mysticism Enters by the Back Door

Logic depends on abstract operations of the mind. Language is needed for these operations. When logic has to deal with a large number of instances under a generalized heading it has to enter into the semantic and syntactical implications of propositions. Mathematics helps to reveal the structure of pure or practical thought in the generalized or much abstracted form of logistic or propositional calculi. Although at one time scientific empiricists thought that they had nothing to do with abstractions, they have admitted the need for logic recently in the revised logico-empirical world of reality they have come to accept.

The Vienna circle of 'Logical Positivists' although they rely on abstract statements largely, are limited to the empirical method of determining what is 'meaningful' to them against what they consider absurd or meaningless. The meaningless is what cannot *work* and prove its use in the progress of science. The tradition of Peirce is continued here. The working of the mind of those who stood for mathematics or logic as strictly limited to the domain of the experimental sciences can be gathered from the following extract:

> This marriage of the empirical and logical traditions was first solemnized by the name 'Logical Positivism' in order to indicate the two families united, but this was changed later to 'Logical Empiricism' when it was realized how bad the odour of the word 'positivism' was for those who associated it with the narrowness of Auguste Compte.[9]

Logical Empiricists like Rudolph Carnap and Bertrand Russell insist on pinning their faith on the *a posteriori* world of demonstrable events or facts of life. They take pride in their scepticism which saves them from all that is 'according to them' meaningless, which latter is often the domain of the *a priori.*

To put the contrast in one sentence, if you ask the Logical Empiricist if the sun will rise the next day he would content himself by saying "It is *very probable*", instead of saying 'sure' as common sense might dictate. Perhaps the common sense position in the matter could be slightly improved and made more scientific if we should say, "It is *very unlikely* that the sun will *not* rise tomorrow." The former way gives primacy to the *a posteriori* while the latter gives primacy to the *a priori.* A science could make use of both these ways and still have the validity of equal certitude or meaningfulness.

When thus the *a priori* is admitted into science on its own right, we have a new approach to wisdom, which at first resembles mysticism although, as we have tried to say, mathematics and mysticism are only two poles of abstract subjective, yet dynamic, thought processes. Through the admission of logic into empiricism, mysticism may be said to have already entered the domain of science as it were, by the back door.

Non-Experimental Mathematics

When we say that the proof of the Pythagorean theorem of a right-angled triangle does not depend on actual measurement, we have made a statement most damaging to experimental science.

From the idea of pre-established harmony and the mystery of numbers through the *Mathesis Universalis* of Leibnitz to the *Principia Mathematica* of Russell and Whitehead and the Fundamental Theory of Eddington, we have a long history of subjectivism in mathematical speculation by which the problem and its solution could be arrived at with eyes shut.

In the meanwhile Euclidean geometry has been superseded by what is called projective geometry and algebra has its new version in sedenion algebra, both of which latter treat the corresponding prior form of mathematics as merely particular cases. In fact the scope of mathematical inquiry has extended. Likewise, Newtonian space has had to be discarded in favour of a time-space continuum which refers to a frame of reference which can speak of a hundred and fifty light years with space attracting or repelling bodies from any point in a universe that expands or contracts or both.

The sense of wonder and consequent vagueness of the import of these great discoveries are not yet over and the language of science has to rid itself of much confusing rhetoric before we can see clearly through the maze of new facts which have to be fitted into a coherent whole. Einstein has been responsible for tempering with mathematics which he sometimes justified and sometimes himself criticized. As Eddington explained: "Einstein has been as severe a critic of his own suggestion as any one, and he has not invariably adhered to it."[10] The suggestion that Einstein made is referred to by Eddington in the following simple terms:

> Einstein almost inadvertently added a repulsive scattering force to the Newtonian attraction of bodies.[11]

Earlier, in the same work, Eddington describes what Einstein did:

> The central result of Einstein's theory was his law of gravitation . . . A year or so later Einstein made a slight amendment to his law, to meet certain difficulties that he encountered in his theory. There was just one place where the theory did not seem to work properly, and that was infinity. I think Einstein showed his greatness in the simple and drastic way in which he disposed of difficulties at infinity. He abolished infinity. He slightly altered his equations so as to make space at great distances bend

> round until it closed up. So that if in Einstein's space you keep going right on in one direction you do not get to infinity; you find yourself back at your starting point again. Since there was no longer any infinity, there could be no difficulties at infinity. Q.E.D.[12]

In the above paragraph we have a close-up of what takes place in the philosophy of science where some 'Absolutist' notions are replaced by 'relativist' ones for the sake of avoiding difficulties in the actual working out of theories. It is a trial-and-error process of revision. A careful study of the modified theories would be seen, however, to have included certain other absolutist notions themselves. The cosmical constant *lamda*, is one such. Many other constants have now been added. The velocity of light is often used as an absolute norm of reference, thus coming back to a form of absolutism. All this tampering with classical notions in mathematics is ushering in a new era of modern mathematics which might serve as the language of physics and metaphysics at one and the same time.

That mathematical thinking, though exact and logical need not necessarily, by itself, lead to the same or similar conclusions is sufficiently evidenced by the fact that Russell and Whitehead, who were joint authors of the work on the principles of mathematics, differed diametrically, in their own philosophical findings. The same mathematical method produced the greatest of modern sceptics as well as perhaps the greatest of modern believers.

Sir Edmund Whittaker, delivering his memorial address on Eddington on August 9, 1951, rightly applauds the philosophical system of the century based on the latest notions of mathematics and science when he says:

> The philosophical system of my old friend and teacher Alfred North Whitehead is justly regarded as the most metaphysical achievement of the present century.[13]

Eddington as understood by Whitehead leads us back through mathematics to a revised form of belief in God which is not without its striking kinship with mysticism of a pure and revised form.

'Subjective Selectivism' and Sheer Mysticism

Eddington has described himself as a selective subjectivist and as being against mere 'crude experimentalists'. His various mathematical constants are meant to reveal a world based on fundamental theory referring to a 'principle of science' of his own as stated in his posthumously published volume bearing the title *Fundamental Theory*. Although there seems, just at the present moment, a tendency among scientists to put Eddington's ideas back into a sort of cold storage, especially by the school calling itself 'Logical Empiricist', about which we have already made some remarks, Eddingtonianism constitutes in itself one of the major challenges to be met by the modern thinker.

It is related backwards to the theorem of Pythagoras which could question the length of the hypotenuse of a right-angled triangle and answer it without recourse to measurement. Both the question and its answer belong to the domain of subjective thought-dynamics. Leibnitzian Universal Mathematics also stressed the qualitative side of reality as against the quantitative side. As Sir Edmund Whittaker has said:

> Leibnitz, however, initiated a new philosophical outlook; he advocated in his own words (Vol. VI, *Mathesis Universalis*) a subordination of a science of quantity to the science of quality — of the science that deals with numerical relations to that which treats of order and similarity. This is Eddingtonianism pure and simple.[14]

The same writer makes the subjectivism implicit in Eddington's mathematical methods very clear when he continues:

> Eddington's Principle depends on the distinction between what we have called quantitative and qualitative assertions; it may be stated thus: *All the quantitative propositions of physics that are the exact value of the pure numbers that are constants of science may be deduced by logical reasoning from qualitative assertions, without making any use of quantitative data derived from observation.*[15]

Mysticism is sometimes defined as the cultivation of the presence of God. It refers to the way of life of the believer. Eddingtonianism which is the latest expression of mathematically understood science, in the light of the above authoritative quotations, refers not only to a form of inner life like that of the mystic, but involves a reference to an entity equivalent to the concept of God or the Absolute Principle. This entity is sometimes referred to as the Eternal as in the following passage from Sir Edmund's analysis of Eddingtonianism:

> We stand in awe before the thought that the intellectual framework of nature is prior to nature herself — that it existed before the material universe began its history — that the cosmos revealed to us by science is only one fragment of the plan of the Eternal.[16]

Mysticism cannot come any nearer that what is implied in the above quotation to join hands with the language of physics which is mathematics. Much as we should not like to see the language of mathematical physics lapsing into one of complacent solipsism, and keen as we are to see mysticism rid of its sentimental vagueness about the notion of the Absolute, which is the central subject-matter of both these forms of activity in human consciousness, it would still be an important day in the history of modern thought to see that mathematics and mysticism though two of the strangest of possible bedfellows, could come together as complementary aspects of the same wisdom that concerns both these approaches to the Absolute.

By a dynamism taking place within consciousness as between two poles of the human personality and joined theoretically by a vertical axis of correlation, mysticism and mathematics represent activities of the psyche that always belong together as expressions of the Absolute which each of us represents within. This Absolute could be referred to as being immanent or transcendent, as psychologically within or cosmologically without. There is a pre-established correspondence between the two aspects thus united. Whether called God, Nature or the Eternal in theological or contemplative language, the subject-matter and object-matter of human thought or emotion must refer to the same central Absolute.

Finally, in order to make it sufficiently evident that scientific mathematics and mysticism could refer to the same high value whether in the *Vedānta* of the East or in the Fundamental Theory of a leading scientist of the West, we shall not in vain conclude here with one more quotation from Sir Edmund Whittaker which must suffice to put the seal, as it were, on the final rapprochement of the two ways of life we have discussed, irrespective of the time or clime of the thought involved:

> In the laws of nature, known and unknown, we recognize a system of truth, which has been revealed to us by the study of nature, but which is unlike material nature in its purely intellectual and universal character, and which if the conclu-

> sions we have reached are correct, is timeless in contrast to the transitory universe of matter. Material nature has made manifest to our understanding realities greater that itself, *realities which point to a God who is not bound up with the world and who is transcendent and subject to no limitation.* The principle that matter exists not for its own sake but in order to help us in bridging the gulf that separates us from the divine, may be expressed in theological language by saying that nature has a sacramental quality, a principle that has long been recognized in religion, and can now be admitted to be note alien to the philosophy of science.[17]

Except for the part we have italicised in the above quotation, which points to the same Platonic tendency which we have noted in the philosophy of Whitehead (see *Values*, Feb. 1959) — a tendency to transcendentalism at the expense of Aristotelian reality — the whole paragraph quoted could pass for the essence of Eastern Vedāntic thought as in the *Bhagavad Gītā* (VII.8-9) which refers to earth and water as sacred side by side with the more abstract idea of the Absolute which is adorable elsewhere in the text. When an epistemology and methodology could be evolved common to the 'sciences' and the 'humanities' and a theory of values formulated, mathematical and mystical abstractions could be made to refer to one and the same central human norm conceived as that neutral Absolute which is the World Spirit both immanent and transcendent at once.

References

1. *The Mysterious Universe*, pp. 166-67, London 1937.
2. *The Listener*, p.555, March 10, 1950.
3. *Ibid.*
4. *The Foundations of Science Relating to Mathematical Creation,* quoted p. 36 in *The Creative Process,* Mentor, New York.
5. *Ibid.*, p. 40.
6. *History of Western Philosophy*, 1946.
7. Cf. *The Listener*, April 10, 1956, broadcast by G. J. Whitrow on *The Mathematicians' Idea of Time.*
8. *Ātmopadeśa Śatakam,* verse 86.
9. *The Age of Analysis,* p. 204, Morton White, Mentor, 1955.
10. *The Expanding Universe* p. 31.

11. *Ibid.*, p. 30.
12. *Ibid.*, pp. 28-29,
13. *Eddington's Principle in the Philosophy of Science*, p. 31, Cambridge University Press, 1951.
14. *Ibid.*, p. 5.
15. *Ibid.*, pp. 2-3.
16. *Ibid.*, p. 31.
17. *Ibid.*, p. 34.

22

Can A Science Be Sung ?

SCIENCE has been considered as dispassionate. There is no room for enthusiasm or emotion in a scientist. It is a cold-blooded investigation of the facts of life, and excitement or exaltation would be a form of prejudice when applied to the matter or method of the scientific way. Such are some of the notions we hold about this branch of knowledge. In spite of this, however, there is still Science that raises its head above this limitation and soars to the sublimity of a song of the soul of man.

The *Bhagavad Gītā* claims to be a song and a science at once. As conceived by its author there is no innate violation of principle in singing of a science in the ecstatic state of wonder. Absolute truth is a wonder and hardly anything more than that. The flash of lightning in the far-off horizon is both a plain fact and a wonder at once. The sunset that a scientist watches is both a glory and a fact. It is not necessary to banish the appraisal or appreciation of one in favour of the other. The plainest of facts could still be a wonder of wonders.

Blending of Values

The scientist need not be ashamed of this element of the emotion of wonder if it tallies with his scientific attitude. The discovery of a new star in the firmament has been referred to as highly exciting in a personal sense to the fact-finding observer who first succeeded in bringing it within the range of vision of his telescope. When Eddington came down from his observatory one night, after seeing a long-looked for astronomical phenomenon, his hair is said to have stood on end. He felt like a sailor who looked at land after the despair of a long voyage.

Song and science can blend, enhancing the value of each other, when the science involved fulfils its highest role. Singing a science would become normal and respectable when the song agreed perfectly with its own high theme. A raving prophet or an angry Jove could meet in the singing scientist a kindred spirit, perhaps of a more normal type. The dancing dervish could only add to the joy of such a happy company.

The blending of the antinomies of humdrum fact and exalted wonder is an art in which great masters like Dante and Milton have excelled. Vyāsa is perhaps the purest example of a poet who was able to sing a veritable Science of sciences without any part of it becoming threadbare. The fabric of poetry that he wove was like some long-lasting homespun stuff whose glossy luxury was enduring.

Gentle sarcasm itself finds its place in some of the verses of the *Bhagavad Gītā* without marring its character as a strictly scientific composition. The attitude of neutral impartiality maintained in some of the verses of this type hidden away here and there in the text of the *Gītā* needs the keen critical eye to discern. Except in the case of the cleverest of readers the joke might be all but missed. Exaggeration, sarcasm, wit and a sense of wonder all blend with different literary devices and idiomatic turns of expression, making the style of the *Gītā* a veritable confection where the figures of speech are most advantageously employed to enhance our conviction about scientific verity or truth of high human value.

The Scientist as Guru

It is a hard fact worth recognizing that the mind of man is so constituted that it seeks to soar into the domain of freedom which dwells beyond mere facts. We tend to shut out our appraisal of verity to the extent that the sense of wonder is excluded from our own personal attitudes, in our common human pilgrimage to the temple of supreme Knowledge. We are obliged to speak of truth with a certain zeal which should not be considered out of place when properly moderated by its own opposite corrective tendency.

Science is or should be guided by our interest in worthwhile pursuits of values in life. In its first phase it seeks objects of satisfaction. When material wants and comforts have been catered for, the mind seeks to satisfy subtler hungers and appetites. These are taken in a certain order of importance and human intelligence then penetrates the whole range of human values till it arrives at one supreme or absolute Value. This is to be sought, not outside oneself but within the range and limits of one's own consciousness. The vision thereafter refers to oneself.

As soon as unitive and contemplative values become thus the normal subject-matter of science, the method of scientific investigation itself has to be reversed. The very instruments of knowledge have to be changed. It is the higher faculty of dialectical reasoning that comes into play. The nature of the reasoning also changes. The dearest object to oneself cannot be anything other than the self and the science of self-knowledge begins to touch the emotions. It becomes alluring and absorbing in its nature.

When the sense of wonder in regard to the Truth that one feels in oneself lures one deeper and deeper into one's own consciousness, the scientist improves, to becomes a poet. Instead of walking, he skips or dances in joy. Rhapsodic or ecstatic states overtake him and the sense of wonder permeates his ways. The true scientist, however, holds the balance between the two tendencies, and sits in the neutrality of the Absolute. He represents the Absolute in himself in a simple and normal way. He can be silent or he can sing of the Absolute in words, and point his finger to the Absolute that is beyond. All these functions combine in him, blending into what he represents in his thoughts, words and deeds. Like Vyāsa of old, the singing scientist pointing his finger to the Absolute becomes both a personal and an impersonal Guru, representing a priceless value to humanity for all time.

23

Towards a Common Speech for Science and *Vedānta*

IT is great to feel small sometimes as it is also great to feel otherwise too. Between godly lordship and human servitude there is a large vertical amplitude within whose range the mind of man can expand or sink into nothingness. Between the poles of the one and the many, the big, the small and the middling, our lives pulsate, basking in alternating sunshine or under the shadow of a heavy hanging cloud. Thus life goes on forever . . .

If Gods and Gnomes Should Be Taboo

All men at all times in all climes have been preoccupied with the notion of a superior being called God. All dictionaries of the various languages of the world have a place for the notion whether all men avowedly own a good for themselves or not.

Perhaps it would not be wrong to say that, though vague in its meaning, the word God is perhaps the most interesting of all the words in any dictionary and the word most bandied about between men from the earliest times, whether for swearing, exclamation or sheer blustering idiotic outbursts of vehement articulation on any provocative situation whatsoever. What would man do without it and, if all the subgroups that come under God, such as fairy, nymph or ghost were to be banned from human speech as disreputable, what a loss it would be for the cause of poetry and art. Many of our best books would have to be put on the index of prohibited literature. That would make humans the poorer forever after.

Poetry and Personification

The richness that we see in poetry as opposed to the comparative indigence of prose comes from the lack of respect for logical syntax as also from the freedom of imagery. Poetic order and diction need not strictly subserve the rigid demands of logic or grammar. Poetry is less public and figures of speech like brightly feathered birds fly freely across the mental space to which poetry pertains. There are figures and figures of speech which compare one thing with another. There are those sustained in the form of allegory or parable. None of these devices, however, can rival the freedom implicit in full-fledged personification of which apostrophe and soliloquy are only applied variations. Literary devices are most effective when addressed to a person present, absent or imaginary. A lover can speak to a parrot his or her most intimate thoughts to set off the effect on the reader. Perhaps the most daring of poetic conceits is that of personification. The self, as it were, communes here with the non-self, and the subtle equation implied gives it more than merely an aesthetic status. Beauty inside one communicates and engages itself *vis-a-vis* a beauty that is in the other as the non-self. The result is the sheer joy of art.

If this equation holds good in the domain of aesthetics it is *a fortiori* so in the context of religion and spirituality in general, not to speak of the ethical implications.

Anthropomorphism in Religion

Idolatry could be looked upon as justified in the context of semantic or rhetoric. Passing from the need for personification to thinking of God with human attributes, will then be seen to be natural to man who is constantly seeking an outlet for self-expression through language. Clothes and jewels for women are similar necessities for the same self-expression which many a foolish husband might strive to stifle in his wife or daughter in vain.

In the great temples of South India elaborate musical offerings are made to the idols which represent anthropomorphic gods. One can call such practices puerile, but as toys are necessities for child life, even the grown-up man or woman cannot do without them. To wean humanity altogether from such forms of idolatry implied or explicitly found in national flag-waving ceremonies or in patriotism itself, would be like trying to clean soap of its stickiness or salt of saltiness.

Anthropomorphism has persisted in one form or another in spite of iconoclasts or puritans. Like pruning a tree or shaving a beard, it only grows stronger afterwards. Nor is it likely to disappear in the near future.

The virtue of a scientist consists in recognizing the given datum as the starting point of all his findings and actions. Here then is a definite datum with which we have to start in trying to reform human nature.

Mechanomorphism

When theology and mythology have given place to positive sciences which mistrust poetry and exalt prose instead, we have come to an age when anthropomorphism has got its rival in 'mechanomorphism'.

Whoever it might be who first used this word, it was Erwin Schroedinger who was able to discover this tendency in modern scientific thinking and gave it a definite meaning. Whether in the classical mechanics of Newton or in the quantum mechanics of Max Planck it is the mechanism of nature that interests the exact scientist or the physicist. A mechanical or experimental set-up must 'work' by natural laws other than what is temperamental, psychological or personal to man as a thinking or feeling being. While the old-fashioned principle of the universe called God resembled man in these respects, the God of the scientist who lives in the laboratory must work his wonders through these uniform forces of nature where his whim or temperament would have no chance at all to enter. As we read in Schroedinger's book *Science, Theory and Man:*

> Let us now turn to the 'exact' sciences. From the procedure followed in these sciences, everything subjective is excluded on principle. Physical science belongs essentially to this category. From all physical research the subjective intrusion of the researcher is rigorously barred so that the purely objective truth about inanimate nature may be arrived at. Once this truth is finally stated it can be put to the test of experiment by anybody and everybody all the world over and always with the same result. Thus far, physics is entirely independent of human temperament, and this is put forward as its chief claim to acceptance. Some of the champions of physical science go so far as to postulate that not only must the individual human mind be ruled out in the ultimate statements of physical research, but that the human aspect as a whole must be excluded. Every degree of anthropomorphism is rigorously shut out; so that at least in this branch of science man would no longer be the measure of all things, as the Greek Sophists used to maintain.
>
> (p. 83-84)

Degrees of Mechanomorphism

Schroedinger himself is against this mechanomorphic tendency in physics, and states clearly, "I think that it goes too far". We know how the observer in relativity physics gains a personal importance and how the uncertainty principle of Heisenberg admits by the back door, as it were, another element which enhances the value of the personal factor inside the domain of exact science.

Just as there are degrees of anthropomorphism we can imagine varying grades of the worship of the totality of mechanical forces operative in the physical world. In quantum mechanics we know further that items of this totality conspire together at close and intimate quarters to operate pulsations and movements of particles, models of which, with coloured tennis-ball-like units, have been used by physicists to aid their imagination. The Bohr model of the interior of the atom with "microscopic tennis ball" electrons which were coloured red, yellow or white, was not based on observation but was arbitrarily conceived to aid imagination. Within the world of physics, conceptual rather than perceptual models are becoming permissible. Shape, form, colour movement are getting, as it were, a hypostatic or mechanomorphic status.

We Believe What We See

The motto of the Royal Society (the British scientific body for the advancement of all branches of science, in London) in Latin means roughly: "We believe what we see". Science pins it faiths therefore on the visible, and when the visible is arbitrary, as in the case of the Bohr atom model that we have jut mentioned, the status it enjoyed in respect of veracity or truth is weak.

In fact it is no better than that of an idol of a god that the Indian peasant woman might be worshipping. Further, it was Hume who pointed out that the relation between cause and effect was not as evident as it is commonly supposed to be. When one enters a physics laboratory the head of that institution might take you as a layman and show you pointers, switches, dials, wheels or adjustments of different kinds of mechanical cr experimental set-ups which have some cause or sets of causes at one end of their sequence and an effect or sets of co-ordinated effects at the other end. They are all complexes of causes and effects and if, as Hume proves, there is no tangible connection between causes and effects the whole mechanomorphic configuration implied has no better status than the functioning of the living human or any other biological organism. Why experimental science should claim greater validity than anthropomorphic analogies is not understandable.

Fable and Fact Meet in Modern Knowledge

Fact is not so different from fable after all. Outside fact and inside faith are complementary in the sum-total of life. What was called superstition once is respectable truth now, and the course of human thinking goes like a cart that never keeps to the correct centre of the road but sways from one side to the other. The progress of thought is like a fish inside a river coming up against the bank on one side or the other as the process of the dialectical revaluation of thought proceeds through the decades and the centuries of history.

Erwin Schroedinger may be said to be one of the leaders of modern scientific thought who is interested to see mechanical and life forces meet in a "unified field theory". Eddington has lifted science altogether from the observatory or the laboratory and made it as effective within his private study for the research of truth even when he sits there with the window curtains drawn shut and perhaps with only a piece of paper and pencil in his hand.

The importance of the point of view of the observer in relativity physics and the indeterminism implied in quantum mechanics, all tend to a new importance to human personality gaining ground again in the domain of what is called exact knowledge. Thus, fact and fable meet again in unitive human understanding.

The 'Morpism' that is Common

The sciences and the humanities have common ground in the proto-linguistic form that is understood in both. Brute idolatry can be fitted back into its implications of the context of pure semantics. The 'unified fields' of life and matter resembling as they do the pulsations of quantum mechanics, serve as a basis for the integrated science that is being talked about more and more at present in circles of progressive thinking.

The form implied in any kind of 'morphism' reveals the same common structure of the Absolute. The Absolute represents a value that is dear, reasonable and existent, and thus covers the fields of aesthetics, ethics, metaphysics and physics with one sweep of its amplitude where life, mechanics, the personal factor and the uncertainty factor meet in a common epistemological and methodological frame of reference. Even the *form* of logic or thought has been recognized from the time of Aristotle and *schematization* and model-making have been employed by Kant and Bergson as well as by Plato and pre-Socratic philosophers.

There is nothing disreputable in the use of proto-language of this kind. The Cartesian co-ordinates are proto-linguistic in essence; so also are the longitudes and latitudes of maps. Graphs and charts with mechanical devices added, of red lights, roller, frames, numbered indices, all use proto-linguistics with great advantage.

In fact proto-linguistics offers to man a vast unexplored field of possibilities in the field of the integration of all thought and could even open up, when treated side by side with propositional calculi that are really meta-linguistic in content, a vast unexplored field of possibilities for unified or integrated knowledge, free from frontiers of tongue or vernaculars.

The 'Form' and the 'Formula' of Unified Knowledge

Truth must be one. There cannot be two rival truths. This is known to us *a priori*. But for the sake of consensus we are obliged to approach truth alternately from the *a priori* and the *a posteriori* ends at the same time. The latter is the method of science and the former that of metaphysics proper. The modern tendency after Mill's formulation of inductive reasoning for the service of science, is for these two methods of approach to overlap or alternate.

Wisdom in fact takes forward strides with both the legs, as it were, without any one-legged programme as some might think. It is really a slow and drawn out dialectical process which is at work in the constant re-statement and revaluation of thought through its history, even when confined in different closed regions or within cultural milieus, parochial traditions or barriers marked out by tongues or vernaculars. Human thought that is perennial goes on forever, depositing a golden dust of Wisdom on its ever widening river-bed.

I have been more keenly than ever before seeking the formula or rather the 'form' of unitive wisdom and have been taking my eyes away alternately from the pages of science to that of *Vedānta*.

There is, when understood properly, much kinship that is at present developing between science and Vedāntic thought. Of course traditional

Vedānta needs to be correctly re-stated in the light of modern scientific thought. On the other hand, Einstein, Heisenberg, Max Planck, Schroedinger and Eddington may be looked upon as conforming to the requirements of correct Advaitic or Vedāntic thought consciously or unconsciously.

Schroedinger's conclusions are seen strangely to come into line with the great dicta (*mahā-vākyas*) of Vedāntic doctrine, and, in the last pages of his book, *What is Life*? where he reconciles the mutations of biology with the quantum pulsations of the atom, he actually makes use of *tat tvam asi* (That Thou Art) to give effect to his conclusions, even remaining an accredited modern physicist of the first order. Heisenberg's uncertainty principle shares its epistemology with the theory of *māyā* which is described as *sad-asad-anirvacanīya* (existent, non-existent, uncertain).

Of course we have to avoid drawing too easy parallelisms, but my own conviction is that there is enough to warrant at least a comparison here. The relativity of Einstein is again acceptance of the non-absolutist standpoint in knowing about the physical world which belongs to *māyā*. The personal factor again takes its place without puerile anthropomorphism. Mechanomorphism itself leads the way to it by its excesses which are valid no more.

Science and *Vedānta*

Further *rapprochement* of physics and metaphysics must still have a future. Both have to be restated in terms of each other with a common normative epistemology and methodology. Doctrines do not matter as long as they refer to any laudable human value if not the highest which cannot be any other than the Absolute. A science of sciences of the Absolute would thus be the basis of integrated wisdom or unified knowledge.

Prof. O. Lacombe of the University of Paris has rendered great service to *Vedānta* in his monumental work *L'Absolu selon le Vedanta* (The Absolute According to *Vedānta*, Paris, 1937), which is a version of *Vedānta* filtered and presented clearly for the first time by a Westerner whose intellectual formation is perhaps of the finest order, whether academic, scholastic or lay, available in any part of the world. The rigour, detail and subtlety with which he has absorbed the difficult subject is surprising. On the other side, scientists seeking a unified field for all knowledge are not wanting, as in the instance of Erwin Schroedinger of the University of Dublin. Science and *Vedānta* can be made to meet in one body of modern world knowledge.

Orthodox and Academic *Vedānta*

The *sannyāsins* of India are the custodians of both *Vedānta* and the Vedāntic way of life. They have followed through the centuries the path marked out by the Gurus of India. Now has come a world interest in the subject of *Vedānta* and colourful *sannyāsins* go to the West to preach each his own version of the Wisdom as each understands it.

On the other side, there is in Western universities a growing interest in this subtle and intricate subject. The masterminds of the West reveal now in applying their intellectual acumen to this subject and after Max Muller, Deussen and others comes O. Lacombe who will surely remain a great name. Although his monumental work is just now out of print and unavailable the few copies that remain here and there in Europe are being studied with much avidity and interest in circles sufficiently interested in establishing *Vedānta* as a discipline desirable both for the thinking Indian and for the Western mind, for just that kind of scientific or unitive training in correct thinking which modernism has so far neglected to its disadvantage.

24

The Travesty of Verbosity

WORDS can mislead and even drive us mad. This has been recognized by Śaṅkara when he says:

> The magic of word is a great forest;
> It is the cause of mental giddiness.[1]

The charge against metaphysics by moderns is also based on this travesty of terminology. It is an evil to be faced. Without it, metaphysics can never be saved from becoming mere 'nonsense' as A. J. Ayer would boldly say. Sense and nonsense, or rather sensible and non-sensible aspects have to go hand in hand, as counterparts, to give convincing meaning to words. Wordiness and verbosity otherwise become as vague as wind let out of a bag.

Words, words, words; they fill libraries and vitiate the air with their constant blare through mega-, micro-, or telephones. Their *blah-blah* or *yack-yack* sometimes becomes intolerable, especially when one is trying to rest one's nerves somewhere in this noisy world.

Too much wordiness is the vice by which silence becomes golden. Salesmen or politicians may be said to be the worst offenders here, filling newspaper pages with columns or broadcast tunes filled with words leading to more words spreading peripherally, till they lash the rocks of cheap opinion in the form of slogans with a briny bitterness or after-taste.

We are ourselves guilty of having contributed to the tribulation of words, for which this article is both an apology and a defense. We can at least avow that we have not been guilty of wilfully indulging in bombast or of using a difficult word where a simpler one would have been sufficient, sweeter or kinder to the reader. Words are public property, and are meant for communication, and serve best this purpose when usage is respected, as also correctness, both semantic and syntactic, not to speak of grammatic etymology. We plead not guilty of verbosity for its own sake.

The Way to Avoid Verbosity

As a social animal, *homo sapiens* cannot avoid being communicative. By mere lack of loquaciousness he need not necessarily be a quietist either, cut off from communion with fellow man.

The confusion of tongues with which God in his consternation punished the proud builders of the Tower of Babel, to disperse them, could have been averted if men could have found a way of communicating precise thoughts by other means than through spoken sound. The written word too depends on the spoken, though maybe indirectly, which again depends on sound rather than on anything more tangible directly.

This terrible travesty of fate implicit in the biblical story of Babelization remains unaltered even to the present-day, after millennia which, in spite of what is called progress, have not helped to find a way to de-Babelization. The eye must take over where the ear has failed to lessen the confusion of tongues, not by mere hieroglyphics, but by a language based on something that is visible.

The mathematics we speak of a graph that 'answers' to an equation, and *vice-versa*. One lends support to the other till they verify each other to yield conviction or certitude, through both intuition based on direct vision and calculation through symbolic logic. Scientific certitude is neither the result of induction nor of deduction in reasoning, but of *both* together. So too is the resultant certitude of visibles and calculables arriving from opposite poles of the same knowledge-situation to a central non-dual, unitive act of understanding intuitive and calculable at once.

The tribulation or travesty of getting lost in the forest of words can only be avoided if we think of sound symbols in relation to visible schemes and *vice-versa*. Having devoted a whole monograph to this subject, and having more than a thousand pages of printed words always with the same scheme in mind, the time is now come to let the reader have a look behind the curtains, as it were, admitting him confidently into some broad schematic features which might save him difficulties in understanding meanings more clearly and also absolve us from charges of appearing grandiloquent or for loving verbosity for its own sake.

The Structure of Word Families

It takes a lot of living to make a 'house' a 'home' is a sentence we have taken from an ordinary dictionary in everyday use. The connotation of a word might here differ from its denotation, so that word games of endless variety can be played, as Wittgenstein has worked out in his last book, *Philosophical Investigations*. "The same word can denote many different things and conversely, many things can unite in a single meaning", says the Guru Nārāyaṇa, revealing in such a possibility a knowledge situation belonging to an absolutist ground or context which is "an ultimate secret of the pandit". (*Ātmopadeśa-Śatakam*)

Vertically, in the pure numinous aspect of the Absolute, word meanings tend to fuse and unite at different levels of the scale of human values, and horizontally, in the world that is the enjoyable (*bhogya*) as distinct from the enjoyer (*bhoktā*) the objective world of values spreads out indefinitely in space. The word 'home' is more vertical in its connotation than the word 'house' which has merely a horizontalized denotation. Both meet in an abstract idea representing a reality where human beings can live their lives.

The same difference can distinguish a wife and a woman, each having its distinct position structurally, and which if mixed up, would be disastrous or nuisable in greater or less sense making life absurd or significant. Fitting words thus into a scheme would help to banish ambiguities and absurdities.

Pragmatic and Semiotic Aspects of Words

When we ask anyone to call a spade we are insisting on the pragmatic or horizontal aspect of a word. On the contrary, when we respect an idol in temple, or admire the original of Mona Liza in the Louvre, it is not the spade or hammer world that we confine ourselves to. In a vertical world of the meaning of meaning, where semiotic processes blend and fuse denotations and connotations of words in ascending or descending processes of meaningfulness or significance, the dead letter comes to life. It lives and moves.

Bread and stones differ and it is not hard to place them in the vertical or horizontal contents. A man who wants to meditate on a rock after his hunger has been satisfied, might interchange the structural positions of each of these words. Contemplatives give primacy to certain values as against mechanistic or earthy ones, and word games are most interesting when played without error according to contexts in any given spatio-temporal situation anywhere by anybody. Like many other games, word games must have a court in which they should be played. The rules of the game should not be violated with impunity. It is the structure of the

Absolute which regulates or lends significance to each word in a given context. It would be like playing football in a tennis court with rules outside that of the game, to mix or violate frames or rules promiscuously. One cannot explore heaven through the help of a sputnik nor mix up hypostatic with hierophantic contemplative values. The actual, the perceptual and the nominal belong each to the four limbs of the semantic polyvalence of words, which, to mistake for each other, without attention to structure, would give disastrous meanings, mechanistically, contemplatively, or both.

Subjective, Selective, Structural Schematism Explained

We should not treat the world as too objectively real, or in other words, there is an adjustment in correct philosophy which moves back into the subject just enough so that the claims of active objectivity and passive subjectivity neutralize each other. This is subjectivism.

Out of the many items of the objective world we select the most important categories, such as space, time or causation. This is selectivism.

Lest such selected items should become disjunct items, we refer them to the Absolute as a normative notion underlying the items, with a subjective and an objective aspect within the Self, as the minus and plus of possible adjustment. When perfect neutrality is abandoned for purposes of clear communication in respect of various problems right or wrong, we create one-sided words or expressions.

The schematism that thus emerges, revealing possibilities with words, is only a form of a proto-linguistic device to enable us to overcome the tribulations that language presents with its paradoxes, antinomies, ambiguities and absurdities, resulting from unbalanced dialectical counterparts.

Any thesaurus will reveal, how, when the alphabetical order is abandoned in favour of any more organic arrangement of words, we can more easily recognize different degrees of depth, saturation, shade, brilliance, tint, clarity or dullness, involving synonyms, and antonyms between words. Difficulties dissolve when linguistic structure is revealed.

The Absolute consists of two sets of entities, namely, words conceptually understood and words perceptually understood. These have a one-to-one correspondence between them, in a sort of tensorial or vectorial space of the world of complex quaternions.

Lest, at this stage, we should be charged with again raising the very word-trouble which by explaining we proposed to avoid, let us only say here that schematism is only a form of language which precedes the spoken or written language which might be called meta-linguistic. As such a basic thought-language presupposes pure thought-movements as also the circulating alternating process of thinking or communicating through concepts or percepts by humans who might be speaking any of the many vernaculars extant in the world, it can be called proto-linguism.

Proto-linguism is meant to offer a graphic frame of reference for words just in the same way as a curve on graph paper explains, clarifies or 'satisfies' an equation expressed in algebraic language. If the latter is meta-linguistic, the former is proto-linguistic. Even to proto-linguistic *schemas* we can add algebraic or arithmetical signs or symbols with discretion by way of thinking of abstract or concrete universals or particulars inter-subjectively or transphysically or both. The scheme is not a new entity outside language, introduced into metaphysics, but is a way of making metaphysics more 'sensible' or tangible and less airy. It thrives at the meeting point of the algebraic and the geometric worlds at the core of the normative notion of the Absolute.

Vertical, Horizontal, Hypostatic, Hierophantic Values Explained

Human life is inserted within a world of values of graded interests, some opposed to the others, so that the problem of "to be or not to be" presents itself to man anywhere and at any time. He is the enjoyer of values and the objective world is a feast spread out horizontally. Sleep and waking, day and night, alternate as does the heart with its diastole and systole. Natural behaviour patterns of organisms from the amoeba to a tiger that hunts or sleeps, show the same ambivalent cycles of alternation. The *Gītā* (III. 16) refers to this as the *evam pravarttitam cakram* (the wheel that is ever in action) in relation to cosmological, psychological, and religious or contemplative events in an over-all world of values.

Those who do not know the two poles, round which there is circulation, involving life values, miss the import of Wisdom in life altogether. The night and day of *Brahman* (the Absolute) as they alternate cyclically, the *Gītā* says again (VIII.17) pertain to the same cosmological structure and world process understood in the macrocosmic context. Microscopic alternation as with the macrocosm, is revealed in quantum mechanics and is implied in Einstein or Eddington.

If we apply the Ockham's razor principle to all these treated together, we get the plain and simple outline of a structure in which words like hierophany, hypostasy, horizontal and vertical values in life, can conveniently be fitted to make meanings of difficult words self-explanatory in the same way as an illiterate contractor of a building would know where the door, the stairs or chimney come in as he examines a building plan which requires only a little training, and that, once for all, to follow. To take another familiar example, the guide to London seen from the alphabetical directory is more easy to use when supported by a map of the roads and buildings actually marked out on it.

The vertical aspect can summarily be said to refer to all pure values, while the horizontal would refer to practical values or affairs in life. Instead of the pair of words 'pure' and 'practical' we can substitute 'intelligible' and 'visible' the 'subjective' and the 'objective', the 'noumenal' and the 'phenomenal', the 'real' and the 'apparent', the 'spiritual' and the 'earthy', the 'mental' and the 'material', in endless couples. The geometrical schematic language can cover many particular instances, irrespective of metaphysical terminology in any philosophy of any part of the world at any time.

Schematism thus is a natural concomitant of perennial philosophy the world over.

Let us now take another pair of words which we have been guilty of using without full clarification so far.

In the *Bhagavad Gītā* (XV.2) there is a reference to the tree with roots up and which further refers to branches that spread both 'downward and upward'. This kind of language is sheer protolinguistics *par excellence*. The upward branches evidently refer to hypostatic religious values in Vedism and the downward ones are the corresponding hierophantic values of the same context of Vedic values, in life. Read and scrutinized correctly in this *Gītā* context, the meanings of these terms will become more clear to any earnest reader.

As particular instances of the same distinction between the plus and the minus limbs of the ambivalent polarity or dichotomy of the vertical axis, we could cite any number of cases, such as the transcendent (plus) and immanent (minus), the teleological and the ontological, the existential and the essential, the celestial and the mundane, and so forth. The thesaurus will give any number of other instances of such pairs or antonyms if the student will take the trouble to look into the respective sections.

Word Families, Clans, Systems, Aggregates

Words can be studied as clustering into natural groups families, clans, systems, aggregates, classes, gestaltic configurations, sets, types or *ensembles.*

It is the Self as knower of words which is the unifying factor, and all words result from apperceptions between prospective and retrospective tendencies in lasting consciousness, resulting in apperceptive masses formed on the plus or minus side vertically, or on the momentarily pleasing or displeasing sides horizontally.

Heat and cold are dual horizontal factors of the latter type, while the attainment of more basic life desires or aims in a purer sense giving pain or happiness, belongs to the vertical context. What is good for one is good for another basically, although in detailed preferences or interests one man's meat is another man's poison. Retrospection is always regretful, while prospective conquest of time with the spirit oriented towards the future of one's life spells joy in life. When the plus and minus are neutralized we get absolute bliss.

Thus 'passion' is to be placed on the vertical plus side and 'tender emotions' such as to children by a mother, on the minus. Extreme tendency to activity as with a huntsman or sportsman is a horizontal tendency. Day-dreaming would correspond to the virtual or horizontal negative aspect of overt activity.

Words belonging to these several contexts can be made to cluster round a centre of origin where pure apperception at the core of the Self resides. It would be a good game for those who want to develop word power to practise making maps of word groups or families with the four-limbed vertico-horizontal plan as the basis of correlation. Meanings otherwise vague and lost in the forest of words, would fall into clarity of self-evident meaningfulness by this method. Serious students could indulge in such word games with advantage to the building up of their word power organically rather than mechanistically as we often see recommended.

The Group of 'Ologies' Considered Together

Theology, cosmology, psychology, eschatology and many other 'ologies' can be treated with reference to the happiness of the contemplative Self. These values normally belong to the human contemplative context. In the mechanistic objective world of sputniks and exploration of outer space, where overt action is involved, the world of value conquered is the horizontal one.

Contemplative worlds in graded order of values range like a Jacob's ladder, touching earth and heaven, which are only other names for a system of values clinging together into a cluster. The ordinary heaven of most religions is a hedonistic and comparatively relativistic system of human values for which the common grade of contemplative men might aspire. At its antipodes we have the negative notion of Hades which is the bed of suffering. Heaven and hell are ploarized vertical sets of value systems, whose bright side represents joy or pleasure, and the dark side pain or infernal suffering universally and eternally understood.

The Sanskrit dictionary called the *Amara-kośa* begins with all words listed in a certain order on the same principle of the thesaurus. The thesaurus' author Roget admits his indebtedness to Amarasimha. To decrease word trouble and increase word power, the grouping of synonyms and antonyms, keeping a revised and more complete scheme than what was used by these two authors, based on the structure of the total situation which we have discussed, could be adopted.

The Idea of a New Dictionary of Contemplative Words

It would be too stupendous a task to think of covering all the words used in the different languages of the world in this way. The walks and vocations of life have increased, and from aeronautics to quiet contemplation there are possible word-systems, each of which demands a separate dictionary of its own.

For our purposes, we have to delimit, grade, arrange and clarify words into families, giving first place to first, keeping absolutist and total contemplative value before us. The plan of a new dictionary must follow the outlines of the double domain of the word schematically understood. Like an atlas usually supplemented by a gazetteer, where latitudes and longitudes serve to relate visible and word realities, such a dictionary must have perceptual and conceptual sides brought together under one reference. Word families can each have a map pertaining to the same linguistic polyvalent ground. Words involving processes must respect the circulation of thought, values taking different positions in the apperceptive thought cycles, making semiosis, syntactics and the pragmatics of language have each their proper planes, zones, lines, cyclic stages or poles sufficiently respected.

Institutions provided with the help of a sufficient staff to collect, collate, classify, arrange, grade and select words must work for years comparing notes and revising decisions to accomplish this grand task meant for a unified language of science which will break through the existing frontiers between one local vernacular and another.

Such is our vision for the future and my apology here is that we have only been able to cover the fringes of the total problem here and there to the best of our ability.

What is Our Defence?

Our justification for employing an abundance of new words, many of which had to be coined or newly combined against prevailing usage, is that we have inevitably to find words that correspond especially as between the contemplative literature of the East and that of the more modern West. Bad translations of Vedāntic expressions, loosely employed such as *sat*, *cit* and *ānanda* as corresponding to 'existence', 'knowledge' and 'bliss' respectively, have been substituted by us for 'Existence', 'Subsistence' and 'Value' as the triple expression more correctly understood in the East and in the West at the same time. Likewise *para* and *apara* would correspond to many pairs of words in the West, such as immanent and transcendent or pure and practical, the intelligible or the visible, the noumenal and the phenomenal, etc. We have preferred to refer them to the two axes, each with a positive and negative, so as to tally more correctly with a scientifically revised theory of knowledge.

Reference

1. *śabdajālaṃ mahāraṇyam*
   cittabhramaṇa kāraṇam

PART V

Hindu Orthodoxy

25

Patterns of Hindu Orthodoxy

INDIAN spirituality is not dead. This is the simple conclusion that emerged in my mind after this significant event of the first *Gītā* Jayantī celebrations in Bombay from November 22 to December 1,1960 which may be said to reflect the temper of the Indian mind at present. More than a century of foreign Western domination has succeeded in many respects in subduing and counteracting the natural expressions of Indian patterns of behaviour and ideals, but anyone who happened to be present at Bombay during the *Gītā* celebrations could never believe that the soul of India had been subdued in any way.

More than ten thousand people, men and women in equal proportion, sat many hours, morning and evening, in perfect orderly silence, listening to discourses from *sannyāsins* who came from different parts of India. The spacious *paṇḍal* (a shelter, usually made of palm-leaf thatch open on all sides), colourfully decorated and lighted with an ample dais which seated the men of renunciation as understood in the last chapter of the *Gītā* itself, with the elite of Bombay humbly occupying the floor, was a sight long forgotten and unseen in modern India.

India's Precious Heritage

The audience included ex-governors of provinces, industrial and business magnates, and even royalties of the previous regime, who again responded to the call of Kṛṣṇa in the battlefield of ancient India. Clans and creeds were forgotten and all listened to the message of the *Gītā* in its various aspects and implications, wrapt, as it were, in a kind of half-mystic trance as the teaching sounded as modern today as it was a thousand years ago.

Vyāsa proved himself the first of all poets and wise men once again in the city of Bombay in spite of the otherwise commercial importance of this city where Maharashtrians and Gujaratis alike still rub shoulders in rivalry in appreciation of the message of the *Gītā*.

There were about one hundred seats on the dais where *sannyāsins* of different orders, denominations or *sampradāyas*, ranging from *sants* to *maṇḍaleśvaras* of the 108th grade, sat in their begging robes as in the days of Jainism and Buddhism. To see the Mahārāni of Gwalior touch the feet of some of those who entered the *paṇḍal,* as if from the street, in half-nakedness, proud of their status as mere beggars, was a sight that touched the hearts of many present, and confirmed in them the renewed belief that modernism had not completely killed out the time-honoured attitudes and ways of life that made India a unique and unrivalled country.

The *bhikṣu* still lives on the streets as the standard-bearer of a heritage that is more than three thousand years old, where the peasant woman is willing to take the dust off his feet without any question about his belief or other status in life. How long this precious sight will continue on this ancient soil with the portent of adverse winds beginning to blow against these pure, simple and human ways of mutual respect and reverence, is still to be seen. In the meanwhile we can only hope that modernism may not pronounce its adverse verdict against the ways of old India and consider it outmoded or even too good to continue.

Orthodoxy and Tolerance

In the way of life of the Hindu, orthodoxy and tolerance enter together in a puzzling manner. The patriot-saint of India, Swami Vivekananda, claimed at the Chicago Parliament of Religions as early as the 'nineties of the last century, that Hinduism was distinguished by toleration above all other excellences. What we saw at the village near Taran-Taran near the frontier of the Punjab does not certainly vouch for this. In the very land of the Five Rivers which itself gave the name to the Hindus, the disciples of Nebi (the Prophet) are not to be seen any more, and their burnt and desolate houses speak of a sad chapter where patriotism and religious sentiments gave rise to an intensely intolerant attitude as between man and man. Simple humanity has been glaringly violated, whatever might be the justification that one group or another might put forward.

Tolerance and orthodoxy cannot live together, and if they do live together, as they seem to do still in certain other parts of India, it is due to a subtle dialectical relation between the two contrary or complementary tendencies present and implied in the two words. The principle of double negation is implied here and sociologically we can watch the rare phenomenon in which orthodoxy sometimes helps tolerance or, at other times, fans the fire of intolerance leading to a general flare-up, disastrous to the rival orthodoxies concerned. Hindu orthodoxy and tolerance have deep-seated secrets which revealed themselves to me in my wanderings in North India which are worthwhile bringing into light for the sake of the socio-religious verities that it can teach in an experimental manner for our guidance.

Each Orthodoxy has its own Central Value

"As is a man's faith that he is himself".[1] This is the subtle dialectical equation with which we can understand each group formation in the name of any religious orthodoxy.

Faith refers to some value that individuals or groups hold dear to them as against others. These value-factors are divisible into two groups: (1) those values that belong to the prophetic context, and (2) those other values of an ontological, hylozoic or hierophantic context.

As one travels from the North-Western Frontier of India towards Benares, a person who is informed about these two sets of values and at the same time is observant, cannot fail to mark evidences of one or the other set of values imperceptibly prevailing over the other. The mild Hindu and the Mohammedan with his zeal verging often on the fanatic (the former compensated only by the puerile forms of value-factors sustaining his rigid orthodoxy) present to the student a picture of contrasting faiths worth closer philosophic or scientific scrutiny.

The Clash between the Prophetic and the Hylozoic

Sikhism present's a blend of the prophetic and the non-prophetic tendencies in religious life. The stern touch of the servere truth that Sikhism implies is visible on the countenance of these people. The glorification of the letter instead of human figures or of persons is the first distinguishing trait. The word and the law or the commandments were important to both, but a closer scrutiny revealed that the waters of the land of the Five Rivers also had some importance with the Sikhs.

Amritsar was a city of immortal waters, and every other place of religious importance to them stressed the bathing in the waters side by side with stressing the *Jap jī*, its teaching and commandments. The childishness implied in the worship of human figures was not favoured by both the groups, Sikh or Muslim. The Sikh is as uncompromising as the Mohammedan in items or articles of belief, although on the side of behaviour, including diet or cleanliness, they were not so rigid in their orthodoxy as their brothers the Hindus, who lived in the same land of the Five Rivers.

Sikh zeal is thus one to be placed between two sets of orthodoxy, the prophetic on one side and the hylozoic on the other. By hylozoism we mean here not only the tendency to endow inanimate factors like water, air, fire or earth with sacredness or life-reality, but the general tendency to consider objects as presences or representatives of aspects of the Absolute. Hierophany and Hypostasy are two tendencies in religion referred to allegorically in the *Gītā* as two branches of a heavenly tree growing downwards and upwards. A whole chapter, the fifteenth, is devoted to this complex structure of holy values, which bind humans in the world of religious ritual or behaviour in general, round a graded series of values.

As we travel from Amritsar eastwards we come across another outcrop belonging, as it were to another stratum of less prophetic but hierophantic-hylozoic values. Instead of the immortal lake-waters, one begins to hear of the waters of the Ganges, than which there is nothing more sacred in the world, to the mild Hindu or more especially the Hindu woman. It is here that the feminine version of orthodoxy can beat all the fervour of the fanatic, whether Sikh, Sanātana Hindu, or Mussalman. Next to Benares itself, Haridvar is the locality where the limbs of the Gaṅgāmāyī interlace and hold in their close embrace a full city in mutual exchange of transferred holiness. Ganges water is not just water (*pānī* in Hindi) to the Hindu, who would correct an irreverent neighbour if he did not refer to its waters by the more Samskritized name of *jala*. I know of the instance too, of a Jain woman who had married a Hindu, who would not treat Ganges bathing as sacred, because Jainism did not attach any importance to such holiness.

While living in Haridvar during the month of November 1960 I had a special occasion to watch the glorification of the Ganges by the people around this city of *sannyāsins*. The Public Works Department wanted to lay the foundations of a bridge across one of the arms of Gaṅgā as it flowed past the city, and had, for about a fortnight, diverted the river along another main channel.

As if by magic, one morning when we looked out of the balcony overlooking the Ganges, that used to roar past through rounded boulders of this area, in view of the foothills of the Himālaya and the woods on the other side of the river, thick with shady trees held auspicious for their fruit or shade, we were surprised to find that Gaṅgāmāyī had disappeared overnight, leaving pools here and there among the pebbles, in which trout and other fish were straded. We first thought that the wonders of the by-gone age or *satya-yuga* were coming back to Āryāvarta ! But it was only the work of the evil Public Works Department, and we realized that the age of miracles had passed forever.

Between fiction and fact I would have preferred to live in the wonder of the former. When, after the fortnight, the Ganges came back, the population stood round at different points of vantage in the city to greet it with jubilation and primitive cries of exaltation, giving vent to a large volume of group emotion. The mass response to the event was unmistakable, and the element of a sense of the numinous that entered into the general feeling, could be guessed by the number of garlands that flowed past on the river surface as we watched them for several days afterwards.

Gaṅgāmāyī's renewed presence coming from the same matted locks of Śiva, the Himalāyan woods, and fed by the snow of the Badrīnāth and Kedāranāth temples was too much for the simple Hindu mind to withstand, because of the ancient hierophantic associations it had from the most ancient days of pre-history. No prophetic note could possibly penetrate into the pressurized sacredness of the situation. Water is just water to the Mohammedan and to the Christian, and although they touch water as they enter a Catholic church to this day and think in terms of baptism with water, the hypostatic sense of the holy has mostly replaced the hierophantic.

The prophetic of the hypostatic go together to constitute the positive side of the sense of the holy, while hierophany and hylozoism go together on the existential, ontological or negative side of the same sense, as known to different religions. Some stress the positive values and others the negative. To understand this ambivalent polarity is the key to the orthodoxies that thrive in different religious formations. Sikh Gurus are open to the appreciation of the holy places of the Mohammedan religion because the Value that Sikhism stresses belongs to the positive rather than to the negative order. Hindus insist on giving due importance both to the positive and the negative values implied in holiness, although in certain group orthodoxies the negative seems to predominate over the positive.

The Place of Kṛṣṇaism in North India

As we travel east still more, the next stratum in religious life that becomes unmistakably evident is the one that refers to the glorification of Kṛṣṇa as a person. Giving a divine status to a human being is repugnant to the true prophetic spirit of Islam and even with Christianity the same tendency is observable though in a less marked degree. Human figures except that of Christ tend to be replaced by doctrines or articles of faith that are generally numbered in order of importance.

Kṛṣṇaism ranges from the exaltation to divine status of the baby Kṛṣṇa, the pastoral Kṛṣṇa of the erotic-mystic context, the king-maker Kṛṣṇa of the *Mahābhārata* and the Guru Kṛṣṇa of the *Bhagavad Gītā*.

Of all these, the erotic-mystic Rādhā-Kṛṣṇa finds popular approbation to its maximum possible extent in Vṛndāban. Here we are going over the same ground in order to extract the content of the orthodoxy implied in these forms of religious growth.

With regard to the Rādhā-Kṛṣṇa cult, the best feature of it seems to be that its appeal is so real and human that it can hold its own, as it has proved by its long history already, against any heterodox onslaughts, ideological or actual, from the outside world. A woman signing a song in praise of a Bāla-Kṛṣṇa (the child Kṛṣṇa) or a man feeling exalted in raising cries about Rādhā (his beloved) and Kṛṣṇa, can never be defeated or browbeaten by any proselytising prophetic religion. They would feel naturally disarmed in the presence of so melting a form of adoration of God. This must be the reason that this cult has survived unaffected after all these centuries and the secret hand of many a brave or beautiful woman of royal harems, Moghul or Turk, must have made their secret contributions to this amazing stability and persistence of this form of religious orthodoxy in the heart of India through the centuries.

Closed Group Formations of Recent Years

The Ārya-Samāja, the Brahmo-Samāja, the Sanītānī Group, the Rāmakṛṣṇa-Vivekananda Group, the Rādhāswāmi Cult, with the Sri Aurobindo and Ānanda-Mayī religious expressions, presented to us, during our stay in Haridvar, ample opportunities for further research in the direction that

Hindu orthodoxies have taken in recent years.

Besides Ganges water which could be used as a criterion of orthodoxy side by side with Kṛṣṇaism, we have to think backwards several thousands of years to the days of Vardhamāna Mahāvīra and Buddha if we are able to get a rough idea of all that Hindu orthodoxy primarily and fundamentally implies.

Nakedness or half-nakedness is to be traced to Jainism. Onion and garlic are taboo in some *sannyāsin* groups, while, at the other extreme today, we have those who go to the extent of eating even beef openly without damaging their orthodox reputation to any appreciable degree. The fish that were stranded in pools when the Ganges was diverted, were not to be touched by anyone living in or around Haridvar, because killing was taboo in that area, while in Bengal the *sannyāsins* offer even fish in their sacramental offerings without any qualms of orthodox conscience. Orthodoxy gets grafted on certain strange taboos or preferences and the complex irrationality which prevails here defies all critical analysis.

In South India, where an orthodox brāhmaṇa would not touch water from a low caste, he could freely drink buttermilk or even toddy if occasion presented itself, without damage to his orthodoxy. Kashmir brāhmaṇas can eat meat and the taboo on fish is less severe. With Sanātanī Hindus I found that, although Dayananda was a staunch adherent of the Vedic way, his rejection of idol worship put him outside the pale of strict Hindu orthodoxy as they claimed to represent it. Caste taboos too prevailed in different degrees and ways among the orthodox.

Ritual was also another factor in determining orthodox conformity. *Ācamana* (sprinkling water round food) before meals is an orthodox observance which some *sannyāsins* keep while others do not consider it essential. In certain circles Vivekananda was taboo while Dayananda was acceptable, in other places it was the other way round, or sometimes both were left out. The real complexion of Hindu orthodoxy thus becomes a puzzle. As a generalized statement which we might however venture to make, it is perhaps hierophantic rather than hypostatic values that decides what is orthodox in behaviour patterns with the Hindus generally. Habits of cleaning themselves, and food habits, ranging from objections to onions up to beef eating, with intermediate taboos on this or that item of food, too many to enumerate in detail, determine the grade of orthodoxy that each person may be said to pertain to.

Other Scruples of Orthodoxy

A respectable Hindu of North India is one who gives great importance to pure *ghee* (clarified butter) and the status of a family is often determined by the amount of this article consumed each month. Generous helpings of butter is normal in the Punjab, while orthodoxy in South India is nominally sustained by one or at the most three small spoons of *ghee* served with rice to distinguish the Āryan from the non-Āryan way.

In the extreme South coconut oil largely replaces clarified butter. The crowning or final distinguishing mark of orthodoxy is also connected with bathroom habits. Much gargling and clearing of throats goes on wherever there are groups of Hindus. In ships where Indians travel I have heard Westerners complain of the horrid exaggerations of the bathroom noises their Hindu cabin-mates when they were just composing themselves to an early morning repose.

Repeating *Hari-Oṁ* or some such sacred formula, starting with the small hours of the day, when many others are sleeping, is no crime in the Hindu world of orthodoxy, while such behaviour would be strongly resented elsewhere. These matters, though trivial, are important in the relations that the Hindu might have to cultivate with the increasing number of outside visitors who are making their acquaintance with India. It is therefore worthwhile to refer to them here.

In the self-righteousness of orthodoxy many of us forget that we might be making nuisances of ourselves to our fellow-men, who too have a right to their different habits. This should not, however, be taken to be a condemnation of these habits which personally I would recommend shorn of exaggerations, to many an outside visitor if he would be willing to listen without disadoption. Early morning hours are referred to in Hindu books, as *Brahma-muhūrta* (time favourable for the contemplation of *Brahman* or the Absolute). Although there is a nuisance value and a humorous side to these behaviouristic exaggerations of Hindu orthodoxy, the value in themselves of these old-time habits is in no way to be minimised. If we add now that the Hindu scrupulously insists on receiving a gift only with the right hand and not with the left, and mention that the *añjalī* or salutation with both palms juxtaposed, is the right orthodox greeting, and refer to full-length prostrations before Gurus, and taking the dust off their feet as the crowning gestures belonging to the context of orthodox behaviour, we shall have covered most of the items that come to mind when we are on this subject of the behaviour scruples of Hindu orthodoxy. Shoes too are taboo in places of worship, but this taboo is perhaps the most primitive of them all, because shoes can sometimes be cleaner than the legs.

Taboo-Counter-Taboo

A Norwegian ex-sailor once told me that the ship's crew discovered a Negro stowaway hiding among the coals in the hold of the ship after it had left a harbour. The head cook took great interest in the find and treated him as a favourite, and all shielded him till one day he was caught in the act of washing himself, using a kitchen vessel in the water-closet. This was enough for all to disadopt and betray him, and he was sent overboard at the next port of call.

Trivial details of habits become taboos and counter-taboos with closed groups in this world with a strange irrationality of their own. It would be equally shocking for a European to see night-dress material used for skirting or if a man wore a sports-tie with a dinner-jacket. If a Westerner in India made the mistake of receiving food with the left hand or touching a pile of food in the hands of the server, all would be lost for him for the rest of his life in the world of closed orthodoxy in India.

There is a delicate balance that scrupulous trivialities of commission or omission could tilt for or against one disastrously. Taboos and counter-taboos exist in all closed formations adding up to the total of separatist and static tendencies in life. What is the shape or complexion of Hindu orthodoxy is the question that we have been trying to answer, and we find that we have landed ourselves into this bog of the sacred and the profane, from whose intricacies we can hardly extricate ourselves. Here we enter into the forest of taboos and bans, injunctions or prohibitions, in which the true complexion of what is Hinduism is lost.

The Mīmāṁsā tradition is what has tried to salvage the shipwrecked remnants of those aspects of behaviour or belief that could stand the scrutiny of critical examination. Between Jaimini and Bādarāyaṇa, some order has been put into this matter, and other Gurus have followed them, trying to throw light in the dark recesses of the world of the sacred or the profane.

Much rationalization still remains to be introduced here before what is called Hindu orthodoxy can stand on its own legs for the benefit of all those attached to this body of belief or behaviour. The *Vedānta* may be said to take care of the doctrinal side, and as for behaviouristic religion, present and future Guru-guidance is needed more than ever before.

Thus we come back to the *Bhagavad Gītā* with whose Jayantī celebrations we entered into this subject of the determination of the true complexion of the face of what we have tried to refer to as Hindu orthodoxy. The task now is to put order into the whole subject from a one-world standpoint, and in this matter there is no textbook that can give us the guiding principles, other than the *Bhagavad Gītā* itself. Belief and behaviour can lead to a new world civilization based on the Science of the Absolute as outlined in this wonderful basic text, on which humanity itself could regulate its behaviour as well as belief on scientific lines.

Reference

1. *Bhagavad Gītā,* XVII. 3.

26

Hindu Philosophical Orthodoxy

MISTY mornings were the rule rather than the usual frosty weather in January 1961. There was unusual rain too for several days before the cycle of the seasons steadied itself. The grass continued green till late this year, on the top of the Nilgiri Hills. Occasionally, as we looked out to the east, the sun rose over what is called *une mer de brouillard*, a veritable sea of mist, effacing the whole of the Keti Valley and spreading its glory over the plains of Coimbatore too. Truth is hidden and falsehood stands revealed and there is nothing much to choose between them as one is as beautiful as the other. Such is the mist of *māyā* that now reveals and now hides what we call 'falsehood' as well as what we call 'truth'. Both are interchangeable terms. The philosophical puzzlement and the corresponding visual puzzlement both lend support to a double mystery in which the awareness of the onlooker or witness is alternately swayed or held.

I have been, within myself, focusing my attention these weeks on the complexion of what is called Hindu orthodoxy. Orthodoxy has its tail end brought up by scruples, interdictions, obligations, taboos or bans, some of which attain to a degree of absurdity. The true face of Hindu orthodoxy however, depends much on philosophical considerations, although it must be pointed out at once that theology, philosophy, science and logic, not to mention ethics and aesthetics, cling together more closely and integrally when we come to examine them in the context of what is called Hindu thought.

Pantheism, pessimism, hylozoism and idealism and existentialism, each with a methodology and axiology of its own, make of the history of Hindu thought a strange blend of the rational and the intuitive. A movement in thought that has thirty centuries for its range or amplitude, with endless currents, cross-currents and ramifications, has to be taken in with one large sweep of the mind, if one is to get a bird's eye-view of the true complexion of Hindu orthodoxy from its tail to its head and, running the gamut of the whole range of human though invisible spiritual values implied. From the taboo on onion or garlic at one extreme, to the hair-splitting and logic-chopping in the *Bhāmati Catuḥsūtrī* which devotes volumes on four small aphorisms of the *Brahma Sūtra Bhāṣya* of Śaṅkara, the complexion of Hindu orthodox thought presents varied tints, black, grey or white mixed with every possible saturation, shade or hue of the spectrum.

Strands in the String of Indian Thought

Sacrifice, gift or austerity are the three strands of the string of Hindu orthodoxy that has continued unbroken through this long span of thirty centuries. These have been distinguished and twisted into one string as understood in the context of the *Bhagavad Gītā* in which the Absolute is referred to as a *sūtra* (thread) that strings successive pearls of value into one garland of values (VII.7).

Yajña (sacrifice), *dāna* (gift) and *tapas* (austerity) are the triple strands of this string as mentioned in many chapters of the *Gītā* (VIII.28 etc.). Just as one strand might pass from right to left when twisted into a string with others, these strands of Hindu orthodoxy change sides, and what was once orthodox becomes heterodox at another epoch. The long history of spirituality in general attains to a strange and complex texture in which the individual strands are visible no more.

Vedic texts which refer to the cutting up of the parts of calf and the libations of intoxicants like the *soma* juice, become taboos in later centuries. Many such changes have been witnessed, so that the complexion of orthodoxy remains variegated and ever-changeful in its hues to the present-day.

Bṛhaspati, the ancient Vedic *ṛṣi*, while being the preceptor to the gods, was associated with a school now considered highly heterodox and materialistic. He laughed at the brāhmaṇas and called them meat-eaters and cheats, just in the same way as Hume compared metaphysicians of his day with bandits and robbers who waylaid and plundered the gullible.

The *Pūrva Mīmāṁsakas* who swear by the *Vedas* are known to believe in no god, although adhering to the very word of the ritualistic parts of the *Mantras* (ritual formulae) and the *Brāhmaṇas* (exegeses) of the *Veda*. Śaṅkara himself has been suspected of being a Buddhist in disguise for his outspokenness in favour of *jñāna* (wisdom) over *karma* (ritualistic action), although Śaṅkara's followers in the various pontifical seats held after him resemble *Pūrva Mīmāṁsakas* rather than *Advaita Vedāntins* in their ways and beliefs. *Sāṁkhya* and *Yoga* have both orthodox and heterodox elements. Pātañjala *Yoga* has changed its complexion altogether after the *bhāṣya* (commentary) on it by Vyāsa and Bhoja. *Nyāya* and *Vaiśeṣika* which started with different authors have come down to our days in a strangely fused form, as found in standard textbooks such as that of Annambhaṭṭa. We can hardly determine nowwhere we stand in respect of its categories, methods or values. Therefore, let those who might have the ambition of mastering Indian philosophy be forewarned against being waylaid by false trails and alluring indications. The volume of available comments variously called *vārttikas, vivaraṇas* or *ṭīkās*, together with other forms of explanation, comment or gloss, are so endless in variety and intricacy that it takes the most way of ramblers the greatest difficulty to come out of the thick woods that Indian thought actually presents. Much academic acumen in the West and heavy punditry in India are being absorbed into the sands of present-day speculation on this subject.

Indian and European Logic

One would expect that precise thinking, in subjects like mathematics at least, would not vary from locality to locality or as between one language and another. "Two plus two make four" everywhere, irrespective of the particular culture. Yet it is strange that to this day we should hear of such subjects as 'Indian' Logic. When two persons discuss or dispute about the validity of a truth or reality or even the preferability of a way of life involving human values, it is normal to presuppose that there should be a universality about the methods employed and the ways in which such truth is appraised or approached.

What is good for one country must be good for another because of the common humanity involved in the benefits of wisdom. All philosophy scientifically conceived must have a normative notion underlying it. Whether wisdom seeks this standard outside or inside the self, it can refer only to the Absolute. Humanity cannot have two truths or two ways of approaching it.

To the extent that such diversity is admitted, the scientific character of philosophy or philosophical character of the science involved must be defective. Bain's textbook of logic happens to be different from Bradley's and Indian logic has its own frame of reference different from that of the West. The case for both Eastern and Western logic must suffer so long as there is no attention paid to normalization of the content of logic and its method.

If we pick up a standard book of Indian logic we find in it subjects that would normally go into a textbook of physics or psycho-physics in the West. Annambhaṭṭa's *Tarka Saṁgraha* starts off with the enumeration of the *sapta padārthas* (seven categories) involved in all discussions of truth or reality. The enumeration covers all things visible or invisible (*dravya* 'substance'; *guṇa* 'quality'; *karma* 'action'; *sāmānya* 'genus or generic nature'; *viśeṣa* 'specificity'; *samavāya* 'mutual inherence'; and *abhāva* 'negation').

Under the first item here we have further subdivisions enumerating the items of the physical world, which imperceptibly merge into such items as time, space or direction and grade still upward, as it were, into the domains of the soul and the mind. It is not difficult to see from the width of the range of the categories thus enumerated, including nothingness and the mind itself, that Indian logic refers to an all-comprehensive notion of the Absolute and not merely to syllogisms or kinds of reasoning.

A Common Method for Science, Philosophy or Reasoning

Departmentalization and over-specialization of knowledge are present-day tendencies, against which there is now actually a reaction in the domain of world thought. If we ignore the absurdities that we have referred to in the name of taboos and bans, orthodox thought or reasoning about the ever-constant Absolute, present in the mind throughout the thirty centuries of its growth and flowering, represents as a whole, the noble aspirations of mankind anywhere in the world.

The zigzag course of speculative reasoning has gone on swaying from one side of the road to the other, but always true to the straight path that bridges the here and the hereafter. One who is keen on tracing the traits of Hindu thought has first to learn to distinguish between the two aspects involved, the lateral sways from side to side on the one hand, and the straight arrow that on the other hand, has always pointed to the high human value of the Absolute. The hopes and aspirations of man have been kept in mind in-and-through the variety and complexity of orthodox speculation in India.

While travelling in the North of India I came against various present-day representatives of this ever-flowering tree of wisdom. The flowerings of this mysterious tree are still reminiscent of the various stages of the origin, development and maturing of wisdom. Some could be traced to the Jaina and some to Buddhistic influence. In the heart of Vedism itself Bṛhaspati, the teacher of the gods, was himself the first enemy of Vedic orthodoxy, although the nickname of materialist as applied to his school of thought is not however false. He only pleaded for a revision of Vedic values and discouraged the heaven-centered self-interest which could be worse than a simple love of good life here and now.

Anti-brāhmaṇaism and even anti-Vedism was nothing new to the most remote school of Indian thought, and the *Sāṁkhya* which had this tendency was considered orthodox or heterodox alternately. Both the tendencies coexisted in the Upaniṣadic texts. Thus the stream of Indian thought has had a strange unity of content and life values of the here and the hereafter entering into its texture throughout its long course.

Sometimes theological, cosmological or psychological, with logic or methodology running through its whole length, with semantics or grammar thrown into the bargain, such is the course of the integrated and unitive content of Indian thought. Practice and precept, from gazing at the tip of the nose or dividing the elements into their real or imaginary constituent particles, both mathematically and experimentally, have all gone into the fabric called Indian wisdom of the ages.

Brahmā and *Brāhmaṇa*

Brahmā is the four or the five faced member of the Hindu pantheon, while *Brahman* (in the neuter gender instead of the masculine) is the Absolute of Indian philosophy. The Masculine has his rivals (both masculine and feminine) who are legion, all of whom figuratively represent one or other aspect of the Absolute.

Monotheism and monism, polytheism, pantheism and henotheism, with pessimistic colourations come into the mystical language of Hindu thought with such variety and vagueness that they are likely to confound and confuse the outside student unfamiliar with the style of Indian thought and expression ranging from the boldest exacting heights to the most puerile of lower limits. Mythological deities, from Brahmā to monkey and elephant gods, multi-headed or many-armed and speaking a composite protolanguage, belong to the background rather than to the foreground of Hindu thought.

The intelligent Indian is not a worshipper of Brahmā and the fact that there is almost no temple dedicated to Brahmā as a god proves that even the common man does not think along these lines. All images have a philosophical meaning articulated or not, speaking a protolanguage of stone, wood or metal symbols or icons. When thought rises above this level where mythmaking tendencies are still operating, we come to the world of doctrines or systems which are known as *darśanas* in India.

Each *darśana* represents a global vision of the Absolute as an existent, subsistent or a value factor, conceived from a definite philosophical or scientific standpoint. Deism or theism become discarded here and Indian speculation attains through its own methodology, epistemology and axiology to very pure heights, and gets lost, as it were, in the fumes or clouds of higher metaphysical speculation, most of which have no reference to simple or common human life here at all. Like scholasticism in the Middle Ages of Europe, speculation has run its full course in India too, making present-day Indian philosophy rather fruitless and sterile.

It is at such a juncture that we have to imagine a dialectical revaluation that it is in the process of taking place in modern India. The invasion of Westerners and the challenge and response that has started in the new normalization of values, has thrown Indian thought into much confusion. Besides noting the complexion of Hindu orthodoxy that prevails in North India at present, I had occasion in recent months to focus attention on the doctrinal aspects of Hindu orthodoxy, and have profitted largely by the personal contacts I was able to make with leading representatives of Hindu thought in Haridvar and Ṛṣikeśa. Added to my own recent studies and meditations on the subject, these have helped me here in taking a bird's eye-view of the general prevailing situation.

New Sprouts from the Heart of Orthodoxy

The history of religions has to be understood in the light of what is called dialectical revaluation. This is subtle process of shifting and selecting new values and ways of life.

What is called primitive religion, steeped as it was in the negativism of ancestor worship and of the hedonistic heaven of Vedism, had to be revalued by writers of different epochs, through the help of legendary heroic poems round the personality of a Rāma or a Sītā as in the *Rāmāyaṇa* and of the five and the hundred heroes of the *Mahābhārata*.

New *Purāṇas* (legendary lore) emerge from time to time with the same end of dialectical revaluation and restatement of spiritual values in mind. In this subtle process there is sometimes the upgrading of prophetic values as against the lower hierophantic ones. New combinations and complexions of orthodoxy emerge and gain primacy in the field of popular religion. The patterns of behaviour are constantly revised and the doctrinal content sways from one extreme limit to the other.

With the impact of Western civilization in cities such as Calcutta and Bombay, the impulse for readjustment was more definitely felt than in the countryside as a whole Calcutta and Amritsar may be said to be two of the centres of change in the North. The South has always remained more conservative and retained old patterns and beliefs through centuries, only occasionally interfered with by such great Gurus as Śaṅkara, Rāmānuja or Madhva. The Brahma Samāja which originated in Bengal and the Ārya Samāja that came out of the Punjab, may be said to be revalued Vedism and Vedāntism respectively. The strong denunciation of idol worship by Ārya Samājists had the paradoxical effect of discrediting, instead of confirming, as one could expect, the status of this group, while puritanism in the name of the Absolute, tended to throw the Brahma Samājists similarily outside the pale, as it were, of conformist ways and beliefs.

These two movements arose at a time when the question was still being asked by missionaries from the West and others whether India was civilized at all. The striking personality of a Vivekananda who raised his voice after these new sprouts of orthodoxy, combined Hindu apologetics with a brand of patriotism into whose composition popular religions of Tantra and Bengal Mother worship also entered. Meat-eating and *ahiṁsā* (which prohibited killing or hurting), was compromised or condemned in the name of manliness. The Ārya Samāja of the Punjab had also, like the Sikhs, to face attacks from inside and outside and developed the quality of bravery in its ranks.

The dose of patriotism tends to prevail over that of religion as we approach the time of Sri Aurobindo who also favoured Vedism and Āryan virtues, while bringing to bear an Indian esoterics influence coming from the Greek and the Bengal *Śakti* cult, in different proportions. The supramental force that can have its effect in the here and now actual world, which may be said to be the keystone of Sri Aurobindo's teaching, gives much place to the Mother principle. It has some elements non-understandable in terms of Hindu thought.

Most of these movements have their institutions in or around Haridvār. The Gurukula University of Kangri on the banks of the Ganges has its rival Sanātanī *Ṛṣikula* on the other side of the same river. The Sanātanī revival supports casteism openly to this day. The Ṛṣikula admits only those who are "born twice" and can wear the sacred thread, to its benefits, although I have been told that these conditions are being applied with greater and greater latitude in present times, to keep pace with a public opinion that is fast discarding the old static attitude to groups within Hindu society.

Outer Marks of Transition

As we travel from Vedism pure and simple to the extreme forms of Vedāntism and try to recognize the various outer marks that distinguish the different kinds of faith that underlie each believer, we find that even within the scope of the various orders of *sannyāsins* there are peculiarities that afford a key to the grading of orthodox thought and behaviour. *Sannyāsins* are fundamentally *parivrājakas* (wandering men), and the recognized means of livelihood is *madhukara bhikṣā* (gathering alms from different persons like a bee taking the nectar from flowers). The rule that they should have no home refers to the *aniketa* (vow of homeless poverty in possession). He is further to be *ayācaka* (one who does not ask or beg), content with what chance brings from day to day, and balanced between polarized attitudes of every kind such as fame or ignominy, etc.

Travelling in North India I was able to observe closely some of the prevailing kinds of *sannyāsin* behaviour patterns. Mīmāṁsaka schools of the Bhaṭṭa and the Prabhākara varieties still seem to have a subtle influence on the modern *sannyāsin* as seen in India now. *Udaka-kriyā* (which refers to oblations with water) *agnihotra* (fire ceremonial) from both of which the *sannyāsin* is supposed to be wholly emancipated, still leave their imprint on some groups or schools of *sannyāsins*. Vedism obtrudes into the pure domain of free Vedāntism in various ways. There are even *sannyāsins* who retain their pigtail or tuft (which belongs to the Vedic context) even after accepting the open absolutist ways of the yellow-robed, who as a rule, are to be clean-shaven. The orthodox priest too may be seen to use this kind or proto-language of shaving to express the austerity or strictness of his inner faith, whether belonging to group or individual patterns of taste in such matters.

The *ācamana* (sprinkling of water round the meal before eating) is omitted by certain orders fully emancipated from Vedism or *karma mīmāṁsā* influences. Even in reading a text like the *Gītā* which categorically denounces all forms of outward holiness, some orthodox persons attach importance to ritualistic injunctions such as *karādinyāsa* (arrangement of hands, etc.) which have sense only according to the *sūtras* of Jaimini and not Bādarāyaṇa, and whose full import in the semantics of Vedism has largely lost its significance at present. The tuft, the marks of sandal paste or ashes put vertically or horizontally on the forehead, and other details of ritualistic behaviour, help us to grade orthodoxy and place each pattern in its proper context, ranging from Vedism with its animal sacrifices to the fireless and waterless context of non-ritulistic wisdom of which Śaṅkara was the greatest of exponents.

The Six Systems and *Sannyāsins*

The various orders of *sannyāsins* in India doctrinally speaking, represent permutations and combinations of the six principal schools of Indian philosophy. The vast majority of them are *brahma-vādins* or those who give prime place to the doctrine of the Absolute. They are followers of Śaṅkarācārya in the main, but interspersed we find those who believe in 'qualified' monism or even in dualism.

Some give primacy to ritual, others give importance to theistic aspects in the name of the demands of the people for devotion. Just as plain living and high thinking go together, so doctrinal aspects and behaviour patterns go together in what the *sannyāsin* tries to represent in his person. Each *sannyāsin* with his group of disciples sometimes to be counted in dozens or in hundreds, may be said to be an ambulatory institution in himself, with various centre in different parts where he will spend some months of the year.

The scale of values which *sannyāsin* adopt determines the grade to which they may be said to belong. Nakedness or semi-nakedness, standing like an *arahat* or a *thīrthaṅkara* reaching from earth to heaven, or sitting with closed eyes like a Buddha or a Śiva under a tree, preferably surrounded by wild beasts, are the various tacit archetypal patterns of behaviour involved.

As for articles of faith, they range from those who believe in materialism, empiricism or realism through those who pin their faith on the various ways of valid reasoning acceptible to each *sampradāya* (traditional hierarchical grouping): The Cārvākas are those who gave primacy to common sense human values and represent the scientific attitude as against the believers in the *Veda*, whose hedonism is more applicable to the life hereafter, although they love the good things of life even here. The Vaiśeṣikas may be said to be neutral or psycho-physical realists, to whom even rainbow colours were interesting enough and not to be relegated merely to the illusion of *māyā*. The *pramāṇas* or the means of valid knowledge are all-important to their sister school of Nyāya, while more abstract reasoning and practice of a special kind of austerity called *Yoga* go together as a pair of values in the next set whose followers are called *Sāṁkhya-Yogins*. They may be said to correspond to the rationalists of the European context, while the Nyāya-Vāiśeṣikas may be said to correspond to the logical positivists or sceptics of the Hume type of thinking. Kant and Hegel come near to the next pair of sister schools,·called the Pūrva and Uttara Mīmāṁsakas. The Pūrva or the Anterior Mīmāṁsakas give absolute value status to *karma* or ritualistic action as a form of language of wisdom, *Karma* thus revalued became for them *Dharma* with a capital letter, not to be known through utilitarian logic alone, but with the aid of higher semantics as based on the meaning, as some moderns might explain.

We enter here into the Wittgensteinian world. *Karma-Mīmāṁsā* has been much misunderstood .as a variety of Vedism, but when we remember that Mīmāṁsakas worship no god but that of *Dharma* itself, the utterly reasonable position that they occupy at the centre of Hindu thought and expression will be evident to any student of comparative religion or philosophy. The philosophical, theological, cosmological and psychological problems or puzzlements that Hindu orthodoxy can present to an academic student or a seeker of wisdom, are thus very intricate indeed.

Speculation may be said to have gone to seed and to be defeating the main purposes of wisdom itself. A dialectical revaluation and integrated re-stringing of the whole range of the values involved is called for at the present moment. The *sannyāsins* of India are the inheritors of this wisdom and it is for them to restate wisdom once again on a world basis and background.

Vedānta Represents Integrated Dialectical Wisdom

Vedānta is no religion in itself but an ultimate consummation of wisdom, with a method, a theory of knowledge and a scale of values of its own. It is fully dialectical and consists of high equations between poles of reality and, resulting from the telescoping of all the previous history of Indian thought, culminates in the well-known *mahā-vākyas* (ultimate great conclusions or dicta) of the whole movement of thought spread over thirty centuries.

Śaṅkara gave it systematized form and others like Rāmānuja and Madhva became famous by supplementing in some way what Śaṅkara himself had implied either in his methodology, epistemology or values. These ultimate dicta point the arrow, as it were, to the findings or flowerings of Indian thought. As the fruit determines the tree, so the wisdom content of *Vedānta* can be seen by the grand dicta which equate the 'I' with the Absolute [*ahambrahmāsmi* "I am the Absolute"; *tattvamasi* "That thou art "; *tvamtadasi* "Thou that art"; *tvambrahmasi* "Thou art the Absolute"; *brahmaivedam sarvam* "The Absolute is verily this whole world", etc.], in the first, second or third persons syntactically or grammatically. The identification of the Self with the Ultimate is accomplished by two distinct sets of reasonings, one referring to Nature viewed horizontally and the other the same viewed vertically. Absolute Nature is no other than the Pure Absolute when the vertical and the horizontal are unitively understood.

Abhinna-nimitta-upādānatva (non-differentiated material-cum-instrumental agency) is the highly technical Vedāntic expression used by the most learned *sannyāsins* when asked in what consists their doctrine of the Absolute. Another way of referring to it as *sajātīya vijātīya bheda śūnyatva* (absence of difference as between its own kind and as between different kinds). Both of these have to be applied to the ultimate notion of the Absolute through dialectical equations of existence, subsistence or value factors, which are the three irreducible categories of the Ultimate viewed from the side of human intelligence.

The Absolute exists, subsists and has value, i.e., *asti, bhāti, priya* (exists, subsists and is dear or interesting). These are also technical terms of the *lingua vedantica* much used by *sannyāsins* and philosophers of India who have a way of blending behaviour patterns with doctrinal aspects, giving to the face of orthodoxy various tints, complexions and expressions.

Through the maze of variety of reasoning sufficient to confound the best of logicians or mathematicians and with varied taboos, bans, obligations, scruples and observances that have different complexions in different parts, one ascends through dialectics to the highest point of wisdom in *Vedānta* which, as the basis of wisdom, as also its crowning point, presents a noble edifice of human thought through the ages.

Through the ancient figure of the naked Tīrthaṅkara of the Jainas, sometimes nearly a hundred feet high reaching from earth to heaven to the Dhyānī Buddha of Kāmakūra, through more than thirty or forty centuries, the same ideogram has been persistently whispered by wise men, and the lispings and mutterings of the formula of wisdom continues to take place even now in revalued and restated forms. They all have their arrows pointing in the same direction. The ideogram is as valid now in the days of a Wittgenstein as it was in the days of Bṛhaspati the teacher of the gods of the Vedic period. Both these names, strangely too, represent the same degree of scepticism or belief which continues with thinking man though separated by long lapse of time.

The Future of Orthodoxy in India

The closed static nature of Indian orthodoxy both in its behaviouristic as well as in its doctrinal aspects, has to be made dynamic and open. Modern knowledge of the West has also made its contributions and arrived at a stage where it can go no further in the same direction as hitherto. Bertrand Russell may be said to present this enigma of modern times and no one who has glanced over his latest volume pictorially and schematically representing *The Wisdom of the West* (as the book is entitled) can ever mistake the nature of Western wisdom that has accumulated there during the ages, nor fail to see the nature of the philosophical blind alley that is at present facing the further progress of world thought.

Semantics, Eastern and Western

The Nyāya-Vaiśeṣikas of ancient India correspond to the logical positivists or empiricists of modern times. The Pūrva-Mīmāṁsakas represented by Jaimini are none other than the Wittgensteinian believers in word games. When Jaimini says that the *Vedas* are *apauruṣeya* (without human origin) and treats it as an Action sufficient unto itself, without need for any other god, Vedic or proto-Vedic he may be said to rise to the pure world of 'meaning of meaning' which has been the subject-matter of much modern speculation.

Between the years 1922 and 1958, during the interval marked by the posthumous publication of his *Tractatus Logico-Philosophicus* and his *Blue and Brown Books* respectively, culminating in his main contribution called *Philosophical Investigations* Wittgenstein has opened up a modern vista for world thought in this very region of the search for the 'meaning of meaning'. This same subject had once engaged the attention of the Pūrva Mīmāṁsakas with whom as stepping stones Śaṅkara may be said to have climbed up to the *sarvajña pīṭha* (the seat of the all-knowledge).

After this effort of Śaṅkara, speculative thought became more or less sterile in India, except for some epistemological or methodological corrections by the Gurus who followed him, such as Rāmānuja and Madhva. The Guru Nārāyaṇa in more recent years, attempted, with a great degree of success, the stringing together of all *darśanas* or points of view in philosophy, in his masterpiece in Sanskrit called *Darśana Mālā* (Garland of Philosophical Views). Unlike the *Sarva Darśana Saṁgraha* of Madhavācārya of the Sṛngerī Maṭha founded by Śaṅkara himself, the Guru Nārāyaṇa gave equal status to all points of view of the Absolute with the common method and theory of knowledge linking them all into a garland, instead of presenting *Vedānta* as a crown or crest jewel.

After the philosophical storms and puzzlements following in the wake of Wittgensteinism, which seem still to raise much dust of controversy in magazines and platforms in the West, especially among those interested in an integrated language for all science, in the name of a Science of all sciences, the time seems now opportune for thinking of a union of *Vedāntic* and Western thought so as to usher into being a new human heritage of integrated unitive wisdom of the Absolute.

27

The Sociology and Psychology of Caste

CASTE is an interesting social phenomena of the Indian soil. It is founded neither on subjective nor objective fact or reality; yet it influences men's minds in a strange way and makes them behave peculiarly, as if possessed by the notion, which becomes sufficiently real to them. The patterns that the notion is able to trace on social behaviour, have strange outlines and persistent and deep origins. Primitive peoples suffer from it more than those who lead an open and dynamic life. Separatist instincts of clannishness, tribalism, parochialism and the fighting instinct itself support it from the negative side. Race and colour provide it sometimes with a semblance of objective reality.

From the positive side of human nature, vague notions of traditional origin and of supposed spiritual value lend it support. Thus nourished it thrives on the tree of life as an epiphyte. Though unsupported by scientfic ethnology, weak people rely on a pseudo-sociology in which they find some consolation. In their minds it is a kind of intermittent and relapsing fever. As it works in favour of some section of the people as against others, those who reap the advantage naturally give it their support. The notion thus enters as a factor in the struggle for life and the very vagueness of the claims of caste superiority keeps it alive from generation to generation.

Outward marks and behaviour give caste an independent objective relaity, as when a policeman wears his uniform. Thus given artificially, the outer reality meets the inner psychology, so that with vague sociological and psychological justifications, the notion of case establishes itself firmly rooted in the body political, economic and social. Its very unreasonableness is its strength, and unwary people get their notions of spirituality moulded by it through its ready-made shapes or forms available in actual society at a given time.

Name and Form

Name and form (*nāma* and *rūpa*) according to the *Vedānta* philosophy, are said to be the twin factors which give support to all reality or creation. The universe consists of name-form (*nāma-rūpa*). The English literary critic William Hazlitt, in his essay on *Nicknames* has put his finger on this very point when he wrote that the more a man objects to a nickname and in direct proportion to its absurdity, the more it becomes tightened on to the person whom it is meant to discredit in public. Likewise, the mud of caste stigma has the power of sticking on to groups or individuals.

Caste is thus to be recognized as a double-edged phenomena which cuts both ways; to some as victims and giving double advantage to others. The knot it ties in the tangled root of the tree of life has also to be cut only by the double-edged sword of dialectics. Such a weapon is referred to in the *Bhagavad Gītā*.[1]

How religion and morality derive nourishment from two different sources and how they tend to create static and closed groups in human society, has been studied masterfully by Henry Bergson in his epoch-making work on the subject,[2] one of the productions of his maturity, after a career of nearly forty years in high academic life in the modern Western world.

Caste thus refers to what Emile Durkheim would call the *choses sociales* (social actuality) whose understanding correctly, and to counter its evil one has to be endowed either with downright comon sense or penetrating dialectical wisdom. In India, caste has taken the best efforts of Western scholars like Emile Senart and the greatest of Indian thinkers themselves like Gokhale to define or explain, and the Herculean efforts of people like Mahatma Gandhi to try and uproot or weed out. So far much success has not attended their efforts. As shouting for silence to a noisy crowd ironically defeats its own purpose, so the efforts by many to get rid of caste only tightens its grip all the more. Instead of avoiding the formation of more closed groups in a given society, both caste orthodoxy and heterodoxy could be blamed equally for fanning the fire of its evil effects. A subtle tact based on dialectical wisdom alone can counter it effectively.

The Guru Nārāyaṇa will be seen to have been unique among the recent personalities of India in having brought an effective antidote to his canker blossom of caste. The unitive approach normal to *Advaita Vedānta* was all that he used to exorcize this complex socio-religious evil which flourishes like rumour is the horizontal no-man's-land of human life-values.

Common Root of Caste and Chastity

The social value called 'chastity', especially the chastity of women, is at the core of this notion of caste. As the *Iliad* and the *Rāmāyaṇa* had a Helen and a Sītā at their core in the long and eventful stories in which men killed each other in great numbers, so caste thrives as a vague fear in the subconscious group mind of peoples lest imaginary cultural or religious barriers should be violated by so-called outsiders. As the queen-bee forms the centre round which the busy live is organized, so tribes tend to form closed units round women. The danger of the confusion of castes to which Arjuna himself alludes in the *Bhagavad Gītā* (I.41) is thought of as arising from unchaste women. It is true that Kṛṣṇa himself, as representing Absolute wisdom, does not support this view, but wholly ignores the plea. In the relativistic context, however, in which the confused Arjuna finds himself, the question of chastity does loom large in his mind, for he has still to be instructed in the finalized doctrine by Kṛṣṇa as his Guru. Vague and confused concern about the chastity of women from which both Menelaus and Arjuna suffered made them partizans (though unconsciously) of wars and sacrifices. Iphigenia's life was offered by Agamemnon to propitiate the gods before the great siege of Troy over the chastity of Helen. The banishment of Sītā by Rāma was based too, on village gossip.

Caste is a word of Portuguese origin currently used in India after the historic connection of the Portuguese with India in recent times. It is derived from the same root as 'chaste'. It refers to the purity claimed by a clan or tribe because of the chastity of the women within its closed and static imaginary frontiers.

Nightmare of Caste in Indian History

Heroic poetry and the mythology that goes with it, have tribal or national wars for their subject-matter. In India they are collectively referred to as *Purāṇas*, and constitute a body of socio-religious literature to which correct thinkers attribute only a low grade of importance as canonical scriptures (or *śāstras*) beside the more serious wisdom literature such as the *Upaniṣads* and the *Bhagavad Gītā*. *Purāṇas* are *smṛtis* (traditional lore) as distinguished from *śrutis* (pure wisdom writings). The latter do not countenance religious or moral obligations as such. The question of caste is thus outside the pale of the highest canonical scriptures of India. Whatever support it might have scripturally is only to be derived from traditional lore (*Purāṇas*) and these are meant for the masses and their approximate guidance in life. Wisdom comes into this only incidentally. The *pundit* and the saint rely on the purer authorities. It is even explicitly stated that the (*Purāṇas*) are meant merely for the edification of women and servants (*śūdras*). However, it is in such *Purāṇas* that the popular mind of the people in India finds vaguely implicit support for the clannish and separatist tendencies to which, as natural humans, they are subject in their crudeness and innocence. The chastity of women became an all the more important factor as soon as people from outside India penetrated into the matrix of the populace of India from the north and from the two flanking coasts of the Indian peninsula. The forests of the Deccan were infested with rough people and bearded sages who lived a life in which the standard of living in terms of getting and spending attained, as it were, to a natural norm of absolute zero. Clothing was hardly a problem, and hunting or fishing gave easy livelihood. It is into such a matrix that we have to imagine arrowheads of penetration of nomads, mostly consisting of men who were interested in both gold and women for booty. On such a soil chastity thus became an important value.

The conqueror soon allied himself with other daring opponents. Between the groups who conformed to the prototypes of the Kauravas and the Pāṇḍavas of the *Mahābhārata*, a dialectical exchange of cultural and religious values, a challenge and response as Toynbee would put it, has taken place throughout the course of Indian history which is at least two thousand years in depth. The Āryan conquering tribes with the priest as centre formed theocratic city states, into which women and servants were admitted from outside the tribe, under sufferance as it were. Merchants had their entry and exit into these colonies under certain conditions. The four castes thus became natural and necessary limbs of such a unit organization as it penetrated with its satellites deeper and deeper into the forests of the Deccan and the South. The long and protracted story of caste is nothing more than the story of alternate conquest and defeat, of challenge and response, in which human values became alternately recessive or dominant as overt values were exchanged for innate ones by one party or the other involved in the struggle.

The conquerors and the conquered were thus equally affected. The result was a constant process of dialectical revaluation. In this process caste became a bi-product. Caste could taste bitter or sweet alternately, like sea water or milk, depending on who was the gainer or loser in the process. Like a bad dream its injustice has disturbed the sleep of Mother India for centuries and is likely to continue to do so unless native common sense or full wisdom is brought to bear on the nuisance that it actually represents.

The Tendency to Rationalize Caste

When caste notions became a chronic nightmare to the Indian mind and an atavistic behaviour pattern imprinted itself indelibly upon the social life of the people with a hierarchy of pseudo-spiritual values attached to and associated with it, various rationalizations were attempted by orthodoxy at different epochs of Indian history. The post-Gupta period was responsible for formulating caste as a social system, and it was then that it got its sonorous title of *varṇa-āśrama-dharma* (duty, based on colour or race and stage or calling in life).

In spite of such a fine-sounding name based on a compromise and an attempted rationalization, however, caste as a system remains vague and indefinable still from any understandable norms or standards, whether ethnological, sociological or biological. It has no objective justification because there are at present as many snub-nosed and black brāhmaṇas as there are fair-skinned and sharp-nosed pariahs, whether in the north or south of India. Schoolboys lined up in scout uniform can never be correctly caste-classified by any objective traits anywhere in India. On the contrary much scientific proof tends to substantiate the unity of the humanity here as belonging to the same one race.

Sub-Conscious Biological Justification

Varṇa-āśhrama-dharma (colour-calling-duty), *kula-dharma* (clan-duty) and *jāti-dharma* (duty as belonging to a kind or species of beings) are to be distinguished carefully if we are to get anywhere to the bottom of the riddle of caste.

We have seen that the first term is a vague attempt at the rationalization of caste for politico-economic purposes after the Gupta period in Indian history. The second term, *kula-dharma* refers to the in-breeding and purity of strain of certain clans. A lower-caste woman could marry a high-caste man but the converse would not be permissible, and so forth. These are features of such a caste-system as prevailed for historical reasons and which no more hold good in modern India. They deserve to be forgotten as a bad dream.

In the dull background of the popular mind of Indians there is the analogy of the species in the animal world which sets the model for thinking of caste as *jāti* (kind), by which each unit is imagined to be a distinct species. As there are many kinds of cows and dogs and many varieties of mangoes or dahlias, caste is sometimes rationalized and understood as an actuality that one has to deal with as a given datum in life. The Guru Nārāyaṇa has directed a deathblow to this form of popular superstition in India in his composition called *Jāti Mīmāṁsā* (Critique of Caste).

Like any other scientific biologist he relies on the law of interspecific sterility well-known to biologists in the determination of a species or distinct kind of animal when examined scientifically. The implications of the law can be explained by two examples. A horse and donkey interbreeding produces a mule which cannot breed any more, being sterile. This is scientific proof of the distinction of the species which exists between the horse and the donkey. But on the contrary, the darkest Negro woman can have fecund progeny when married to a White man. This proves that the species, kind, or *jāti* of the Black and White peoples is one and the same. Caste which is referred to as *jāti* (kind or species) in India stands exploded as a justification of the existing divisions in society which are referred to under this caption. The objective or scientific validity of caste from empirical standards is thus null and void. It belongs to the limbo of horizontal absurdities in human life persisting more as a nuisance value than anything else.

Caste and Vertical Norms of Value

When referred to the norms belonging to the vertical scale of human values, the validity of caste brings us to more speculative ground. Here a strict empirico-logical approach soon leads us to a blind alley. The open question for us here is how far caste is to be justified as normal to thinking man. The claims of sociology, ethics and religion to order human relations intelligently on the basis of what is natural or in accordance with what is often called the will of God are what we have to examine here.

It would be futile and disastrous to try to deny or violate what is necessary and in keeping with the laws of nature. On the side of contingency which rises above obligations, to the domain of free moral or spiritual choice, we have to postulate natural grades among men striving for the goal of emancipation to see if any of these grades would correspond to or justify the notions prevailing especially in India in regard to the four main castes and their respective duties and privileges. Between these necessary and contingent aspects of human life, a revised and revalued notion of human types and patterns of behaviour which go with them could be imagined as justifiable, not as hereditarily fixed and static castes, but as stages in the progress of man towards emancipation or freedom.

The ethical, religious and sociological view thus taken would then be poles apart from the origins of caste as found in the notion of women's chastity in the tribal context. Its *raison-d'etre* would refer to a contemplative normative principle related to perennial philosophy and its validity would have reference to a normative principle belonging to a true science of the Absolute. Instead of being related to chastity and to closed and static social groups, caste would then refer to quite another notion altogether based on open dynamic groupings tending to abolish 'caste' rather than to its establishment. The foundations of such a revalued notion of the four castes have already been laid in the *Bhagavad Gītā* by its author Vyāsa. Open and dynamic groups in society can be used intelligently to abolish closed and static castes.

Manu's and Vyāsa's Divisions Contrasted

Hitler had anti-Semitic feelings and called himself an Āryan as against the Jews, whom he persecuted. When this can be true in modern times, it requires very little stretch of imagination to see that the penetrating Āryan hordes as they drove their arrows deeper and deeper into the proto-Dravidian matrix of the Indian population of the time, should have had a social outlook which they believed justified their treatment of non-Āryans as slaves (*dāsyas*). The *Manu Smṛti* is a compendium of obligatory laws belonging to this period. Just as post-Hitlerian justice is different from that of Hitler, or as the law of Jesus bears striking contrast to that of Moses, the former being open and dynamic as against what was closed and static, so there is a wide gulf of difference between caste as understood in the light of the teachings of Vyāsa in the *Bhagavad Gītā* and caste as understood by Manu.

The *Bhagavad Gītā* has two main references to caste, one at the end of the ninth chapter and one in the eighteenth chapter. Earlier the attitude of Vyāsa to caste is stated as a paradox in the following words:

> The four divisions (*varṇas*) were created by me based on type modalities (*guṇas*) and aptitudes to action (*karma*) divisions. Know me to be their maker as also their unmaker. (IV.13)

No sooner is the obligatory character of caste conferred on one hand than it is taken away by the other and characterized as a free and contingent factor in life. The same open spirit is found in chapter XI, verse 32, which throws open the door of the high spiritually recommended in the *Gītā* to women, merchants (*vaiśyas*) and even to those outside the Āryan pale (*śūdras*). A further comparison of the implications of the sequence of verses (chapter XVIII, 41 *et seq.*) confers a revalued status to caste free from all obligatory character altogether. When this is read together with the verse in the same chapter which says:

> Abandoning all (obligatory) duties come unto Me along for refuge;

I shall liberate you from all sin; sorrow not. (XVIII. 66) the thorough-going non-obligatory character of the caste duties as conceived in the *Gītā* and its striking contrast to the position taken in respect of the same question in the Laws of Manu should be quite patently evident to all.

The Caste of the Sages Vyāsa and Parāśara

If, even after the revaluation of caste notions in the *Gītā*, which thus makes it thoroughly non-obligatory and takes all the sting out of it, leaving it only with the status of a cancelled cheque or like *cafe sans cafeine,* if then, any value should still be attached to the notion of hereditary caste, especially in the minds of Hindu orthodoxy, such last vestiges of caste become effaced when we remember that the central personalities Vyāsa and Parāśara, of this great religion, if it might be called so, are themselves out of caste. Their birth was not through adherence to but by violation of the rule of caste chastity or purity, not to mention the sex morality involved therein.

In Nārāyaṇa Guru's *Critique of Caste* he tellingly refers to the classical cases of Vyāsa, the most important of the sages of antiquity connected with integrated Hindu spiritual thought, and of Vyāsa's own father Parāśara. The latter was born of the lowest pariah woman, although he is respected as superior to any brāhmaṇa in his authority and status. Parāśara became father of the central figure of Hindu orthodoxy through illicit relations with a fisher maid as mentioned in the various episodes at the beginning of the *Mahābhārata* itself. Caste orthodoxy thus receives its death blow from the very core of Hindu thought itself, and to Nārāyaṇa Guru and to Chattambi Swami of Kerala goes the credit of giving the notion of caste its long-deserved burial.

These two figures of Nārāyaṇa Guru and Chattambi Swami who rose on the geographical toe of Mother India more than a thousand years after the great Śaṅkara who was born also in Kerala, were legitimately fitted to do so as belonging to the vertical line of Gurus of India who are born again and again to set going again the course of true wisdom along the path of absolute purity and righteousness.

The Moral Imperative and the Doctrine of *Sva-dharma*

When all vestiges of caste notions based on the idea of chastity have been effectively effaced from the mind of the person seeking to find justification for at least broad divisions among men, based on moral, sociological or psychological considerations, we can examine if any moral imperative factor is involved to spport such divisions that books like the *Gītā* condescend to refer to in the contact of contemplative wisdom. Ontological considerations have to be treated hand in hand here with those that are teleological, while the demands of human nature have to be respected side by side with the high hope, dignity and destiny of mankind.

The categorical imperative of Kant presupposes a moral urge pointing to what is morally right. The doctrine is only an elaboration of Rousseau's dictum that Nature is always good. He even refers to the verticality of growth of a plant as a natural inclination which, even when the plant is titled at an angle maintains its heliotropic verticality. To think of a vertical line or scale of moral and spiritual values natural and legitimate to man is not repugnant to the spirit of the best theories of ethics. More particularly, Aristotle's ethics gives to whatever is most specific in any species of animal as the line where what is right in behaviour also lies.

When one conforms fully with one's own nature as a human being in such matters as are legitimate at once with the inclinations of every other normal human being, the requirements of right conduct are *ipso facto* fulfilled. The golden mean in which right conduct lies produces and joins the line on which legitimate human instincts also lie, while it points to the goal which marks the highest hope of perfection of which each man is capable. Obligatory or necessary duty joins thus the contingent course of right activity specifically peculiar to each individual. Thus we arrive by a long detour to the doctrine of *sva-dharma* (naturally right action) found in the *Bhagavad Gītā*:

> Man attains to perfection through action that is naturally right for him; hear thou from Me how conforming to one's natural course of action one attains to the target of contemplative life (*siddhi*). (XVIII.45)

The line of conduct that joins the innate tendencies in man with the perfection which is his goal in life is the same as the coruse that right action has to take. Such a course, in which the innate dispositions in an individual and the high goal are dialectically treated as counterparts together in determining what constitutes right action for him is what *sva-dharma* implies. This has nothing to do with chastity or heredity, and depends on type psychology only.

The sociology and ethics compatible with such a theory of *sva-dharma* need not necessarily be thought of in relation with the history of geography of India at all. Plato outside India also divided men into four groups such as the priest, soldier, etc. To the extent that scientific sociology which is yet to be formulated can sustain such a classification, the justification for the division of men into groups may be validated. Barring this possibility, which is still remote, notions such as caste could not be justified even in any extended theoretical sense.

The Revised Status of Caste

The scheme of the four castes recognized by Vyāsa in the *Bhagavad Gītā*, although they do not have any validity in the context of social obligation based on chastity or hereditary tribal notions, are meant by him to be used diagnostically in the pure contemplative context.

There are no pure Āryans or Dravidians in India any more, but there are men and women who are emancipated or bound in various degrees. Degrees of emancipation and bondage, as between contingent freedom and necessary restrictions imposed on freedom can be found in individuals or in groups within any society. The proletarian bound to his factory and wholly dependant on wages to be got in a certain locality for any particular kind of work could be the modern *śūdra* or slave. A brāhmaṇa who begs from many or receives gifts and fees for officiating as a priest to various families in an Indian village is not bound to the locality or to one master or capitalist. The *sannyāsin* is freer still and need not please any economic or social master at all. Women are held in the clutches of social necessity to a greater extent than men. The merchant has freedom to the extent that is stock-in-trade attracts a narrower or a wider range of clientele. The soldier enjoys a greater measure of leisure when life is normal around. He commands the goods of life by his power. A philosopher king like a Janaka of India or a Marcus Aurelius of Rome enjoys a degree of inner and outer freedom which is most favourable to the balanced contemplative life that could be considered as a model or norm of spiritual perfection.

If we should visualize the spiritual progress of man in the most general terms, the four great divisions mentioned in the *Gītā* could serve as symbols for the nomenclature of four of the principal stages in the evolution or emancipation of man from the status of a mere cog-wheel to that of an individual with free choice in the matter of ordering his life. As signs, to be used as Greek letters are used in science, the names of the four castes, if they have to be used at all, may be used to represent diagnostic stages in the scale of emancipation in contemplative life. They have then to be conceived in open dynamic terms rather than in any closed static sense. The *śūdra* of the *Upaniṣads* as in the episode of Janaśruti and Raikva (*Chāndogya Up.,* IV. i.1-IV.iii.8 and see *Brahma-Sūtra Bhāṣya* of Śaṅkara, I.iii. 34) is a man who is given to grief because of his concern about his state in life, and the perfect model of an emancipated Āryan as represented by a Rāma or a Kṛṣṇa is the lotus-eyed gently smiling person who is unruffled under difficulties. They are free from inner conflicts. Rāvaṇa and Arjuna as represented in the traditional lore would bring up the rear end in such a picture of dialectically contemplative progression visualized as an eternal procession of men seeking wisdom.

The *Brāhmaṇa*-Pariah Axis of Caste Dialectics

Caste is a state of mind with a long history. When examined objectively or even subjectively it melts into nothingness. In spite of this verity, however, it remains indelibly imprinted as an idiom in human consciousness and on the Indian soil does continue to affect the behaviour of peoples even when they know it to be unfounded and happen to be wise in other respects.

The terms *brāhmaṇa* and pariah have become incorporated in the language of the world. The latter is the generic name for someone despised and rejected while the former refers to one respected and welcome. Between the two there are distinct sets of contemplative values which attain to reciprocal polarity. The *cheri* or region where the pariah lives is not open for the brāhmaṇa to be welcomed according to the strict tenets of the orthodoxy of the pariah. Likewise the *agrahāram* of the brāhmaṇa does not admit the pariah. There are pure and holy pariahs as well as pure and holy brāhmaṇas. Śiva himself, the God of the South, was not a brāhmaṇa, and spurned the Vedic sacrifices. Indra, the typical God of the Āryans of the North, on the contrary, was known for his immorality and lust, and did not have a high status in the scale of contemplative spirituality. Greed and lust are even today associated with high castes, while the lowest castes are known for their spirit of detachment and renunciation. Social refinements might go to the credit of the high caste, but absolute standards of spirituality have ever remained with those at the opposite pole of the dialectical axis of values.

Although brāhmaṇa and pariah could justly be used as interchangeable terms referring to the two ambivalent aspects of contemplative spirituality, the purer form of absolutism still remains recognizable on the side of the pariah rather than on the side of the brāhmaṇa. The latter swears by the four *Vedas* while the pariah saints who have abounded in South India from times prior to the Christian era have remained true representatives of the Vedāntic way of life. When we remember that the *Gītā* itself refers more than once to the *Vedas* depreciatingly and that in a certain verse the *Gītā* sets at rest all questions of holiness in the context of the Absolute, the case for caste even in the context of spiritual values may be considered as abolished and closed. The unmistakable spirit of equality implied in the Absolutist outlook of the *Gītā* is revealed in the verse under reference here:

> The wise man considers with equality the brahmin endowed with learning and humility, the cow, the elephant and the dog as also the dog-eater. (V.18)

Caste as an 'Objective' Social Factor

The *Gītā* refers to the four social divisions in two distinct contexts. At the end of chapter nine it is subjective state of mind to be absolished. In chapter eighteen castes are treated as having an objective status of their own. The subtle distinction that is thus made is very important to notice.

Although caste may be abolished mentally by thinking people, it persists as a social phenomena non-subjectively. The outer marks and names that persons employ give reality to it and when the group mind takes the name and form of caste for granted and uses these for regulating human affairs in everyday life, caste attains to a rigidity or a reality all its own independent of its real foundations in truth. It becomes an actuality and a regulative factor in human conduct. Like the grafting of name and form and like the tightening of a nickname on one to be held up to ridicule, the less founded on fact the notion is, the more binding it becomes through the mind which is ever engaged in myth-making. The instinct of myth-making is ever active and takes hold of the least little suggestion or name or form to crystallize fibs and fables as entities that are real.

In sociology the group mind lends further support to such figments of the imagination. To counteract the fissiparous tendencies that the notion of caste lets loose in society to mar human solidarity and freedom it is first of all necessary to omit the use of caste names. Titles or marks that help to prepetuate invidious differences between man and man must be carefully avoided. Instead of thinking of a multiplicity of castes it would be in keeping with the spirit of science to think of the human race itself as belonging to one kind. Instead of the methods sometimes recommended by reformers that one should ignore caste to kill it, it would be more reasonable to reduce it as applying to one human species with the full concurrence of scientific evidence.

Thus the demands of the group mind to think of caste as a reality could be made to agree with the actuality of the case. Marks that help to distinguish the castes may for the same reason be avoided. Incidental differences that are bound to exist between man and man could be treated as such and their importance minimized. The barriers for social intercourse might be removed. Insisting on recognizing one and only one human kind should be what teachers and government alike should practice in regulating the day to day intercourse of man with fellow man.

Nārāyaṇa Guru's Attitude to the Caste Problem

Guru Nāryāṇa may be credited with having discovered the correct formula for countering the evil of caste. It would be too much to expect those who reaped the benefits of caste to abolish it themselves. The roots of caste lie buried deeper than what mere reformers can reach. The apartheid that prevails between Whites and Blacks in South Africa and the trouble in the Little Rock educational institutions in the United States have at least visible difference of colour to lend a semblance of justification for distinctions to be imposed between man and man. In such cases the strong hand of law and order might find a solution.

When, however, subtler apartheid prevails as in caste in India, not based on anything visible, the ailment may be said to be chronic and have its roots deeper still, so that what is called for is a root and branch revision in the whole attitude to the question.

The method of Nārāyaṇa Guru was first to take away the support of caste names. He advised his followers constantly not to ask the caste of man, and if asked for it, not to tell the name and to forget all about it. Social intercourse and equality of treatment were recommended in the name of human justice. Religious places were to be open to all people without caste discrimination and all civil rights were to be guaranteed.

As he emphasizes in the very first line of the *Critique of Caste* composed by him (see page 69) the caste of a man consists in the humanity and in the human qualities he represents. To be a human being in the fullest sense was to be really taller in superiority than titles such as brāhmaṇahood could ever confer. Referring all human beings to the normative principle of what is unique or specific to the human kind itself, the Guru was able to reduce the possibility of caste to unitive terms. Religion and God which also regulated human relations were also similarly brought into unitive treatment. In fact such a unitive treatment was quite compatible with the non-dual attitude of the *Advaita Vedānta* which he represented in his own philosophical teachings. Thus preserving what was most precious in the heritage of India and without offending orthodoxy and so becoming heterodox himself, he discovered a formula by which the evil of caste could be effectively countered.

Man's Humanity Distinguishes the Human Kind

Nārāyaṇa Guru's approach to the problem of caste was neither accidental nor unconscious. In the first line of his composition he evidently addresses himself to Hindu orthodoxy when he insists in the Sanskrit language of Hindu orthodoxy itself (the other verses being in his regional Malayalam language) that man's humanity is what should give him superiority. In other words the good man is one who is more human and who recognizes the humanity in his fellow men.

The requirements of social justice, of morality, and for the superiority in the name of one's caste are all thus referred to the same central and unitive principle in the value called Humanity. Likewise when human and godly values are treated unitively in the religious context we get the same result of an absolute human value at the core of human affairs.

On a certain occasion the Guru went to far as to say that if his devoted followers insisted as they sometimes did, on considering him as an incarnation of God, they could do so only on condition that such a status was conferred on him because of his opposition to caste as it prevailed.

The unique status of Nārāyaṇa Guru implicit and explicit in his attitude as one who wished to abolish caste barriers as between man and man is a matter that needs greater and greater recognition in modern times not only in India but the world over. The poignant complaint of the Guru is expressed at the very end of the very first verse of his composition:

Alas ! This truth no one understands !

These words put the seal as it were on the uniqueness of the discovery of the Guru in his own words. The unity and solidarity of humanity was what was most dear to the heart of the Guru.

References

1. (Guru) Kṛṣṇa said : They speak of an unexpended (holy) fig. - tree with roots above and branches below, whose leaves are sacred verses; he who knows it is a *Veda*-knower.

   Below and above spread its branches, nourished by the modalities of nature (*guṇas*), sense-values its buds, and downwards also there are ramified roots which bind to action in the world of men.

   Nor is its form comprehended thus (as stated) here, nor its end, nor its beginning, nor its foundation. Having sundered this holy fig-tree of strongly-fixed root with the weapon of decisive non-attachment.

   Then (alone) that path is to be sought, treading which they do not return again (thinking) I seek refuge in that Primordial Man from whom of old streamed forth active (relativist) manifestation.

   (Ch. XV, Verses 1-4)

2. *The two sources of Morality and Religion.*

Glossary

Abhāva : Non-existence. The opposite of *bhāva* in a vedāntic-category. Non-existence has two main divisions :

(1) The absence of one entity in another, (*Samsarga-abhāva*) which is of three kinds :

a) prior non-existence (*prāg-abhāva*),

b) annihilative non-existence (*pradhvamsa-abhāva*),

c) absolute non-existence (*atyanta-abhāva*)

(2) One object not being another (*anyonya-abhava*) or reciprocal non-existence.

Adhyāsa : Superimposition; false attribution; illusion.

Adhyāsa is of two forms : *Svarupa-adhyāsa* and *Samsarga-adhyāsa*. The former consists in superimposing an illusory (*mithya*) object on something real. Example: Seeing a snake on a real rope, or of superimposing ignorance (*avidyā*), the empirical world upon *Brahman*, which is an example of a foundational error. *Samsargaadhyāsa* is the superimposition of an attribute on an object. This relation is false (*mithya*). Example: A transparent crystal placed on a red silk appears to be red.

Advaita : Non-duality, the transcendence of experiencing every form of reality.

Āgama : A synonym of any ancient scripture, particularly the *Vedas*. There are non-vedic *agamas* also, like *Śaivāgama, Vaiṣṇavāgama, Jaināgama* etc.

Ānanda : Value dynamics which is sometimes equated with a christian concept of bliss. In an absolute sense, the same as the Kantian concept of summum bonum.

Annam : Food, that which is consumed, especially to appease hunger.

Apara : Relativistic, conditional.

Ardha-Nārīśvara : The androgynous concept of Śiva, both as male and female.

Arivu : A malayalam word meaning knowledge. Nārāyaṇa Guru uses it as a synonym for Self, Consciousness and sometimes on par with Subsistence (*Cit*).

Bhāva : Existence.

Bhedābheda : The doctrine of difference as well as non-difference, propounded by Bhartṛu Prapañcha.

Brahma Vidyā : The science of the Absolute. Another name for *Vedānta*.

Cit : Consciousness. The second attribute of *Brahman* as in *Sat-Cit-Ananda*. That which substantiates truth as well as value-dynamics.

Dakṣhināmūrthy : An aspect of Śiva as the supreme teacher, who imparts his wisdom in silence, showing on the sign of wisdom-gesture with his right hand.

Dvaita : Duality. The philosophy of maintaining dualism.

Gaṇesa : The Lord of both the shining ones and manes, the departed souls. Symbolically, he is figured as an elephant-headed god, riding on a mouse.

Guṇas : The triple modalities of nature, originally conceived by Kapila in the *Sāmkhya-pravachana-sūtras. Sattva-rajas-tamas.*

Guru : Derived from the root '*gu*'-meaning darkness and the root '*ru*'-meaning destroyer. A wisdom teacher.

Īśvara : The principle of control which (who is maintaining) the integral law that sustains each entity as a specific mode in the totality of the being.

Karma : Action. All actions are included under this term, more especially ritualistic actions.

Kṛṣṇa : Chief of the Yādava tribes and an incarnation of Viṣṇu. The *Guru* of the *Bhagavad Gītā*.

Kṣetra-kṣetrajña : Field and knower of the field. Field or ground can be psychological or spiritual as well as actual. These terms correspond to the actual and perceptual aspects of reality. The entire XIII chapter of the *Bhagavad Gītā* is devoted to this discussion, and the distinction between these two aspects of field and knower, in itself constitutes one of the central problems of philosophy.

Kuṛal : The Tamil work by Tiruvalluvar who belongs to the first century AD. Ethics, philosophy and mysticism blend in a wholesome perennial form of wisdom in this work which may be said to be a continuation of wisdom of the 'pre-historic' India, more or less independent of the Vedic tradition. Thiruvalluvar was not a brāhmaṇa but a non-caste Indian, who in spite of this circumstance still holds a high place among the authoritative sages of India.

Liṅgam : Literally, anything that constitutes a sign or symbol. The male sex-organ as a symbol is referred to as *liṅgam*, The *Śivaliṅgam* which is the phallic symbol of Śiva is a spherical stone which is an object of worship in India from pre-historic times. It is dressed up, annointed or washed with ablutive waters by way of respect or adoration in memory of the antique god Śiva.

Mahāvākyas : Literally, the great sentences. Applied to the conclusive formulae of Vedāntic wisdom, such as *tat tvam asi* (that art thou), *Aham brahma asmi* (I am *Brahman*), *Prajñānam brahma* (consciousness is *Brahman*) *ayam ātma brahma* (this Self is *brahman*) *Auṁ Tat Sat* (AUṀ that is what is real); *sarva-khalvidam brahma* (everything here is *Brahman* indeed).

Maheśa : Another name of Śiva. Literally, the Great god.

Mantras : A stanza of Vedic hymns. Literally, those words, which save the person who contemplates on them. Also meant to be recited beautifully. The ritualistic part of the *Vedas* also known as the *Mantra*.

Māyā : Connotes a factor of epistemological and methodological importance in Śaṅkara's *Vedānta*, especially, and in the Upaniṣadic lore generally. Whatever is postulated as the cause of the unreal, spoken of in the most generic of categorical terms in philosophy, as against theology, is to be laid at the door of *Māyā*. It is the basis of duality or synergic antinomies. The nearest Western equivalent is the *Negativitat* of Hegal's system.

Mīmāṁsā : A critical enquiry. Two Indian Schools of philosophy are called *Mīmāṁsās*. See *Sāṁkhya*.

Muni : A silent recluse.

Nārāyaṇa : One who sleeps on the primordial waters. (*Nara*, water: *ayana*, to lie in repose). Creation, before Brahma gave it the four directions, symbolized by his four heads, has the indefinite nature of all-pervading water ("God moved upon the face of the waters" as *Genesis*, 1, 2, puts it) on which the numinous principle of life or creation was supposed to recline. This image of creation formed the background of the later Viṣṇu tradition which itself suffered many changes through history and become the Vasudeva cult of the Bhagavata. In the original Nārāyaṇa scheme, Śiva, Viṣṇu and Brahmā met without distinction as the *Ādi Nārāyaṇa*, the first divinity of creation or the primodial Man or *Nara*, when called Nara-*Nārāyaṇa*.

Nirvāṇa : Extinction of all desires in a kind or pure void of the Absolute consciousness.

Nivṛttimārga : The path of withdrawal. This is related to *neti, neti* or the *via-negativa*. It means, sinking into one's own true nature by withdrawing the mind from outward going attachments, the final culmination of this process being *Nirvāṇa*.

Padārtha : A philosophical category. Literally, the meaning of a word.

Pāra : Beyond; pertaining to the ultimate or Supreme; as opposed to the immanent here and now aspect of reality which is *apāra*. It could mean the transcendent.

Para-Brahman : The higher *Brahman*. Śaṅkara conceives of two aspects of *Brahman*. The lower *Brahman* (*Apara Brahman*) is the ultimate Reality as having form world for its attributes. The higher *Brahman* is attributeless, and hence is inconceivable.

Param : The Supreme, the Transcendental. An epithet of *Brahman*.

Pārvatī : The consort or *śakti* aspect of Śiva. She is the daughter of the Himālayas and is also a huntress, and known under various aspects in mythology and inconography.

Paśu-pati : Both these terms and *pāśam* are basic concepts in the ancient Śiva religion. *Paśu* is creation in the sense of beasts or animals of all kinds, while *pati* is the master or creator. *Pāśam* is the bondage in which all life is trapped. *Paśu-Pati* is Śiva visualised as surrounded by animals, thus bringing together dialectical counter-parts belonging to a situation which is typical of the spiritual attitude cultivated by the Śaivites.
(Literally the lord of Beasts)

Prajñā : Consciousness.

Prakṛti : Nature. Literally, that which is always in an active state. This activeness is inherent in the Ultimate Reality or *Brahman*. *Brahman* in its active state is called *prakṛti*.

Puruṣa : Literally 'person'. The word is used both in the universal and particular senses. In the universal sense. He is the cosmic person who has the entire cosmos for his body. In this sense He is often called *virāṭa puruṣa*.

Rasa : The essence, juice. Aesthetic enjoyment.

Ṛṣi : A seer. A wise sage of ancient India who live generally in the seclusion of the forests. They wrote all the hymns of the *Vedas* as well as the *Upaniṣads*. They were not necessarily monks and many of them had their wives living with them.

Śakti : See Pārvatī.

Saṁhitā : Literally, those which are enjoined inseperably. Name of the initial part of the *Vedas*, dealing mainly with rituals. Also called *mantra*.

Sāṁkhya : One of the six systems of Indian Philosophy. The other five are *Nyāya*, *Vaiśeṣika*, *Yoga*, *Pūrva Mīmāṁsā* and *Uttara-Mīmāṁsā*. The last one is also known as *Vedānta*.

Saṁsāra : Worldly life that passes through a succession of states causing sufferings. Often considered as an ocean. Transmigration of souls is also considered part of it.

Ṣaḍ-ādhāra : Six bases, six physiological centres between the tail end of the spinal-column and the fore-head. Six such centres or zones are imagined by certain *yoga* schools for the sake of meditation. They are *Mūlādhāra*, *Svādhiṣṭhāna*, *Maṇipūra*, *Anāhat*, *Viśuddhi* and *Ājñā*.

Ṣaḍ-Darśana : Six systems of Indian Philosophies namely, *Nyāya*, *Vaiśeṣika*, *Sāṁkhya*, *Yoga*, *Pūrva Mīmāṁsā* and *Uttara Mīmāṁsā*.

Sat : That which exists always. The subsisting reality in all the transcient forms of the visible world, even as gold is the subsisting reality in all ornaments. *Brahman* as this subsisting reality is designated as *Sat*. (see *Ānanda* and *cit* also).

Siddhi : Attainment. Certain *supra-mundane* attainments gained through certain yogic practices. Eight such attainments are referred to by Patañjali in his *Yoga Sūtras*.

Śiva : The ancient hero-god from the times of pre-history, associated with radical virility and renunciation. He is an unconventional god like Dionysious, wearing skins and dancing in ecstasy, drunk with cosmic consciousness. He is the most ancient and the most important figure of the Indian Pantheon, and occupies his seat in Banaras in the plains and Kailas in the Himālayas.

Smṛti : Learning or scriptural lore remembered by a student when he applies pure wisdom-teachings to his practical life. Obligatory conduct and works of religious duty belong to this catagory. Also known as *Dharma Śāstra*. What is taught in them are subject to alterations according to time and clime.

Sphoṭa : The name of the Indian theory of semantics. Literally, bursting out. A meaning bursts out in the mind just on hearing the utterance of a word.

Śruti : That which is heard. The words heard from a Guru. The recorded writings of Guru is concerning pure wisdom teaching. All the *Upaniṣads* are considered *śrutis*. What is taught in the *śrutis* is of eternal value.

Śūdras : The lowest of the four castes. The other being *Brāhmaṇa, Kṣatriya* and *Vaiśya*.

Syād-vāda : Name of the philosophy of Jainism. Literally the doctrine of may be, may be not.

Tapas : Austere Self-discipline. Literally, 'heating up'.

Tripuṭi : The aspects involved in the event of knowing something, namely the knower, the known and the act of knowing. Literally the three-petalled one.

Tulasī : A kind of basil plant of the labiate family and considered holy. It is planted in front of orthodox Indian houses.

Upaniṣad : When the chapter of *Karma* or ritualistic action has been transcended by a religious student or *Brahmacārin*, he is ready to receive the posterior philosophical teachings which constitute the *Vedānta* (i.e., "the end of the Vedas"). The *Vedānta* is non-theological; concerned with the Absolute or the *Brahman*. The word is said to be derived from *upa*, beside and *niṣad*, sitting near, so that it is a teaching received by a disciple when he is allowed to sit and listen to philosophical teaching near or by the side of the *Guru*.

Uttara Mīmāṁsā : See *ṣaḍ darśana*.

Vaiṣṇavites : Those who consider Viṣṇu as the Supreme or the Absolute.

Varṇa-āśrama : A term loosely applied to refer to the caste system and the four stages of life in the society. *Varṇa* literally means colour. Originally it signifies the four psychological types of human beings.

Āśrama refers to the four stages of human life, viz. as a student house-holder, forest-dweller and renunciate (*brahmacārin*, *gṛhastha*, *Vānaprastha* and *sannyāsa*). These two contents are often mixed up and the orthodex Hindu way of life is often referred to as *Varṇa-āśrama-dharma*.

Viśiṣṭa Advaita : The qualified non-dualism of Rāmānuja. It considers the world and the numerous souls as qualifying the Absolute or *Brahman* forming Its or His body.

Vyāsa : The son of Parāśara born of a fishermaid. Otherwise known as Veda Vyāsa. He was also the author of the *Brahma Sūtras*. Also known as Bhādarāyaṇa. He is the most important of the personalities in Indian spirituality.

Yoga : Is harmonization. In all organic structuring of organisms two opposit principles are employed. Such as the psychic and somatic, the chemical and electrical, the sensory and the motor, the sympathetic and parasympathetic. In the functional aspects also we see such complimentarities which can also prove to be contradictories, if the law of harmonization is not properly maintained. Number of functions in the body are autonomus, regulated by the opposits of control and release. The principle of harmonization is very much like a principle of ambivalence going from plus to minus and arriving at a neutral point of homeostsis. The overall science dealing with this is yoga—always with a middle ground. There are many levels of finding such homeostsis, such as between the spiritual and the social in which the middle ground of morality, crime and punishment in which the middle ground is theraputic correction. A similar ambivalence is between the psychological and physiological in which the middle ground is awareness of harmony and a sense of ease.

There are different systems of Yoga in India. Three contemporary systems are Patañjalis *Yoga sūtras*, based on the *Sāmkhyan* epistemology called *Sāmkhya pravacana sūtras*. Two other moderate systems are of the *Sapta-bhūmika-yoga* of the *Yoga-vasiṣṭha-Rāmāyana* and the *Yoga* of *Karma Yoga* and *Karma sanyasa-Yoga*, which suggests many modalities such as *Jñāna Yoga, Karma-Yoga*, and the attainment of stabilized aspects such as *Stita-prañja, Guṇātīta, Brāhmīstiti, Bhakta, Sanyāsi, Tyāgi* and the state of *Yogārudha*. Two complimentary systems founded by Yogendra and Matsyendra are today called *Haṭha Yoga*.

Index